OUR JOURNEY TO EL DORADO

TWO WOMEN, TWO IMMIGRANTS, TWO WORLDS COLLIDE— A TRUE STORY OF FAITH AND FREEDOM FROM HUMAN TRAFFICKING

M.F. RENÉE

THE CULTURAL STORY-WEAVER

ISBN 978-1-7367253-7-5

TABLE OF CONTENTS

To my beloved Habiba and all the women and girls around the globe who carry the same story—the same story of brokenness, trauma, and pain. To all the women and girls around the world who are still secretly enslaved. You are not forgotten. We will find you. We will rescue you. Stay strong while we tell your story, while we plead with people to help, while we scream loudly from the mountaintops the truth and sad reality of what happens in the darkness behind closed doors. I will be your voice—the voice of the "Silent Ones." Most importantly, I dedicate this book to God, "the Author and Finisher of our faith"—our story, our journey to El Dorado. I trust Him to write the last chapters and the end of this story.

"Speak up for those who cannot speak for themselves,
For the rights of all who are destitute,
Speak up and judge fairly;
Defend the rights of the poor and needy."
Proverbs 31:8-9—The Bible NIV

THE PEOPLE IN THIS BOOK HAVE GIVEN ME PERMISSION TO TELL THEIR STORY. NAMES AND LOCATIONS HAVE BEEN CHANGED FOR EVERYONE'S SECURITY.

"Jesus left the ninety-nine to go and rescue the one."
Luke 15:4—The Bible NIV

ARABIC TEARS

With that one phone call, the threads of our lives intertwined —forever.

"We heard you speak Arabic. Can you help us with some translation? We have a new Moroccan girl who can't speak a word of Spanish."

"Yes, I love Arabic."

I'd heard about these women, the work—the difficult, heart-breaking work. I'd also heard the statistics in Spain—some of the highest in Europe. Alarming . . .

I wasn't sure what I was getting into. I wasn't sure if I wanted to walk through the door that day.

It didn't take me long to love you—a broken, hurting woman who had left everything—your parents, your son, your land, your culture, your language, your life . . . your broken life in North Africa. Like all the other women sitting next to you in the boat that day, you crossed the Mediterranean to pick strawberries in the fields of Spain.

It was no El Dorado.

Sitting in that room, you begin to tell your story—in Arabic, the language I love.

Arabic. The onslaught of your pain, your trauma, your grief slam me in the face.

Arabic. It stings. I feel sick to my stomach.

Arabic. You speak so fast, sob so loudly. At times, I can hardly understand you.

Arabic. I don't want to ask you to repeat. I don't want you to say it again. I don't want to hear it again.

Arabic . . . But there's no one else. I am the only one in the room who can hear and understand your story, your words, your pain.

Arabic . . . a blessing, a burden.

Arabic . . . a language I love, a language I hate.

I try to listen, but your pain hits me hard. Tears stream down my face. I reach across the table and take your hand. I lean over and hold you.

You weep. I weep. I have never seen so many tears. I stroke my finger across your cheeks to wipe them away. I hand you a tissue. I hold one too.

The emotion is raw—yours, mine.

Arabic . . . I listen carefully to your words, absorb your pain, your sorrow, your story.

Strawberries, promises, darkness, streets, alcohol, drugs, men, money, Mafia, secrets, torture, death . . .

I swallow hard. I breathe deeply. I turn to the other two women sitting at the table with us.

And I speak.

Arabic.

English.

Spanish.

Your sacred story travels around the table. I hear the trauma once, twice, three times—in three different languages. My head spins. My mind is foggy.

I weep. I hold your hand.

When I walk out the door that day, I carry your story with me. It's a story that is more than I can handle, more than I can hear, more than I can bear, more than I can carry.

The pain and grief are heavy. I can hardly breathe.

I beat my fists against the steering wheel, tears streaming down my cheeks.

"God, I didn't ask you for this! I don't want to do this anymore! I don't want to use my Arabic like this! Find someone else!"

But there's no one else. Arabic. I'm the only one who understands your story.

Arabic . . . it feels used and abused . . . just like you, my sister.

I cry Arabic tears.

THOSE ON THE FRONT LINES

I sat alone in my car. It was April 2020, just after the COVID-19 pandemic had invaded the world. Spain was still in a period of total confinement. I had already been in lockdown with my husband and four sons for almost forty days. It felt like Noah's Ark; however, the rain was still pouring, and the waters were not receding.

It was only the second time I had been out of the house, the second time I had driven my car in over a month. It felt strange. I could finally breathe. I went to the pharmacy to pick up medicine for my son. After removing my face mask and washing my hands thoroughly with antiseptic gel, I sat in my car to escape and read for a while. No one at the house needed me.

I had just downloaded a new book onto my phone, "Half the Sky" by Nicholas D. Kristof and Sheryl WuDunn. The subtitle intrigued me: "Turning Oppression Into Opportunity for Women Worldwide." By the time I got to the dedication page, I was already in tears. After a message to the authors' children, these words jumped off the page and straight into my heart.

"And for all those on the front lines around the globe, saving the world, one woman at a time."[1]

Choked up, tears welled up in my eyes and slowly trickled down my cheeks.

The authors wrote this book for me—FOR ME. In 2009, when they published and dedicated their writing, they already had me in mind. They didn't know me, and they still don't. But, there I was, in 2020, in Spain, on the front lines. I didn't choose this battle. I didn't expect this. I wasn't trained for this war. I was just thrown onto the battlefield with no boot camp or military armor.

My only weapons—love, prayer, and a mind and a mouthful of Arabic.

As I read those words, I thought about the many others I know personally who stand courageously on the front lines with me. I thought about Karen* and Andrea,* the two directors I work with. They regularly lunge head on, smack into the middle of danger— into the dark and evil streets—to rescue helpless girls. Although typically accompanied by undercover police agents, they risk their lives and the lives of their families to find and free women held captive in slavery.

I thought about Jessica* and Paola,* the psychologists I work with. They sit for hours with these broken and traumatized women— listening to them, caring for them, loving them as they share their stories. They hope that somehow they can guide them towards hope, healing, and redemption in their journey. I thought about Maria* and Chris,* the persistent lawyers who fight for the human rights of these women—seeking justice and help for the oppressed. I thought about Beatrice* and her team in the south of Spain, rescuing exploited migrant women from the agricultural fields. They, too, stand on the front lines, "saving the world, one woman at a time."

That's all we can do—stand, pray, and journey alongside one woman at a time.

Two unlikely women were about to cross paths—a tall, fair-complected, light-haired woman from the deep Midwest of America and a petite, dark-skinned brunette from the desert mountains of Morocco. We were both on a journey . . . a journey to a better life . . . a journey to El Dorado. We were both searching . . . searching for deeper meaning and purpose.

If the only reason our family came to Spain was for me to meet this one woman, then it was all worth it.

"Jesus left the 99 to go and rescue the one" (Luke 15:4). The ONE is worth it all to Him. The ONE is dearly loved by Him.

Here I am, today, on the front lines of the battle in Spain, walking alongside ONE woman. This woman's name means "Beloved" in Arabic. This woman's name is Habiba.*

*Names are changed to protect the identity of the individuals.

PART ONE

Her Dream

MOROCCO ROOTS

Morocco—our homeland, our family, our culture, our language, our life.
Morocco—the land we left behind.
Morocco—the place we still call home.
Morocco—the country to which we can never return.

CHAPTER ONE

MY MOROCCO

We are a "globe-trotting" family—always on the move, always packing our suitcases. Travel is in our DNA. We have hauled our children across the world to live on three continents, raising our four boys across borders, across languages, across cultures.

Sometimes we forget who we are or where we are.

Two of our children were born in the U.S., and two were born in France. They like to argue about which of them is eligible to run for President of the United States—only the two born on American soil. In our years of marriage, we have spent little time in the United States. Most of our life has been overseas in France, Morocco, and Spain. Two of our sons went to boarding schools in Germany and Senegal and universities in England and Germany. I guess you could say that the world is our home.

Although born in different countries, we all carry two passports—American and French. Our four children also bear the label of "Third Culture Kid" (TCK), a term coined by David Pollock and Ruth Van Reken to mean "a person who has spent a significant part of his or her developmental years outside the parents' culture. The TCK frequently builds relationships to all of the cultures, while not having full ownership in any."

Loss, goodbyes, disconnect, confusion, transition, loneliness, suitcases, moves, travel . . . that describes our family of nomads.

In all of our early global travels, Morocco wasn't on our horizon. I don't even remember hearing about the country before I moved to France at nineteen to study abroad. Given that Morocco is a former French colony, crossing paths with Moroccans on French soil was quite common.

After graduating from university, I spent a year teaching English in a high school in the south of France on a Fulbright Teaching Fellowship. One of my fellow English teachers, from Tunisia, invited me and another colleague to visit his country and his family during our spring break. We gladly accepted his invitation to explore his homeland.

I fell in love with everything about North Africa—the crystal turquoise Mediterranean Sea, the bright blue and white handmade pottery, the rich ethnic spices, the warm and friendly locals, the daily doses of sunshine, the busy outdoor markets, and the cheap prices that were always open to the art of negotiation. And the Arabic language . . . I loved the way it sang in my ears and danced in my heart.

I decided then that one day I would go back to that land—the land of North Africa.

When I met my French husband, Vincent, during my first year in France, I discovered that he also had a fascination with foreign lands, people, languages, and cultures. Many of his university friends were from Algeria, the Ivory Coast, La Réunion, Morocco, La Martinique. No doubt, we were made for each other, and travel would become a significant part of our shared life story.

While living in Paris a few years later, I taught French to immigrant women at our local church. Every Tuesday morning, we met together for sweet mint tea, homemade treats, fun and games, and free French lessons. It was the highlight of their week and mine. Women from predominantly North Africa and the Middle East—Morocco, Tunisia, Algeria, Iran, Lebanon—gathered. We were friends who quickly became family to one other.

We were all foreigners, all immigrants, all people from another land. We were all separated from our family, our friends, our cultures, our languages, our worlds—the ones we had always known. Our babies nursed side by side, our toddlers crawled on the floor and played together. We shared stories. We shared pain. We shared laughter. We shared tears.

Living in the international business quarter of Paris, La Défense, my husband and I quickly discovered that over eighty percent of the people living among us in the high-rise apartments were from North Africa. Everywhere we turned, we saw dark-skinned hands decorated with rust-colored henna, inhaled the pleasant odors of stewed *tagines* and couscous in the hallways, crossed paths in the elevator with veiled women, heard the scrambled dancing of Arabic all around us, purchased homemade specialities at the local grocery store downstairs, and watched our children play soccer in the courtyard with the immigrant children.

North Africa. We were surrounded by it, and we loved it. Our kids did too.

Many of our oldest son's preschool friends were from Morocco, Tunisia, and Algeria. When Timothée went to their homes to play after school, he didn't realize that he was playing with the "outcasts" of French society. For our son, these immigrants were his friends. That's all he knew. That's all he needed to know. Another son, Robert, went to the neighborhood nursery where he shared toys and sippy cups with those from North Africa—another world.

North Africa. We didn't know it then, but their world, their land, their culture would one day become ours.

In 2001, a company invited us to visit Morocco. Vincent was a finance and business consultant, and there was a job opening in his field. We grabbed the opportunity to travel and explore. Leaving the two boys we had at that time, ages five and three, with Vincent's parents in the village, we couldn't wait to fly across the Mediterranean Sea to discover this unknown country.

We fell in love. We fell in love with everything—the land, the people, the culture, the language, and the food. Everything. By the time we arrived back at Charles de Gaulle Airport in Paris two weeks later, we had already made up our minds. Morocco would be our next home.

In 2003, with only our two oldest boys in tow, ages seven and five, we moved to Morocco. It quickly became our home. The people, the neighbors, adopted us. Vincent worked for an American company selling electric transformer maintenance. I taught English to parents at the boys' school, as well as French and health to illiterate women in the local community center of our small, rural seaside town.

Vincent and I both studied Arabic intensively during our first two years in Morocco. Hearing the local Moroccan dialect, *Darija*, still makes my heart leap for joy. Savoring a bowl of chicken couscous, a plateful of *s'fa moudafouna*, a beef, prune, and grilled almond *tagine, cornes de gazelle*, and sweet mint tea . . . just thinking about these Moroccan delicacies still makes my mouth water.

"*Bledi*," I often say in Arabic, "My country."

When native speakers hear me speak Arabic, they know by my accent and my vocabulary where I've been, where I'm from.

"You're Moroccan," they always say.

Morocco is my country, my children's country, our family's country, our country.

We dreamed of one day retiring in Morocco, purchasing a small, simple home in the south, near the water. We wanted to live there forever. It was our home, our land... until one day.

Morocco was stolen from us.

In 2010, our company asked us to leave the land we love. We packed our bags, loaded up our van, and said our teary goodbyes to friends who had become like family. We knew it was time to go, and there would be no turning back, no coming back, no return. With broken hearts, our family crossed the border of Morocco into another land ... Spain.

We didn't stay long in Spain, only landing there a few weeks before driving on to France. The further we drove north, the further away we traveled from the land we loved—Morocco. As we looked back over the Mediterranean, its beauty, its welcome, slowly faded .. . until it disappeared completely into the horizon.

———*eee*———

Our hearts continued to long, continued to yearn, for that land, for those people. While living in France, working among immigrants and refugees from North Africa and the Middle East, we found a reprieve when we stumbled upon a *hanoute*—a Moroccan grocery store, when we strolled through the Arab market, when a Moroccan neighbor invited us to his home for tea and couscous, when our children brought their Moroccan friends home from school, when we ate at a favorite Moroccan restaurant, when we heard Arabic music blasting on the local radio, and when we spoke Arabic with our immigrant friends.

But the deep longing remained. Longing for Morocco, longing for *home*.

France would also not be our home forever. In 2017, another land began to call us, to woo us. It took us by surprise. We didn't understand why . . . why this new land? Was there something waiting for us there?

Spain.

The location was a surprise, but the move wasn't. We were nomads, after all, always loading up our camels, always on the move. Our family seemed to dance to a seven-year cadence. Seven years in Morocco, seven years in France. Perhaps things were getting too monotonous and familiar. Perhaps it was time for a change. Strangely, our family seemed to thrive on the thrill of transition and upheaval.

There was a new and exciting open door for us in Spain. Our organization was starting a project among immigrants and refugees. Multiple times a day, "dreamers" were arriving by boatload along the Mediterranean coastline. Men, women, and children who were looking, hoping for a better life. Just like us, they were people on the move—the diaspora—imagining a life that would be better on the other side of the border.

Unfortunately, our last two moves—from Morocco and France—had been painful, challenging, and unexpected. We were weary and wounded. At times, we considered throwing in the towel, wondering if perhaps our days of living abroad were over. Deep down inside, we longed for a better life—a land flowing with milk and honey, a place to settle and rest. Perhaps, like those dreamers, we were searching for El Dorado and didn't even realize it.

Our family loves Spain. During the past decades, it became our favorite vacation spot. While living in Morocco for seven years, we would often take the boat up north. We called it a "cruise," even though the ride across the Strait of Gibraltar from Tangiers to Algeciras lasted only forty-five minutes. It was long enough to get seasick on especially stormy days.

Likewise, while living in France, whenever the boys had school vacation, Spain always topped our list of destinations. Living in the south of France, we were only a few hours' drive from the border, and we didn't hesitate to cross.

Spain. We loved everything about the country—the climate, the language, the food, the people, the culture. The moment we crossed the border from Morocco or France, we knew we had arrived in Spain. Everything was different—the air, the colors, the fragrance. Our family couldn't wait to move there.

After a long wait, much patience, and a lot of preparation, we boarded the plane on June 1, 2019. Looking out across the Atlantic Ocean towards Spain, we expected warm weather, never-ending sunshine, a relaxed way of life, friendly people, fun language learning, and amazing paella. We got all that.

Immediately, our new life in Spain captivated our family. Compared to the stress and exhaustion of our last season in France, it felt like El Dorado—this ideal "dream" land, this better life.

But there was more waiting for us in Spain. There was the unexpected. One day, one phone call, one conversation, one invitation would change me forever.

Once I walked through the door, there was no leaving. Once I saw, once I knew, once I heard, once I felt . . . there was no turning back. I could no longer close my eyes, no longer forget, no longer plug my ears, no longer ignore. I could never remain silent.

CHAPTER TWO

HER MOROCCO

F rom the moment Habiba took her first breath, life was hard. She didn't stand a chance.

Born and raised in a poor, rural family in the south of Morocco in 1978, Habiba could never climb the ladder out of poverty and into a better life. For most Moroccans, poverty was a state that one must accept. There was no choice.

Unfortunately, Habiba's family wasn't the only poor family in Morocco. The statistics were astounding. Even though Morocco had made significant economic progress, half of the rural population still considered themselves poor. There were over four million people who lived on less than $4/day. Three million of those people lived in rural areas.[1]

That captured the perfect picture of Habiba's family—rural and poor.

───ele───

When I first met Habiba, I remembered her crying a lot when we asked about her family in Morocco.

Had something happened back in her homeland, something that was too raw and painful to talk about? Or perhaps she simply missed her family, missed her country. We didn't know what made her cry, what made those many tears fall.

The first time they called me in for translation, we met in the downstairs room of the safe house with the psychologist.

Paola* asked Habiba how she was doing, and her answers were filled with worry and fear about her family.

What was she afraid of? Did she fear for their safety? Their well-being? Did she wonder if they would have enough money to eat? Did she question what their future would hold?

The first day I met Habiba, I asked her if she had any children. When she told me about her son, I asked his age.

She shrugged and said, "I have no idea, maybe twenty."

When I heard "twenty," something slammed me hard in the pit of my stomach. My two oldest sons were nineteen and twenty-one. Habiba and I were roughly the same age, and we both had sons in their twenties.

I could be in Habiba's shoes.

Coming from the Western world, it might be shocking to think that Habiba didn't know her son's age. How could you forget when your own child was born? I can still remember the exact date, the exact hour, the exact minute, and the detailed events surrounding the births of my four boys. I could never forget.

Yet, Habiba did not know how old her one and only son was . . . Zacharia.*

In Morocco, it was common for people to not know their age or birthdate, especially those coming from rural, uneducated, and illiterate families. Perhaps the family simply didn't know the date on which the big event took place, or the family didn't understand the significance of birthdates and didn't think to recall the date. Maybe the family didn't have a means to record the date, through either written or oral form.

For national identity cards, passports, and driver's licenses, every person in Morocco has their birthdate clearly marked on the document. However, people often randomly choose a date, typically January 1. It's amazing how many Moroccans are born on the first day of the year.

When Habiba told me she didn't know her son's age, I was not surprised. I was only sad.

Habiba's husband—the father of her son—had died two years after Zacharia's birth. Based on Habiba's story, that would have been twenty years ago. Twenty years since her husband died, since she became a disgraced widow, since her son turned two. Twenty years since her level of poverty drastically increased.

Twenty years . . .

When Habiba was born forty-three years ago in that small Moroccan village, who would have known how her story would be written, how her life would unfold? Who would have known that forty-three years later she would live in Spain? No one knew. No one could have imagined. No one could have seen these parts of her life coming.

Although only separated from Spain by a small body of water, the Strait of Gibraltar, Habiba's dearly beloved Morocco now seemed long gone. From the city of Gibraltar on clear days, one can look across the sea to see the beautiful, faraway land of Morocco. That may be as close as Habiba would ever get to seeing her country again. She had made her choice to uproot from her homeland two years before, and now she could never go back.

Never.

—— *ele* ——

"How old were you when you got married?" I asked Habiba as she ate her *patatas fritas** on the terrace of the tapas bar.

"I have no idea. I don't know."

It was hard for me to fathom. How could I ever forget my wedding day? That beautiful celebration is forever etched in my mind. I remember the date, the hour, and the weather. I recall my age and the dress and shoes I wore. I could never forget.

But Habiba did. She could not even recall the age at which she became a bride.

"Were you young—fifteen, sixteen, seventeen?"

"Something like that. I don't know."

Whenever we went grocery shopping with Habiba, we noticed she couldn't count well. It made sense that she couldn't count the years of her life.

I wanted to ask Habiba about her life in Morocco before coming to Spain. It had been almost one year since I had met her. During our first meetings with the psychologist and the human rights lawyer, I listened to most of her story. However, Habiba shared very little about her life back in Morocco. When the lawyer asked her questions for the file, her answers were vague and distant.

"I can't tell you. I can't tell you," she repeated over and over again through her tears.

It was obviously too painful, too shameful.

Then one day was different. We weren't sitting in a meeting room with the director and the human rights lawyer. That day, we sat alone—just the two of us—next to a large fountain, under the shade of a tree, in the cool evening breeze.

I had picked up Habiba at 6 pm, knowing it would be cool enough for a short walk and a bite to eat. After a few minutes of strolling down the cobblestone streets in the still blazing Spanish sun, we found a tapas bar, where we stopped to have a drink and an evening snack.

"What was your husband's name?" I asked Habiba, hesitantly, unsure how sensitive she would be about sharing her past life. There was still a lot of pain there, and I didn't want to stir the pot.

"Abdelwahed."*

I smiled at the familiar name—it was common in Morocco.

"How long were you married?"

If she didn't remember her age for their wedding, perhaps she could tell me how long they were together before he died.

"I don't know. But, I know that it's been twenty years since Abdelwahed died."

Staring at my french fries, I tried to do the calculations quickly in my head as I listened to her story. The tapas bar began to get crowded. The cool evening air was enticing to all the locals.

After further questioning, Habiba continued to walk me through her story. As a young girl, she didn't want to get married. It was a forced marriage—common in Morocco.

"Did you ever love Abdelwahed? In all your years of marriage?"

"No," she said bluntly. "He beat me. He beat me a lot. I had to stay home and couldn't leave the house."

I reached across the table to touch her hand. My heart was ripping in two.

"I'm so sorry."

Habiba went on to explain to me that her husband had worked as a trashman. They lived in a small, simple house in a rural area with her sister-in-law. Habiba had wanted to take birth control pills, but her husband didn't allow it. After a year of marriage, Habiba became pregnant with their only son, Zacharia. Just after Zacharia turned two, Abdelwahed died suddenly.

"How did he die? Was he sick? Did he have an accident?"

"I don't know. The *j'nun*—evil spirits—attacked him. He smoked cigarettes, marijuana, and drank a lot."

Habiba fidgeted in her seat as she recounted the earlier years of her life, then took a sip of water.

Shortly after Abdelwahed died, his family members came to see Habiba at the house.

"Your husband is dead. Now you must leave," they told her.

Habiba had no choice. She escaped to her parents' home—faraway—and dropped off her son, not feeling capable of caring for him and working at the same time. She then traveled to a nearby coastal city looking for a job. Searching was hard, and it didn't last long. Picking up her son a few months later, Habiba returned to the rural area where she had lived with her husband in an isolated area in the countryside.

She described her home. "It wasn't really a house. It was made of dirt, with no furniture other than a few old mattresses on the floor for sleeping."

As I listened to Habiba's story, I realized her experience of Morocco was drastically different from my experience of living in her land. During our seven years in Morocco, our family lived in a nice house by the beach. We owned two vehicles, our boys went to private schools, and we had a local woman who helped us full-time with cooking and cleaning. Our days were filled with dipping our toes in the cool ocean water, basking in the sun's warmth, enjoying the savory local food, and living off the goodness of the land.

Habiba's Morocco story was different—vastly different. She was born and raised in the deep pit of poverty. From a distance, I had observed the poor, lived among the poor, and helped the poor. Yet, I could never fully understand what it was like to be one of them.

In desperation, Habiba had found what work she could—begging on the streets or making fresh pastries. She sold her fresh *m'simmons*, *b'rir*, *bataboute*, and *hersha* for two dirhams a piece. In her home, Habiba got up in the early morning hours to mix and knead the dough, wait for it to rise, bake the traditional treats, and then set off walking to the pastry shop to sell them at sunrise. Zacharia was always with her for those early morning deliveries.

Habiba worked other odd jobs, like cleaning houses and cooking for wealthier families. In Morocco, these are called *r'dema* and have a lower, almost shameful, status as a servant or slave in her culture. It did not matter to Habiba. She took any job she could find. They had no food to eat. They had nothing.

When I heard that Habiba had cleaned houses and cooked, I suddenly saw the faces and recalled the names of the women who had worked in our home in Morocco for many years—Fatna, Rabia, Amina . . .

Hearing the chattering voices around me woke me up to my new reality. I was now sitting in a tapas bar in Spain. I wasn't in Morocco. Those days were gone.

I looked across the table at Habiba, who brushed her dark hair off her forehead. She always wore her hair the same way, pulled back in a bun.

"Did you ever consider getting married again?" I asked her while we nibbled on our *patatas fritas*.

"No one wants to marry a widow with a child," she murmured, her gaze turned down towards the table. "There's so much I can't tell you about my life. We had so many problems. Zacharia was in jail for a while, but the village leader bailed him out."

She didn't want to tell me why her son went to jail, and I didn't pry.

In Morocco, Habiba had no life, no hope, nothing . . . until she heard about the beautiful strawberry fields in Spain. It did not take long for her to imagine her dream job in El Dorado.

"You came here to Spain to feed your family, didn't you?"

Rather than answer my question, she replied, "Do you know what the first thing I want is? I want a house. I want to build a home."

Habiba had never had a home of her own. She wanted a house— for her, for her son.

"Zacharia's House," she said, looking off in the distance with dreamy eyes.

When Habiba left for Spain, she took her son back to her parents in their village.

"Has it been hard for your parents to take care of Zacharia?"

"I try to send them money regularly to feed him."

I knew that Habiba's parents were poor. Living in a rural area, they most likely fell in the half of the Moroccan population who lived on less than $4/day.{1}

"Does your father still work?" I asked Habiba, wanting to know more of my friend's story.

She was silent and looked away uncomfortably.

"My father can't work anymore. He's too old. He was a beggar," she said quietly. I could hear the shame in her voice.

I reached across the table again and took her hand in mine.

"Your life was hard in Morocco."

"Yes."

"Thank you for trusting me and telling me your story. I'll carry it in my heart forever," I told her with tears in my eyes.

We sat in silence and cried for a few minutes.

I paid the bill for our half-eaten meal, and we headed back to the apartment.

"I'm starting to know you more, Habiba," I told her, with my arm draped gently around her shoulder. "You're my friend, and I want to know where you came from."

"You want to know my story."

I nodded and told her how much I loved her. I hugged her goodbye as I dropped her off. She entered the large wooden door leading up to the apartment.

No one on the streets of Spain knew who had just been among them. No one knew who she was. No one knew her name.

But I did. Her name was Habiba.

I was finally starting to fill in the missing puzzle pieces of Habiba's story. With each visit, I saw her life tapestry more clearly. I was beginning to know who she was.

"Yes, Habiba, I want to know your story. I want to tell the world your story," I whispered to myself as I made my way back to my car.

*patatas fritas—french fries

CHAPTER THREE

A WAY OUT

B orn into poverty. Trapped. Stuck. No way out.
Until . . . one day, Habiba heard about the strawberries . . . the strawberries in the fields of Spain.

Could it be her El Dorado? A way out of poverty? An open door to escape the devastating life into which she had been born?

I wonder what went through Habiba's mind when she first heard about the opportunity to pick strawberries in the fields of Spain. Did it sound like a dream come true, a long-awaited chance to buy that house she had always dreamed of?

There was no upfront investment, no cost to make the journey. It was an all-inclusive, all-paid trip to paradise. Upon her return from Spain to Morocco, they would require Habiba to pay back the cost of her passport, visa, and boat tickets. She did not know how much money she would make or how much she would have to pay back. Would she have any money left for her family?

Habiba didn't know. She didn't think about these things. She didn't ask questions.

Habiba wasn't the only one making the "dream trip" to El Dorado. There were others, other young women like her, chasing their dreams . . . their dreams of the other side, a better life, a brighter future. Perhaps it was possible to not have to live day-to-day, wondering if there would be enough food on their plates. Perhaps it was possible to have more than enough.

Yes, I wonder what went through Habiba's mind when she first heard about the strawberry fields of Spain.

Did she imagine what it would feel like to say goodbye to her parents and to her only son? Did she question if she would one day see them again or if it would be a final adieu? Did she imagine what it would feel like to board the boat and sail away from her homeland? Did she question if she would one day be able to return to the place of her birth? Did she imagine what it would feel like to leave her country, her culture, her religion, her language? Did she question if she would one day be able to find her roots again?

Did she count the costs?

I don't think so. I think she heard about a chance to feed her family, an opportunity to provide for their needs. I think she thought her choice would lead to a better life, a brighter tomorrow for her and for her family.

I don't think she thought beyond the present moment. I don't think she considered what could happen. I don't think she asked herself, "What if . . . ?" I don't think she pondered these things. I don't think she took time to reflect. I don't think she waited before deciding.

I think she said, "Yes!" without hesitation.

I can't imagine saying "yes." I can't imagine being so poor, so desperate, so hungry that I would be willing, be able to turn my back and walk away from it all. I struggled to hear her story and understand her decision.

Other girls, other women, were also talking about the strawberry fields of Spain. The El Dorado of their dreams was about to come true, if they would only say, "yes."

Habiba said "yes" that day.

I wonder what her parents and her son thought when she came home to tell them that she was leaving for Spain. Were they dreaming too, imagining a better life, a brighter future for their family? Were they hoping that Habiba would be their savior, the answer to their desires for more than enough?

Perhaps they put pressure on her to go, encouraging her to go to El Dorado and make money to send back to them for food and clothing. Perhaps they pushed her to get on that boat.

Or did they?

Perhaps they pleaded with her not to leave, begged her to stay, and feared what could happen on the other side of the sea.

Or did they?

With paperwork in hand—passport, visa, and a boat ticket—it was time to say goodbye. It was time to say goodbye to her family, time to say goodbye to Morocco.

How could she walk away? How could she? I listened, but my heart and body ached. I tried to imagine myself in her shoes. I couldn't.

⎯ℓℓ⎯

It was May 16, 2019, the first day of Ramadan—the thirty-day fast for Muslims around the world.

Habiba did not know what the other side of the sea looked like. She'd only seen pictures of Spain and parts of Europe on television.

It was another world, a foreign land, different from anything she had ever known.

Did she cry when she said goodbye to her parents, when she kissed her only child for the last time? Was there a knot in the pit of her stomach? Was her heart pounding?

Habiba told me she planned to leave for only six months. In her mind, it was a brief trip to Europe. She imagined carrying a stack of euro bills back home with her. Her earnings—although small in Spain—would go a long way in Morocco.

Her family would no longer be poor, no longer live in shame, no longer be trapped in misery. She would save them, rescue them. She would be the answer to their many prayers and pleas for help.

Habiba was the chosen one to go, the only one who could go, the open door to their better life and brighter future. Habiba would provide a way out. Habiba was on her way to El Dorado.

THE CROSSING

It's time to say goodbye.
Goodbye to those we love.

It's time to depart from our families.
Our families who have loved us.

It's time to leave everything behind.
Everything we've ever known.

It's time to board the boat.
The boat that carries us faraway.

It's time to cross over the sea.
The sea that will forever separate us.

It's time to imagine our new life.
The new life that we've always wanted.

It's time to leave poverty behind.
The poverty that has forever defined us.

It's time to look toward the future.
The future that will be as bright as the sun.

It's time to chase our dreams.
Our dreams that live in our hearts.

It's time to meet new friends.

New friends in foreign lands.

It's time to start our new work.
New work that now awaits us.

It's time to make some money.
Money that will provide for us.

It's time to pick strawberries.
Strawberries that will nourish us.

It's time for the crossing.
The crossing that will change us.

Yes, it's time for the crossing.
Yes, it's time for the crossing.

—ℓℓ—

Note to Reader: Throughout the telling of Habiba's story, I have included my own personal reflections. Poetry was often the only way I could process the sadness and brokenness of what I was experiencing as I journeyed alongside her.

CHAPTER FOUR

A FAUSTIAN BARGAIN

D id Habiba see beyond today? Could she see beyond today? Could she see she was making a Faustian Bargain?

"A deal in which one focuses on present gain without considering the long-term consequences."[1]

I had never heard of a Faustian Bargain until I read *Enrique's Journey: The Story of a Boy's Dangerous Odyssey to Reunite With His Mother* by Sonia Nazario. The book tells the journey of a young immigrant boy from Honduras, determined, at all costs, to find his mother who had abandoned him years before to follow her dream of El Dorado, just beyond the border.

In the opening remarks, Ted Conover described this book as "an empathetic glimpse into the Faustian Bargain made by immigrants who leave family behind for a bet on the rewards of life in the north."[2]

"What's a Faustian Bargain?" I thought to myself.

Curious, I began searching for the meaning and was intrigued by what I discovered. It comes from the medieval legend of Faust, who was said to have made a deal with the devil. In exchange for unlimited knowledge and worldly pleasures, he exchanged his very soul.

At first, I thought that described Habiba. But was it in exchange for world pleasures, or was it in exchange for survival?

What exactly convinced her to sacrifice everything, to leave everything—her son, her parents, her country? What drove her across the Mediterranean Sea to Spain? What did Habiba see beyond the water, that shiny dream she was chasing?

What was she running after that could be worth abandoning everything—everything she believed, everything she valued, everything she cherished, everything she loved? What did she long for that was more important than her family, her country, her culture, her religion, her dignity, her self-respect, her values, her person, and her identity?

Those were the questions I kept asking myself as I listened to more and more of her story. I couldn't grasp what could drive a woman to do this. I kept wondering, kept asking, kept searching, but I had no answers.

A Faustian Bargain, is that what happened to Habiba? Is that what happened to all the dreamers out there?

When Habiba first heard of the opportunity to leave Morocco to pick strawberries in the fields of Spain, did she consider the long-term consequences of her decision? Did she think about how it might affect her son and her parents? Was she aware of the potential legal ramifications of being an illegal immigrant in Europe? Did she think about the hard physical labor, what it would be like to bend over in the strawberry fields all day under the blazing summer Spanish sun? Did she think about the dangers, the risks she might face in this new land?

Could she see beyond her family's immediate need to eat, her family's poverty that stared her in the face day after day? Could she see beyond the few euros that she would make picking strawberries for six months?

A Faustian Bargain—"A deal in which one focuses on present gain without considering the long-term consequences."

As I read those words again and again, it suddenly made sense. For months, I had been struggling to understand, struggling to see how Habiba could have left, how she could have walked away from everything. When I understood the Faustian Bargain, it matched her story perfectly. On one hand, it brought me relief to understand. On the other hand , it uncovered more confusion and more sadness in my heart. There was obviously something greater, something deeper that propelled Habiba forward—forward into the dark abyss.

As I searched for more meaning, I soon realized that Habiba's focus on the present, not on the future, was cultural. For Habiba, this perspective and way of life were innate. When you live in poverty, you live day to day. It is hard to plan for tomorrow, or next week, or next month. You don't know if you will survive today. You don't know if you will have enough food to sustain you . . . today. You don't plan, or project, or look forward. You just live in the present. You live today.

I can remember, during our years in Morocco, having conversations with our local friends about the future. Up on the hilltop, near the neighborhood where our family lived, there was an old rundown shantytown. The small houses were made of grey cement bricks with silver tin roofs. Each house had a small courtyard where the chickens ran wildly. They were simple homes, usually comprising a small living room, a separate bedroom, and a little kitchen. We called these clusters of homes *douars* in Moroccan Arabic.

Our neighborhood was in full-blown development, and the government and construction companies were bulldozing down all the *douars*. They were making room for more fancy houses, for more people with money.

Many of our Moroccan friends had lived in their *douar* for years, for decades. For many, it had been home for generations. We knew the bulldozer was coming for our friends and their homes. They knew it was coming. Every time we went to their home to visit and have a glass of hot mint tea, we always asked what their plans were.

"Where will you go when the government official shows up at your door and tells you to leave? Where will you live? What will you do with all your belongings? How will you build a new home? How will you pay for a new place to live? How can you begin saving money now before they kick you out of your house?"

These seemed like logical questions for us to ask ourselves as Westerners. In our culture, we plan, wanting to be prepared for what is coming. However, for our local friends, who only lived in the present moment, these questions seemed unnecessary and meaningless. They lived day to day, with little regard for tomorrow and the future beyond. They were existing and surviving in the moment. Our friends never had answers to our questions about their future—their family's future. They simply received each day, with its potential bad news, as it came.

Hearing this perspective on life disturbed me back in Morocco, and now it was disturbing me again in Spain. How could people not plan for tomorrow, if not for themselves, at least for their family, their children? I wanted to respect that people of other cultures had different views on life, but this lack of forward thinking and future planning made absolutely no sense to me then. It makes no sense to me now.

Habiba's story was exactly the same. I always hate to lump all the people of one nation and culture together. However, the crossover and the similarity were striking. When they offered Habiba an opportunity to leave for Spain to pick strawberries in the fields, she most likely didn't see beyond the immediate, promised salary that she could provide for her son and her parents. She could see only today. That is what called her from the other side of the sea—a means to survive. It was money, provision, and food that beckoned her to cross over. Those were the "rewards of life in the north."

A Faustian Bargain can also be called "a deal with the devil," "the selling of one's soul," or "an agreement in which a person abandons his or her spiritual values or moral principles in order to obtain knowledge, wealth, or some other benefits."

Habiba didn't realize it then, but she had just struck a Faustian Bargain. With whom? With the devil—the enemy of her soul—or with herself?

The day Habiba left Morocco, she agreed to abandon everything. What she didn't realize at the time was she was even abandoning her values—spiritual, moral, and cultural. The life to which she would be exposed in Spain would eventually drag all of her core beliefs through the mud.

Habiba, born and raised as a Muslim woman, would abandon her Islamic faith and belief in God on this journey ahead. All moral, spiritual, and cultural values of purity and modesty would be trampled underfoot. Habiba's cultural values as an Arab woman to honor and respect her family would be neglected, as she turned her back on her son and her parents and walked away.

Habiba didn't realize what she was getting into or where she was going, but there was no turning back once the deal was made.

CHAPTER FIVE

THE STRAWBERRY FIELDS

H abiba and the other women boarded the large ferry boat in Tangiers, Morocco, and set sail across the Mediterranean Sea. Habiba was nervous as she watched a number of women on board presenting false documents to the authorities and getting arrested.

Habiba wondered if her papers were legal. She did not know.

After a forty-five-minute ride, the ferry boat arrived on the southern coast of Spain in the port city of Algeciras. A nameless man greeted Habiba and the other women, then put them on a bus to the city of Palos de la Frontera. It was nearly a three-hour drive.

Habiba couldn't speak a word of Spanish; neither could the other women. They were lost in the unknown language that swirled about them. They just followed and blindly obeyed.

Most of these Moroccan women and girls couldn't read and write. And even if they had been literate in the Arabic language, the Spanish road signs—written from left to right—would have looked foreign and backwards to them.

Habiba and the other women were vulnerable, naïve, innocent, ignorant.

Where were they going? Where were the promised strawberry fields?

Their Spanish boss greeted them when they arrived. Habiba described Ricardo as a nice older man with a fat stomach. His kindness and care for them crossed language barriers. The women ate well and had a decent place to rest their heads at night. They all slept together on the floor in a large shared room.

Ricardo seemed honest and innocent, with no ulterior motives. It was summer, harvest time, and he needed a lot of extra hands and cheap labor for his strawberry picking season. Through his extensive network in Morocco, he could quickly and easily hire foreign women and girls to do the hard work for a few months. He probably did this every year. Ricardo hired the "Strawberry Girls" from Morocco.

Few local Spanish women or young girls would accept a job picking strawberries in the fields—too much hard work for too little pay. That grueling, physical labor was known as "slave work" for illegal immigrants. Most of the women working daily with Habiba in the strawberry fields were from Morocco and Romania. Thankfully, the Moroccan women didn't have any language or cultural barriers between them. They were united, like a family.

Habiba wasn't young, though. She was forty-one years old, and leaning over all day at the waist to pick strawberries off the ground was horribly intense physical labor. It didn't take long for her back to feel like it was shredding in two. The scorching Spanish heat in the middle of summer was unbearable.

Habiba didn't complain. Being a strong, resilient woman meant suffering and sacrificing, not for herself, but for her family back in North Africa. There was nothing she wouldn't do to help them, to provide for their needs.

Ricardo regularly gave them money to send back to their families —money they had worked hard to earn. When the months of strawberry picking were over, there was one logical assumption, one clear understanding, one clear agreement with Ricardo. These women would leave his fields, leave his country, and return to their homeland in Morocco.

The story seemed simple and straightforward.

That is, until only two weeks after arriving, one of the Moroccan women asked Habiba if she wanted to leave the strawberry fields for a better place, a better job, a better life. The woman told her, "You've got nothing in Morocco. You've got nothing waiting for you back there. You've got nothing to send back to your family."

The woman's words rang true in Habiba's heart. She was right. What did she have to show for all those long, hot hours bent over picking strawberries? She was sending her family what little money she was making, but maybe there was more out there? Maybe the grass truly was greener on the other side. And, it was true, Habiba had nothing to go back to in Morocco. Why would she want to return to her life of shame and poverty?

The woman told Habiba that she knew a Moroccan man who could provide legal papers for her to stay in Spain long term. She wouldn't have to return to Morocco when the six months were over. This man would provide a good salary for her, so she could continue to send money back to her family.

When Habiba heard the woman's story, she was filled with hope that maybe her dream could come true after all. Maybe she *would* reach El Dorado. She felt nervous about leaving the strawberry fields, but when she heard this man was Moroccan, she was reassured. Surely she could trust him. After all, he was one of her own—a brother, like family.

This man promised her everything. This man promised her a way out—a way out of poverty, a way out of the strawberry fields.

Lots of promises . . .

Ricardo did not seem to know that another man had arrived on the scene. He was oblivious to the man luring his workers off his land and away from his strawberry fields.

As Habiba shared the story, she seemed sad.

"We didn't even tell Ricardo goodbye. We fled in the night."

No one knows for certain the identity of the woman who enticed Habiba and the other women to leave the strawberry fields. Perhaps she was paid to work in the agricultural industry so she could meet the new girls, gain their trust, and then lure them away. Perhaps she was part of a larger network recruiting women from Morocco into another line of work.

Habiba wasn't the only one invited that day to leave the strawberry fields for a better life. They promised four other Moroccan women the same things. They all believed the story they were told and agreed to go with the strange Moroccan man. Each of them paid him fifty euros to set them up with a good job, a nice place to live, and Spanish residence papers. The arrangements were made quickly, and they fled in the night. None of them had any idea where they were going. They innocently believed the woman and trusted the man.

Upon entering the car, the man confiscated their telephones and hid them in one of the seat cushions. They drove to a certain location and then changed vehicles before continuing on their way. At one point, the police stopped them and motioned for them to pull the car to the side of the road. Habiba shuddered. Terrifying thoughts flooded her mind of what could happen if the police caught them. The fearful women whispered to each other in the backseat.

"Don't speak! I'm the only one who will speak!" the man commanded them frantically.

He then assigned roles to each of them—his fiancée, his sister, and his sister's friends. Habiba was "his fiancée." Being that they were all Moroccan, the story was believable. The police asked the man for his papers and asked who the women were. Habiba held her breath.

"She's my fiancée. She's my sister, and they're her friends," he said.

The officer waved them on. Habiba sighed, her heart still pounding in her head and in her chest. Sweat beads dripped from her brow. The four women looked at each other nervously, communicating silent words of fear.

Several hours later, in the early morning hours, they finally arrived at their destination. Habiba did not know where they were. The man dropped her off at a house—the "nice place to live" he had promised. She felt relieved to finally get out of the car and step into the new life that awaited her. She could feel hope and excitement rising. The man told her she would be cared for by the Moroccan woman there. Her name was "Madame."

CHAPTER SIX

DRINK, DON'T FEEL

"I had no light," Habiba told me as we sat at the table in a church. The safe house director and the human rights lawyer sat opposite us.

"I had no light," she repeated. "They made me stay in the dark all day and all night."

Habiba was shaking as she spoke, tears streaming down her face.

"I kept asking for a lightbulb, but they wouldn't give me one."

I reached across the table to touch her hand and give her a tissue.

"You must have been so scared."

She nodded. I could see terror in her eyes.

Madame was a Moroccan who always wore a veil on her head, tightly covering her hair, like many of the women in her homeland.

"She was mean. She yelled at us all the time. I don't like women who wear veils anymore."

Once again, I saw that fear in Habiba's eyes as she described the woman.

"Drink, drink, drink, so you don't feel," Madame told her over and over.

Food was scarce, but alcohol and drugs were plentiful. Men often hung out in the living room smoking marijuana.

"Drink, drink, drink, so you don't feel," Madame told her over and over.

"So I wouldn't feel anything when I was with the men," Habiba explained to us.

Tears filled my eyes. I squeezed her hand gently.

"Go out into the street, go to the bar next door, have sex with the men, and bring me back the money," Madame demanded.

The scene she described was horrendous—every day, seven days a week.

"Sundays were the busiest days," Habiba told us. "The bar next door was full of men."

"Sundays," I thought to myself. "That's the day I go to church with my husband and my children. It's a special day, a family day, a holy day."

The human rights lawyer wrote frantically in her small orange leather notebook, documenting the information to build her case for sexual exploitation.

"How many men would you see in one day?" the lawyer asked.

"It was different every day. There were regulars, and there were men I would only see once."

Five, six, seven, eight, nine, ten . . . the numbers were alarming. How was it possible for one woman to have intercourse with that many men in one day?

I gasped inside, maybe out loud. I don't know. My heart felt sick. I thought I might vomit. Anger and rage rose violently inside me. I wanted to scream, "Stop! Don't say anymore! Stop!"

I felt stunned, powerless.

"How much money would each man give you?" the lawyer asked.

"It depended on how long I was with them. For something quick, five euros. Others would give ten, fifteen, twenty."

My fingers touched my lips to hold back my shock and sickness.

To prove that this woman was running a sex trafficking business, the lawyer needed more information.

"How much of your money from sex did you have to give to Madame?" she asked.

"Most of it. I never had much left."

As she talked about the amount of money, she gave the figures in Moroccan dirhams, not in euros.

To make sure that we were all understanding the amounts correctly, I asked the safe house director for a piece of paper.

I drew pictures of tiny rectangles representing euro bills. It grieved me to draw the images, as tears welled up in my eyes. I didn't have the courage to look at Habiba, feeling the rumbling of an outburst brewing in my heart. We counted out loud as she described the average day, each man giving her a certain amount of money—five, ten, fifteen, twenty euros. Habiba grabbed the pen from my hand and quickly began drawing more and more rectangles. Together, we counted and added up the bills one by one.

Habiba could vividly remember receiving the money from the men. She could remember feeling the dirty bills in her hands and the numbers written on the face of each one. Even if she didn't understand euros and the exchange rate between the local currency and her familiar Moroccan dirhams, she remembered.

She remembered everything.

Together, we counted out loud the amount of money and the amount of men represented on that little piece of white notebook paper.

With each increasing number, a tear fell.

Habiba then counted the amount of the bills that would go to Madame. Habiba saw very little of her hard-earned money. She had to pay for her room and board . . . with sex. She had to pay for her pitch-black bedroom with no lightbulb . . . with sex.

Habiba then told us another story about a "regular" she would often see. He would take her to the local grocery store, where she could pick out and buy whatever she wanted—in exchange for sex. This man never gave her money, but he fed her well.

There were other Moroccan women living in the house with Habiba. They were all treated the same way.

"Drink, drink, drink, so you don't feel," Madame told them over and over.

It is well known that drinking and drugs are common in brothels. Sometimes, women are required to take a "happy drug." Men prefer women who smile and appear to be enjoying the sexual act, rather than those who look and act miserable, in pain and agony.

Habiba drank to survive, to numb the overwhelming pain. A woman of conservative Muslim background, in which alcohol and drugs are considered *haram** and of the devil, laid down her religious values and beliefs in an act of self-protection. In order to survive emotionally, Habiba had no choice but to drink.

Maybe that was better.

Wouldn't it be best not to feel, best not to feel what those men were doing to you, best not to feel what was happening to your body, best not to feel your emotions—your sadness, your shame, your disgust, your fear, your anxiety, your pain?

Wouldn't it be best not to feel, not to feel anything at all?

Habiba had most likely never had a sip of alcohol in her life before she arrived at that brothel in the south of Spain. Now, Habiba didn't care. She followed Madame's orders and began drinking—a lot.

Habiba didn't want to feel.

haram—sinful

CHAPTER SEVEN

MAFIA TERROR

"She's seen death," I translated in English for the safe house director and the human rights lawyer. "This woman has seen death."

My heart raced, and I felt a knot growing in the pit of my stomach as I listened intently to Habiba's story.

"I can't tell you. I can't tell you. I've seen horrible things. I can't tell you. I can't tell you," Habiba repeated, with a trembling voice. That all-too-familiar terror invaded her eyes.

I reached over and placed my hand on top of hers on the table, trying to connect.

"You're safe here, Habiba," I told her reassuringly. "They can't hurt you."

"I can't tell you," she continued. "They'll kill me."

I turned to the other women at the table and translated.

"She's scared. She's afraid to talk," I told them.

"They're all afraid to talk. It's the Mafia," the lawyer said. "They make sure they won't talk."

Habiba described two tall, heavyset men who arrived in a big, fancy car in front of the house. She was terrified of them.

"They took one of the women, one of my friends," she said in tears, her voice shaking. "She never came back. I don't know what happened to her, but I never saw her again."

I squeezed her hand gently to comfort her somehow. I felt impotent and sick to my stomach.

"I think they killed her," she said.

As I listened to her story, my heart and my head were pounding. I felt scared—scared for Habiba, scared for all those women who still lived in that brothel.

I also wondered about that woman they took away, that woman who never came back. Where did they take her, and what did they do to her? What had she done that had angered them? Did she seek help or try to run away?

The lawyer asked me to continue questioning Habiba about what had happened and what she had seen. I translated the questions in Arabic.

"I can't tell you. I can't tell you. I can't tell you. It's too horrible to tell. Please don't make me tell," Habiba pleaded over and over.

"She's seen death," I translated again in English for the other two women at the table. "This woman has seen death."

It was too much for Habiba. It was too much for me.

Pale and nauseous, Habiba looked down at the shredded white tissue in her hands.

"I think she might pass out," I told the other women. "We have to stop for today. It's too much, too much."

I wanted to scream at the top of my lungs, "Enough! Enough! Stop!" I couldn't bear to hear another word.

The lawyer closed her orange leather notebook. I felt relief flood my body, relief that the story was over, the book was closed . . . at least for today.

We got Habiba a glass of water and gathered around her. We hugged her and asked if we could pray for her. There was nothing else we could do. Only God could comfort her and bring her peace in the midst of so much trauma and suffering.

I prayed for her in Arabic, and the safe house director prayed in Spanish. Afterwards, Habiba tried to stand, but she almost collapsed into our arms. Her body was weak.

"She's sick with grief," I told the other two women. It was as if the pain and brokenness of her soul had overtaken her.

As Habiba was unable to walk, we all sat back down and waited with her for a few minutes at the table. Several of us cradled her hands in ours. When she was finally ready, she stood up, and we slowly made our way to the car.

We had been meeting in a room at a local church. Because we were getting to a tough place in Habiba's story, the lawyer felt it was best to go to a neutral location. Without the other women around from the safe house, Habiba would be more comfortable talking, unafraid that others might overhear. They didn't trust each other. They didn't trust anyone.

How do they ever trust again when they have been betrayed and broken by so many?

Habiba's story of horror is common in Spain, perhaps even common at a global level. It made me shudder to think of all the other women living in this extreme terror around the world.

Fear. They live in daily fear.

A few months after hearing Habiba's story, I was called to a different safe house to translate for another rescued Moroccan woman.

From the street, the apartment complex appeared discreet and simple. No one would have known it was a safe house for women. As I walked through the entryway and climbed the stairs, I trembled in fear and dread.

"We can't understand her story," the director had told me on the phone. "Can you come and listen to her? We need to understand what happened."

I had already heard about this woman. Some colleagues in the south of Spain were involved in her initial rescue.

"It's one of the most horrific stories we've heard," my teammate wrote in a text. "And we've heard a lot of horrible stories."

Was I prepared, ready to hear another story of pain, darkness, torture, and death? Did I want to go, want to hear, want to know? Wasn't Habiba's story enough? Did I have to listen to another woman's trauma?

I had no choice but to go. I knew God was calling me. There was no one else.

As I approached the door of the apartment, I prayed for strength, wisdom, and the ability to understand Arabic beyond my human abilities. I asked God to shield me emotionally and to be by my side. I felt His presence. It often came as a strange peace amid my fears and the unknown beyond the door.

I walked into the office of the safe house and saw her. She wore a tight, sleeveless dress that was cut high above her thighs, probably one of the dresses she wore on the streets. I walked over to her and kissed her—Moroccan style—on the cheeks, her right and then her left. It surprised her to hear me speaking her mother tongue, *Darija*. She smiled timidly, her gaze lowered.

The black-haired woman sat on the desk chair, and I sat down on the couch in front of her. The human rights lawyer sat next to her in another chair. I attempted to make small talk with the woman, trying to make her feel comfortable with me. She didn't know me at all, and she was going to have to tell me her story—her dark, painful story.

Did she trust me—a perfect stranger? Probably not.

As we started to talk, there was a knock at the office door. A young boy walked in and approached the woman.

"Is this your son?" I asked.

She nodded.

"What's his name? How old is he?"

She told me the name of her five-year-old son. I greeted him in Arabic and smiled. Another worker from the safe house came in and asked if she could take him to the park. When they left, I continued translating the words of the human rights lawyer.

"Do you want to turn in those who hurt you?" I asked her. "The police and government here in Spain will protect you."

The woman cried, "I can't. I can't. I can't."

I leaned over and placed my hand on top of hers.

"They'll kill me," she said, motioning with her hand a knife cutting her throat. "They'll kill me, like they did the other women."

I could see, hear, and feel her terror. It filled her eyes. I shuddered when our eyes locked for a moment.

"One woman they cut into tiny pieces."

I closed my eyes. I didn't want to see anymore. I didn't want to hear anymore. I didn't want to know anymore. I didn't want to feel anymore.

I translated for the human rights lawyer what the woman had seen.

The lawyer understood. She knew. This woman would never tell. Her story was all too common. The sex trafficking Mafia in Spain made sure that women wouldn't tell the deep, dark secrets of the trade.

It didn't matter how convincing the lawyer was. It didn't matter how much the lawyer could reassure this woman of police protection for her and her son if she turned in her traffickers. This woman wouldn't tell. She was scared to death.

"I want to get my daughter to Spain with me," she continued with her story. "She's back in Morocco, and I want her to come here with me."

Her three-year-old daughter was living with her parents. She hadn't seen her in two years, since she had left home.

"How old are you?" I asked her. She looked so young, yet she had two children, ages three and five.

"I'm twenty-one."

My heart sank. I felt like someone had stabbed me in the chest. That was the age of my oldest son. How was it possible that this young woman already had two children and had seen such horror in her short life? It suddenly occurred to me that her five-year-old son had probably witnessed the same atrocities. He would be marked for life. It crushed me to think of the consequences of that kind of trauma in the mind of a little boy. Tears welled in my eyes, and I couldn't hold them back.

I didn't.

The human rights lawyer explained to this woman that if she didn't turn in her perpetrators, it could take up to three years before she would receive her legal residence papers for Spain. Only then would they allow her to live and work legally and bring her daughter from Morocco.

"You can think about what you want to do," the lawyer told her gently, but I knew she was discouraged. I could hear sympathy and compassion in her voice. However, this woman's story was the same as the other thousand she had heard that year, and the lawyer knew it was unlikely that this victimized woman would turn in her perpetrators.

This woman and her five-year-old son were being transferred to another safe house in the city that same night. I would never see them again. I would never know the next chapters of their life and the end of their story.

But, one thing I knew, this woman—just like Habiba—had lived a nightmare. It wasn't a horror movie; it was real-life terror, and it still had a powerful grip on their hearts, minds, and souls.

ALL FOR THIS?

All for this?
Did I give it up all for this?
Did I really give up everything for this?

Did I really give up my family,
My parents, my son?
All for this?

Did I really give up my country,
My language, my culture?
All for this?

Did I really give up my tragic life
In North Africa?
All for this?

Did I really trade my broken life
For another broken life?
All for this?

Surely there is more,
More than this broken life,
I now hold in my hands.

Surely there is more,
More than the sadness and suffering,
I now hold in my heart.

Surely there is more,
More than the vivid memories,
I now hold in my mind.

Surely there is more,
More than the pain and abuse,
I now hold in my body.

Surely there is more,
More than the strawberry fields,
More than the darkness and men.

Surely there is more,
More to my life than this,
More to my story than this.

All for this?
Did I give it up all for this?
Did I really give up everything for this?
All for this?

PART TWO

Her Rescue

CHAPTER EIGHT

KNOCK AT THE DOOR

There was a knock at the door that sounded like hope . . . sounded like freedom.

From time to time, a Spanish woman and a Moroccan woman visited Habiba's house, bringing bags and boxes of donated food from their nonprofit organization. Habiba especially remembered all the cartons of milk they carried through the door.

The two women were always kind and joyful, a refreshing change from the people with whom Habiba usually interacted. She didn't know why, but she liked these two women. She felt safe and comfortable with them.

"Don't you have a light?" one woman asked Habiba as she showed them her small bedroom. There was a tiny window in her bedroom with covered glass panes. No light could enter.

"No, they won't give me a lightbulb."

Suddenly, Habiba had an overwhelming desire to tell the women her story. Madame was not home, so she discreetly slipped them a piece of paper with her cell phone number and told them to call her if they could find her a safe place to stay.

Habiba didn't have to say much. These women knew. They knew exactly what was going on behind those closed doors.

Their nonprofit organization, along with several others, worked in the neighborhood. Habiba described prostitutes, women selling their bodies, day and night, lining the streets day after day. The local bars were full of men looking for sexual pleasure, and nearly every house, every room, every apartment in that neighborhood was a secret brothel.

"The police were always there too," Habiba told me. "They all knew what was going on, but they didn't stop them. They couldn't."

Those two women knew they were walking into a brothel to deliver food and milk. They knew that the women they crossed paths with in the kitchen were used, abused, trafficked, and exploited. They knew that there were women inside that house who needed to be rescued.

When they saw Habiba's small, dark room, when they saw her grief-stricken face, when they saw her worn-out body . . . they knew. When Habiba told them her story and slipped them her phone number, they knew. This Moroccan woman needed out. She needed out quickly.

Habiba didn't know if she should trust them, especially the Moroccan woman. What if they told Madame? What if they were a part of the same group, the same Mafia? Maybe one day, they would take her away too—never to return, like her friend.

But something deep inside of Habiba saw light, hope, love, and salvation in these women. Habiba's life was miserable and destitute. She didn't see any way out. These two women might be her only chance, her only hope, her only bridge to freedom.

A few days later, Habiba received a phone call. The woman's voice on the other end of the line told her they had found a safe place for her. She needed to meet them at a certain location, at a certain time.

Habiba thought quickly and pretended to be talking to an acquaintance. "Let's meet together. I'll see you soon," she said cheerfully and calmly.

She walked out the door of the brothel that day, knowing that she would never return, but unsure if she was walking into freedom or another deadly trap. Habiba walked as fast as she could to the meeting place, constantly looking behind her. She found the two familiar women waiting for her next to a car. Habiba still didn't know if she could trust these women. She was taking an enormous risk. She opened the door and got into the car. There was a pregnant woman behind the steering wheel who smiled and seemed harmless.

"She'll take you to a safe place," the woman told her. "Don't be afraid. She'll take care of you."

They drove for hours. Habiba did not know where she was going. She just had to hope and trust. Upon arriving in a large city, she was taken to a house and greeted by a friendly woman with blonde hair. She welcomed her and told her she would be safe.

"But *will* I be safe?" Habiba thought to herself. "That's what I was told when I trusted the man who took me from the strawberry fields. Is this woman another Madame?"

Habiba entered the house with only the clothes on her back. She was scared. She didn't know the women who were there, lounging on the couches in the living room, sitting at the large wooden dining table.

"Where am I? Who are these women? Am I in another brothel? Are these women prostitutes like me? They don't look like prostitutes."

The blonde woman introduced her to the other women at the house. They were all from different countries. They welcomed her and smiled, then led her to her new bedroom.

The first thing Habiba noticed was the light. Her bedroom had a large window, and the sunshine beamed through the sheer white curtains. In the center of the room, just over the bunk beds, was a simple light fixture. She looked up and could see the lightbulb shining inside, giving radiance to the entire space. Another small lamp sat on the desk in front of the window.

There was light in her new bedroom—lots of light.

Habiba felt a peace, a warmth, a safety like she had never known.

There was light.

Habiba was still scared, but she continued to trust and to hope.

That evening, she sat in her bedroom on the desk chair, in a state of shock. Just the night before, she had been in the streets, in the bars, and in the beds of multiple men. She had slept very little that night.

It was only that morning that she had received the call from the women of the organization. Now, just hours later, she was in a new house, a new bedroom, with new women.

She felt disoriented and lost. Where was she exactly, and who were these people? Why would they take care of her? They didn't even know her. Could she trust them?

Exhausted after a long day of driving and wondering, she joined the women for dinner that evening. Hesitant, she spoke little. The women were kind and asked her a few questions. She was afraid to answer, afraid to tell the truth. So, she didn't. What if they told someone?

After dinner, the blonde-haired woman who seemed in charge gave her some pajamas and some toiletries—a towel, soap, a toothbrush, and toothpaste. Habiba went to her bedroom, changed into her new pajamas, brushed her teeth, and then crawled into the lower bunk bed. The flowered sheets were soft, warm, and cozy.

She kept the light on. She didn't want to turn it off. She didn't want to be in the dark again.

OVERWHELMING LOVE

It was a shift . . . a radical shift.
From darkness to light.
From abuse to care.
From force to choice.
From sex to affection.
From giving to receiving.
From fear to peace.
From isolation to community.
From men to women.
From nothing to everything.
From starvation to abundance.
From cruelty to kindness.
From abandonment to welcome.
From numbness to feeling.
From hurt to help.
From rejecting to accepting.
From shame to honor.
From dirty to clean.
From rundown to modern.
From messy to organized.
From wickedness to holiness.
From black to white.
From mourning to dancing.
From sadness to happiness.
From depression to joy.
From loneliness to family.
From curse to blessing.

From hate to love.
It was love . . . overwhelming love.
She had never experienced this before.
It felt heavy, suffocating.
She didn't know what to do with it.
It felt foreign, awkward.
She wasn't sure if she wanted it.
Yes, she wanted it.
Yes, she needed it.
Yes, she accepted it.
Overwhelming love.

CHAPTER NINE

HOW COULD I SAY NO?

A knock on my door was coming too—unexpected, inviting, irresistible.

Upon arriving in Spain, we explored our town; visited the outdoor market near our house on Wednesday mornings; enjoyed tasting local foods like tapas, paella, churros and chocolate; had fun learning Spanish; and got to know our new neighbors and work colleagues.

September arrived, and our family quickly found ourselves pulled into the hustle and bustle of school runs for the kids several times a day, as well as to and from daily soccer practices in the city. We were also working and studying Spanish several times a week. Life and the stress of our transition overwhelmed us.

It didn't take us long to get to know some parents at our boys' school. One day, they invited us to have coffee in one of their homes. It was nice to be with a larger American expat community. It felt comforting, like home.

Upon leaving, one mother approached me. "You used to live in Morocco, didn't you? Do you speak Arabic?"

"Yes, I love Arabic. Our family lived there for seven years. We didn't want to leave."

My heart and mind quickly scanned memories, reminiscing back to our sudden departure from the land we love. I felt robbed, the life we loved stolen from us. Even today, hearing the word "Morocco," fills me with sadness and longing, right alongside joy. Our family still loves everything about that place. I was lost in my thoughts while the woman continued talking.

"I volunteer at a safe house in the city, working with rescued victims of sex trafficking. There are several Moroccan women there who can't speak Spanish. Would you like to come with me one day and meet them?"

I got into the car with my husband and told him about the conversation.

"I'm not sure if I'm ready to dive in. We just arrived. I need to get settled, help the kids get adjusted, and learn Spanish."

Life was full, and I was in no hurry to get busy with volunteer work—especially in sex trafficking. I love Morocco. I love Moroccans. I love speaking Arabic. It was all quite tempting. I missed that country, those people, that language. Even so, it didn't seem like the right timing, maybe not even the right fit. I'd heard about human trafficking, and it honestly sounded terrifying. It seemed to be the new buzz around the world, but I knew absolutely nothing about it.

A few weeks later, she contacted me again. There was a need. The safe house had just rescued a Moroccan woman who couldn't speak a word of Spanish. Could I help with translation with the psychologist of the safe house? I'd always heard that a need doesn't constitute a call. I had wisely followed that advice throughout the years. My habit was to always ask God for a clear open door and confirmation before saying yes to something and committing for the long-term.

When I got the call, I didn't sense a no. I also didn't hear a clear yes. How could I say no? There was a need. There was a need I could fill. These poor Moroccan women couldn't tell their stories. No one could understand them, hear them, listen to them, feel their pain, walk beside them. No one should have their story stuck inside of them, with no place to let it out, no place to release it. For these women, there was a major barrier—a language barrier. Perhaps I could be a bridge—a translation bridge.

I told them I was willing to visit the safe house, meet the women, and see how things went. It was a test—for me. I would try it and see what happened, but I would not commit to anything. Humanitarian work is draining. It had worn me out for over fifteen years—in Morocco and in France—and I didn't even realize it. Painful circumstances and tragic situations had ripped our family out of both beloved places that we had called home. We were uprooted overnight from the lands, the people, the cultures, the languages that we loved. That included our work among refugees and immigrants.

Now that we'd been out of humanitarian aid work for two years, I honestly wasn't sure if I ever wanted to return. Our family was just beginning to find peace and stability again after several years of transition and chaos. The last thing I wanted to do was disrupt that and be pulled away from my newly found El Dorado. That was what my human mind, my logic, told me. My heart, my soul, however, spoke a different message. My heart felt a tug, a pull, an attraction. It was as if something higher, something greater, was inviting me. Even if I wanted to say no, I couldn't.

"Sure, I'll come," I replied on the phone. "I'll come and help with Arabic."

I couldn't say no, so I didn't.

CHAPTER TEN

YOU SPEAK MY LANGUAGE

"I 'm just going to check it out," I told my husband, feeling torn inside. I was curious and wanted to know what a safe house was. However, I wasn't sure if I wanted to walk through those doors.

That morning, I prayed silently, "God, please give me a sign if you want me to invest my time and energy into this work right now. Make things really clear. I will only say yes if you want me to."

Meeting up with three other American volunteers, we drove into the city together. It was a long drive, allowing me plenty of time to think. What was I getting into? Did I want to walk through that door? What would I find on the other side? Who would I find on the other side? Was I ready? I felt ill-equipped, with no training in trauma and sex trafficking. Perhaps nothing could have prepared me.

When we walked through the door of the safe house that morning, we went straight to the director's office.

"You're a miracle, an answer to prayer," the director told me. "Our team has been praying for months that God would send us a woman —a Christian woman who speaks Arabic—to help us with the Moroccan women we rescue."

When I heard the director's words, I could not believe my ears. I could vividly remember how we had felt God clearly leading our family to this city for several years. After much prayer, our family felt an even stronger confirmation. We had shared with the leaders of our organization how we sensed God directing us. Up to this point in our faith journey, God had always made the location of our work and lives clear. We sensed strongly that He was doing that again, but we didn't know why.

Why this country? Why this city? A French-American family, fluent in Arabic, moving to Spain. In human logic, it made absolutely no sense.

The safe house director's words that morning confirmed in my heart that we had not misunderstood God's leading to move to Spain. He was also answering my prayer from that morning. Perhaps this was the right time for me to invest my heart—my entire being —into humanitarian work again.

We walked out of the director's office and into the living room. Six women sat at the dining room table making jewelry—stringing charms on bracelets and attaching clasps to necklaces. We greeted them, and the women responded with timid smiles. I followed the lead of the other American volunteers who had lived in Spain for quite a few years. They knew what to do culturally. We all introduced ourselves and went around the room kissing each other on the cheeks—Spanish style.

I'm not sure what I expected to find on the other side of the door that day, but I had been wondering . . .

What does a safe house look like? What do the women look like— these women off the streets? How will I feel? Strange, uncomfortable? How will I perceive them? How will they see me? What will I say? What will I do? How will I react?

It pleasantly surprised me to find these women to be just like me. They dressed, talked, and acted like me—like typical women.

They were from all over the world—Nigeria, Venezuela, Russia, Colombia, Morocco—different ethnic looks, different accents, different styles of dress. However, there was one woman who stood out to me. Her brown, tanned skin, sleek, black hair pulled back in a bun, and her deep, dark eyes drew my attention.

It was her.

Since falling in love with the Moroccan people decades ago, I have always said, "In a room full of women, if there is one from Morocco, I will beeline towards her. It's almost as if I don't see the other women in the crowd. I only see the Moroccan woman."

I felt that same way upon entering the safe house that day. There were other women in that room . . . making jewelry, chatting, listening to faint background music. For me, however, there was only one woman in the crowd. Our eyes met. We smiled at each other. She was Moroccan, no doubt. I could hear, smell, taste, see, and feel it. I greeted her in the typical Arabic way, with one kiss on her right cheek and two on her left.

"*Salaam*, my sister," I said to her in the Moroccan dialect, *Darija*. I felt like a little girl, unable to contain myself, bursting with joy.

I will never forget the look in her eyes and the grin on her face. It was as if she was screaming at the top of her lungs . . . "You speak my language?!" She didn't have to say anything. I could hear her silent, unspoken words. I could feel her happy, dancing heart.

She returned my greeting in Arabic and spoke the traditional blessing of peace upon me.

"*Salaam*."

I continued with the typical greetings and exchanges and then asked her what her name was.

"Habiba. My name is Habiba."

Habiba—my favorite Arabic name. It means "Beloved." While living in Morocco, my local friends had given me that same name.

Vivid images carried me back to that small neighborhood village in that dry desert land. We were gathered around a small wooden table with the women, drinking thick, creamy buttermilk, *l'bin*, and strawberries. It was a hot, muggy afternoon, when my best friend, Aiysha, christened me. She had just heard my story of how I had met God.

"Your name is Habiba," she said. "Because you are the Beloved of God."

We had the same name—Habiba. I already felt deeply connected to my new Moroccan friend at the safe house. We were so different —our backgrounds, our families, our physical appearances. Yet, we were so much alike.

After asking her name, I asked Habiba how she was—her health, her mother, her father, her children. She gave short answers to my string of questions, then asked me the same. Conversation with Habiba felt natural to us both. It felt like home.

I sat next to her at the table, where she continued to make jewelry. We chatted about Morocco, about Spain, about the weather, about food, about parents, about children, about everything. She was happy to have found someone who could speak her language—her heart language.

As much as I enjoy learning and speaking other languages, Arabic is still the foreign language that I love most. It feels like a heart language to me too, because something comes alive in me when I hear and speak it. This powerful feeling is hard for me to explain. The way Arabic dances out of my mouth, the way it flows on paper —weaving elegantly and intricately from right to left. I love it. Arabic is far from being my native language. However, I feel comfortable speaking it, or rather stumbling and fumbling through it. I've heard it takes a lifetime to master the Arabic language, and I believe it.

For Habiba and me, Arabic would become the first of many bridges. This fascinating language would connect us, unite us, and lead us. Arabic.

"You speak my language?" Habiba asked.

"Yes, I speak your language. I love your language and your country. I lived there for seven years."

Habiba radiated with joy. There was an instant connection between us. I knew her land. I knew her culture. I knew her language.

As I looked at her, I no longer saw a victim of sex trafficking, I saw a human, a woman, a friend, a sister.

My mind flashed back to my life in North Africa. All the women called me *"b'nti," "r'ti," "a'mti."* It did not matter if I was Moroccan or not. It did not matter if I was one of them or not. I was immediately adopted as their "daughter," "sister," "aunt." In Morocco, you are rarely called by your first name. Rather, your name is quickly replaced by a family term of endearment. You cannot live there without being adopted by the whole community.

That was the connection between Habiba and me. It didn't matter if I was tall with pale skin and light brown hair, and Habiba was petite with a dark complexion and coal black hair. We were sisters—Moroccan sisters.

⁓ℓℓ⁓

When I walked through the door of the safe house that day, I expected to meet broken women. I expected to see sadness and pain on their faces.

But I didn't expect this.

After finishing the jewelry making and cleaning up the dining room table, they served us a simple lunch of roasted chicken and potatoes.

Habiba and I continued in conversation. Although there were other women eating with us at the table, we were in our own little world. Just the two of us, enjoying each other's company and speaking *Darija*.

It didn't take me long to notice that Habiba wore jewelry on her neck and ears—gold crosses.

It was shocking. In all my years living and working in Morocco, I had never seen a local wearing a cross. There is no religious freedom in Morocco. We knew Moroccan Christians, but they lived out their beliefs and faith behind closed doors, often fearing persecution of family, friends, and neighbors. We had heard stories of those who had been divorced, kicked out of their families, fired, imprisoned, tortured, and even faced death for their decision to follow the way of the cross.

"Tell me the story behind your crosses." I asked Habiba, curiously.

Her next words took me back to her little village in North Africa when she was a little girl.

"I watched a movie on TV. It was about the man, Jesus. I loved him the first time I saw Him.

I ran to gather all the other little girls in my village. We sat in my living room together watching the movie . . . until someone walked in and chased us out. They told us to stop watching Jesus.

I hadn't thought about Jesus until I arrived in Spain, when I came to this house. These 'Jesus People' take care of me. They feed me. They give me clothes. They give me a place to live. They love me."

As I listened, I continued eating my chicken and potatoes, but I was in shock and disbelief. Habiba's testimony of learning about Jesus sounded too crazy to be true. Habiba had been introduced to Jesus as a young girl through satellite television in her home in a remote village in the south of Morocco. She had even tried to share her excitement and her passion for Jesus with her neighborhood friends. Decades later, God brought her all the way to Europe to be rescued and loved by "Jesus People." Only God could work out all those intricate details and orchestrate that kind of redemptive plan.

"After all these years," I thought to myself. "Wow! What an incredible story!"

I often pray I will have an open door to tell people stories of God's love. That day, however, God surprised me by using Habiba to tell me His story. I knew then that God had answered my prayer for a sign. Before walking through the door that day, I had asked Him to make it clear to me if I should volunteer at the safe house and help this woman.

"Ok, God," I whispered in my head. "I heard you loud and clear. I'll come back again. There's a bigger reason you've called me here."

Before leaving the safe house to drive home that day, I pulled up an app on my phone with some oral Bible stories in Moroccan Arabic. I pulled Habiba aside in the living room and told her to listen to one of them.

"Can you understand the story?" I asked her.

She nodded, smiling as she listened. She didn't have her own phone, so I sent the Bible stories to the director of the safe house to give to her. Now Habiba could listen to more stories about Jesus—freely. No one could stop it. No one could silence it. No one could turn it off.

CHAPTER ELEVEN

FIRST BIRTHDAY PARTY

"I don't know how old I am," Habiba said.

The first time I had heard a Moroccan say this, it shocked me. How was it possible to not know your own age? With Habiba, however, it didn't surprise me at all. Her words reminded me of all the Moroccan women I knew. Rarely did they know their age. It was a common story.

"My parents don't know how to read and write," Habiba said. "They never went to school."

Habiba had a Moroccan identity card and passport. They both said the same date, January 1, 1978. Was that her actual birthdate? Was it the right month, day, year? She did not know. No one would ever know. Not even her own mother knew.

The custom of the safe house was to celebrate each woman's birthday, a time to make them feel special and loved.

"Next week is my birthday," Habiba told me one day when I went to visit.

"Wow! Are you going to have a birthday party?"

"Yes, it will be my first birthday party ever!"

"You've never celebrated your birthday?"

"Never."

My heart leapt with joy and sank with sadness at the same time.

"How is that possible?" I thought to myself, calculating in my mind Habiba's age based on the date on her passport. "Habiba is forty-two, and no one has ever celebrated her birthday, her life."

"Well, in that case, we are going to have a very special first birthday party for you!"

The following week, we all gathered at the safe house. Habiba was nowhere to be found when I arrived.

"Where is she?" I asked the volunteer from the house.

"She's upstairs in her room getting ready."

I ran up the stairs and knocked on her bedroom door.

"Where's the Birthday Girl?" I whispered, as I opened the door.

There she was, dressed in her finest clothes. She had on blue jeans and a white blouse. Her long, dark hair flowed down her back and shoulders, almost to her waist. It was the first time I had seen her hair down. Habiba was wearing light makeup and some jewelry she had made.

"You're beautiful," I said.

She blushed and lowered her gaze. Tears slowly trickled down her cheeks. It felt like a wedding day for a young bride. I hugged her and wished her "Happy Birthday!"

I brushed her hair gently and then asked her, "Are you ready? Are you ready for your first birthday party ever?"

Habiba smiled and clutched my hand.

"Everyone's waiting for you. It's your special day, and you're the honored guest."

We walked slowly down the stairs, and Habiba entered the dining room. More than twenty women—volunteers and women from the safe house—applauded and cheered loudly as she entered the room. Habiba glanced down, embarrassed. She wasn't used to having all this attention. She wasn't used to feeling loved like this. She wasn't used to people celebrating her . . . her life. She simply wasn't used to this.

Habiba took her seat towards the middle of the table. Her joy was uncontainable, seeping out of her pores. She was radiant. Beautifully wrapped presents were piled high on the table before her.

"Is this all for me?!"

She unwrapped each gift slowly and carefully, as if to savor every moment—jeans, tennis shoes, fluffy socks, shirts, pajamas, gloves, a scarf, and a warm, thick, black winter coat with a fake, fur-lined hood. Everything was new. Nothing was used. Nothing was donated. Nothing was "handed down."

Her eyes welled up with tears as she drowned in the blessings.

"*Choukran! Choukran! Choukran!*"* she repeated over and over. Arabic flowed like a river out of her mouth as she naturally expressed her love and appreciation for those who had gathered. I translated into English for one of the house volunteers, who then translated her message into Spanish. Habiba couldn't thank everyone enough for being her family, for loving her, for caring for her, for giving her more than she could have ever asked or imagined.

Everyone clapped and cheered, then we sang "Happy Birthday" to her in multiple languages—English, Spanish, and Arabic. She sat in tears and in smiles, absorbing the moment and the abundance of love and joy that flooded her.

Next came the homemade birthday cake with candles—all forty-two of them. Habiba beamed in front of the light, like a little girl having her first birthday party. There it was again—light. They had brought her into a lighthouse, and she never wanted to leave. She never wanted to live in the dark again.

Making a wish, she blew out the candles, and more cheers and applause echoed throughout the room.

A first birthday party at age forty-two is one that Habiba will never forget . . . and neither will I.

Choukran—Thank you

CHAPTER TWELVE

FREEDOM TO CHOOSE

I t was nearing Christmas, our family's first in Spain.
We had heard about an Arabic-speaking church in the city, but
had never visited. We all love the Arabic language and culture, so we
thought it would be fun to celebrate Christmas there. It would be a
nice and exciting change from the English- and Spanish-speaking
churches we usually attended.

My husband contacted the pastor and asked for information
about the day and time of the service. Shortly after, we received a
text inviting us to an upcoming baptism.

I love baptisms. They are full of testimonies—real, personal
stories of transformed lives. We were excited—a baptism in Arabic
in Spain. The woman getting baptized was from Morocco. She had
moved to Spain several years ago, where she found freedom of
choice, freedom of religion. She eventually became a Christian. The
pastor asked if we would like to join them for the celebration,
followed by a luncheon. We eagerly accepted.

A few days before the big event, I had an idea. Perhaps we could
invite Habiba to come with us. She was obviously interested in
knowing more about Jesus, fascinated with him since her childhood
back in Morocco.

As a young girl, Habiba was forbidden to inquire, forbidden to
ask questions, forbidden to seek, forbidden to be curious, forbidden
to follow anything outside of Islam. However, now she was free. She
was in an open country where she could ask questions, seek, and be
curious. She could now choose and follow her own beliefs.

I wasn't sure if Habiba would be comfortable going with us to a
church, but she eagerly accepted the invitation. I tried to explain to

her what baptism was, so that she was prepared to see them dunk this woman in an inflatable swimming pool set up in the front of the church. If you don't understand what baptism is and what it means, you have to admit this is a strange sight to behold.

In the car, after picking Habiba up from the safe house, I tried again to explain to her again the symbolic meaning of baptism— identifying with the death and resurrection of Jesus—and the person's public proclamation of his or her decision to follow Him. Habiba was intrigued and excited to experience this.

I sat watching her throughout the service. Everything was in classical Arabic, more of an educated, literate form of her dialect. However, she could still follow and understand. There were two pastors, an Egyptian and an American, who spoke Arabic fluently. Their message was clear and insightful, once again explaining the public act and celebration of baptism.

Their informative message, however, paled in comparison to the story of the Moroccan woman who stood up next. I sat enthralled with her testimony, and so did Habiba. I couldn't help but turn my head regularly to watch Habiba's facial expressions and body language as she listened, mesmerized. She seemed to hang on to the woman's every word, each spoken in Habiba's heart language—the Moroccan dialect, *Darija*. There was absolutely no language barrier between them.

Habiba and I were both captivated by the true story of this woman's life transformation. This Moroccan woman had walked from darkness to light, from bondage to freedom, from fear to peace. Her life had radically changed, and the new life she had found was irresistible.

After hearing this woman's journey of life change and courage in the face of persecution, we were all invited to stand and draw near to the front of the church. A large blue inflatable swimming pool awaited the big moment. Habiba walked quickly to the front, curious. It was as if she couldn't get close enough, fast enough. She didn't want to miss a thing. She wanted to catch every detail of every moment—every word, every sound, every sight, every movement.

The Moroccan woman, dressed in a long white tunic, followed the Egyptian pastor into the water. He shared a few more words and asked her some questions. The woman answered, confirming her decision and commitment to follow Jesus. Sitting in the water, the pastor slowly and gently leaned the woman backwards into the water until her face and long, dark hair were completely immersed. She emerged dripping wet, yet smiling, radiant.

Everyone broke out in cheers and clapping. Habiba joined the celebration with the rest of the crowd. What was going on in her mind? She was fully present in the moment, absorbing it all. It was exciting for me to think that this experience could be life-changing for Habiba. Perhaps one day, she might decide to follow Jesus, too.

After the closing prayer, we made plans to carpool to the Turkish kebab restaurant for lunch. Before walking out the door, Habiba pulled me aside.

"I need to talk to you," she whispered.

We went to a private area at the back of the church.

"What is it? Is everything alright?"

"Yes, but I have to confess something. I'm sorry. I lied in the car."

She told me the details. I knew she had lied. In the car with us that day there was another woman from Morocco, a Christian friend we had also invited to the baptism. After picking up Habiba from the safe house to go to the church, our friend was kindly making small talk in the back seat of our car to fill the time and space during the long ride. Since they were both from Morocco, this woman asked Habiba a typical get-to-know-you question.

"Where are you from in Morocco?" she asked.

Habiba was scared. She didn't know this woman. She didn't know if she could trust her. She didn't know if this woman might know her story, know about the safe house, know the sex traffickers. Perhaps this woman in the car, our friend, was even from her same hometown in Morocco. Maybe she knew her family or was a distant relative. Habiba didn't know. She didn't know what to do or what to say.

She panicked when she heard the woman's question. Lying, she told her she was from a city far from her hometown in Morocco. Her answer seemed to satisfy the woman's curiosity. She didn't ask anymore questions, and Habiba sighed in relief.

"I understand," I told Habiba. "It's okay. God understands too, and He forgives you."

"I'm sorry that I lied," she said.

Considering that lying was common in Habiba's culture, in order to save face and save honor, I knew this confession was a big step for her. Something was taking place in her heart that was bigger than her culture. I hugged her and reassured her that God still loved her and so did I. She smiled, clearly comforted. I could see the burden lifted from her.

"Are you hungry? Shall we go to lunch?" I asked her.

We walked to the car joyfully, talking about the baptism and the Moroccan woman's unforgettable story.

"I've never heard or seen anything like that," Habiba said with fascination.

On our way to the kebab restaurant, our seven-seat van was packed to the brim with people, most of whom we didn't know. There were two other Moroccans in the car. Habiba was enjoying the conversation and the community experience with others from her homeland. She didn't have many opportunities to speak her dialect at the safe house.

In the car, the other women told their own stories—their personal journeys from Morocco to Spain, their journeys from Islam to Jesus. Habiba asked them a lot of questions, and their answers satisfied her wonder.

"Get whatever you want on the menu," I told her, upon arriving at the Turkish restaurant. "We're buying."

We knew that she didn't have any money. We didn't want to bring shame upon her—knowing that shame was such a huge part of the Arab culture. Rather, we wanted to honor her, to bless her, to care for her needs.

I thought to myself, "I wonder when Habiba last ate in a restaurant."

In Morocco, coming from a poor, lower-class family, she probably never stepped foot in a restaurant. That was a luxury for the privileged upper-class. Picking strawberries in the fields of Spain, living under the terror and reign of the Mafia of human trafficking . . . I'm sure there were no restaurants in her life during that time either. Since living at the safe house, government funding and donations from humanitarian organizations were scarce. It was hard enough to feed the mouths of all the women and children staying at the safe house, let alone have extra funds for splurging on restaurant meals.

I wondered . . . was this the first time Habiba ate in a restaurant—in her entire life? Maybe it was a first-time experience like her birthday party. Habiba gladly accepted our offer to buy her lunch that day. She ordered a cold beverage and hot BBQ chicken wings and fries. The plate arrived, and there were at least twenty wings covered in messy hot sauce. She only ate a few.

"You're not hungry?" I asked. "Why aren't you eating?"

"I'm not used to eating big meals."

She didn't want to take the chicken wings back to the safe house with her, so she told me to take them home to my boys. Not wanting to waste them, I asked for a box to go and wrapped them up. My twenty-two year old son would be especially happy. He loves hot wings.

"I'll tell my son that you sent them home for him," I told her, laughing.

She smiled. In the car, on the way back to the safe house, Habiba was glowing, radiating with joy. Clearly, the day's events had filled an empty place in her heart, and I was glad that we had accepted the pastor's invitation and that Habiba had joined us.

I prayed for Habiba that night, prayed that she would know peace, prayed that she would know God's love, prayed that she would find the answers to all of her heart's questions, prayed that she would know which way to walk, prayed that her life could be transformed too—just like the baptized woman, prayed that she would find freedom, healing, restoration, redemption, and transformation in her broken life story.

Only God could heal Habiba's broken heart, restore her shattered soul, and free her plagued mind. Only God had the power to save Habiba, change her, heal her. I prayed, "God, have mercy on Habiba. Help her, heal her, restore her." I walked by her side, listened to her heartfelt cries, wiped her tears as I held her in my arms. I prayed with her, offering comfort, hope, and life. But only God provides deep soul care and heart healing. Habiba needed more than I could provide. She needed God.

ele

"I decided to follow Jesus!" Habiba screamed loudly on the phone.

"What?!" I answered, surprised by this unexpected news.

"I wanted you to be the first to know."

I had a million questions firing off in my mind like popcorn.

"What happened? When? Where? How?"

I was confused and delighted at the same time.

Perhaps Habiba was allowing God to enter into her heart and life. Perhaps she was welcoming the soul care of the Father. Perhaps she was experiencing the peace and comfort of Jesus, the Prince of Peace.

When we dropped Habiba off at the safe house the day before, after the baptism, I remembered how happy and excited she was. I had never seen her like that—so light and free. Her smile beamed from ear to ear.

Something unexplainable had happened that day. There was an obvious change, a transformation taking place in her heart.

On the phone that evening, Habiba explained to me she had gone to another Arabic church on Sunday, the day after the baptism. She had a lot of questions about baptism and wanted to understand. She asked the Moroccan pastor, who answered her questions thoroughly. Habiba quickly became convinced that day that this was the path she wanted to walk. She was determined. There was no coercion, no force. Habiba had decided, and no one was going to stop her.

After hearing the testimony of the Moroccan woman who had been baptized the day before, Habiba now desperately desired what that woman had found—joy, peace, and love in Jesus. Habiba needed a savior too, and she found one. Habiba encountered someone who loved her unconditionally, someone who could mend her broken heart, someone who could free her from slavery, someone who could rescue her from the pit of hell, someone who could restore her shattered soul, someone who could fill her mind with peace, someone who could gift her with unspeakable joy.

Habiba found Jesus, and this time, no one could take Him away from her.

Over thirty years before, Habiba had watched the Jesus film in her living room in Morocco. Now, living in Spain, Habiba had the freedom to choose. Habiba chose Jesus. Habiba means "Beloved." That day, Habiba became a beloved child of God.

As I listened to Habiba's excited voice on the phone, something occurred to me. God had brought Habiba all the way to Spain— chasing after her El Dorado. She didn't find the streets of gold that she expected.

She found something even better.

CHAPTER THIRTEEN

HER CULTURE OF HONOR AND SHAME

I t was all about honor.

When she made that decision, when she boarded that boat, when she crossed that ocean, when she picked those strawberries . . . it was all about honor.

Habiba wanted to bring honor to her family. She wanted to provide for them. She wanted to be their way out—their way out of poverty.

It was all about honor.

"*Sharaf*," "honor" in Arabic, has a strong meaning. Everything one does, everything one says must be for honor—the honor of one's family.

How you walk, how you talk, how you dress, what you eat, what you drink, where you sit, how you enter a room, how you greet people, who you know . . . is all about honor.

You can lie, you can kill, you can divorce, you can abuse, you can steal. You can do anything, and everything is acceptable, if it brings honor to your family.

Roland Muller, in his study on honor and shame in the Arab culture, tells the following story from his time living in the Middle East. He was driving in a taxi that came to a sudden halt. In the middle of the street, a teenage girl was dying. Her brother had shot her in the head four times. He told the police, "There she is. I killed her because she was in an immoral situation with a man." The laws of that country protected this young man and his innocence. "He had not committed murder but had preserved the honor of his family." [1]

During our seven years living in Morocco, we never knew if people were lying to us, because lying is culturally acceptable if it "saves face" and brings honor.

In our Western culture, guilt and innocence, right and wrong, are deeply ingrained in our way of thinking. For us, telling the truth is the right thing to do. If we don't, we feel guilty. It's not about honor and "saving face," it's about doing what we believe is the "right" thing to do in any situation.

There is a big difference between a society that values honor and shame and a society that values innocence and guilt.

When Habiba left Morocco to come to Spain two years ago, when she made that Faustian Bargain, she was willing to give up everything. Why? It was all about honor—honor for her family.

The flip side of honor is shame. Everything must be done to avoid bringing shame to your family. "Saving face" is critical.

In Arab countries like Morocco, one regularly hears the word, "*Ashouma*," which means "shame" in Arabic. Parents begin speaking this word to babies so they know the power of shame and the importance of honor.

It's all about honor.

Habiba would have heard this word, "*Ashouma*," repetitively from her earliest days of life. This strong Arabic word has largely constructed her mindset. Honor and shame are now deeply ingrained in her—in the deepest part of her being.

When she made that decision, when she boarded that boat, when she crossed that ocean, when she picked those strawberries . . . the last thing Habiba wanted to do was bring shame upon her family.

When she was taken from the strawberry fields to the brothel, she did not know that she was heading into a place of shame. She thought that her decision to stay in Spain long term, to get her papers, to find a job, to have a place to live, to make more money to send back to her family in Morocco was a decision of honor.

Little did she know that her own honor, the honor of her family, the honor of her name, the honor of her country . . . would slowly be stripped away.

Along with her clothes, her modesty, her religion, her dignity, her self-respect, her identity . . . Habiba's robe of honor was removed and replaced by a cloak of shame.

Drinking alcohol, taking "happy drugs," sleeping with strangers, selling her body to the night were all "*haram*" and "of the devil" in Islamic religion and Arab culture. These scandalous acts heaped heavy stones of shame upon her body, her heart, her soul, and her mind.

I wonder if Habiba could hear the echo of her mother's voice and her father's words, "*Ashouma a'lik!*" "Shame on you!" When she stood on the street waiting and luring clients, when she lay in the bed of one more nameless man, when she drank another glass of hard alcohol so that she didn't have to feel—so her body, mind, and emotions would be numb—did she hear their words resounding in her ears?

"*Ashouma*" were words of curse from her family, her community, her culture, her country.

Now, not only was her world and her life filled with shame, but she also had no money to send back to her family. The El Dorado she had dreamed of was nowhere to be found. It was all just an illusion, a mirage.

Trapped. Poor. Abused. Exploited. Shamed.

"Do your mother, your father, your son, and your family know what happened to you? Do they know everything?" I asked Habiba one day while sitting next to her on her bed at the safe house.

"They know everything," she said. "I told them everything."

I wondered what that phone conversation had been like. What did her family think? What did they say? Did they speak those all-too-familiar words to Habiba, "*Ashouma a'lik*"? Or did they have compassion on her? Did they cry? Were they sad or worried about her—her health, her safety? Were they angry with those who had done this to her—with those who had exploited their daughter, their mother?

"My mother wanted me to come back home. She wanted me to leave Spain right away," Habiba told me.

"Why didn't you?" I asked her.

"I couldn't," she said. "I could never go back to Morocco."

She didn't say, but I knew exactly why Habiba could never step foot again on the soil of her home country, why she could never step foot back into her community.

Shame. It's all about honor, and it's all about shame.

In her community, before leaving Morocco, Habiba was already a woman in a position of shame. Her husband had died when her son was two-years-old.

Although widows are not shamed in the same manner as divorced women, the fact that Habiba had never remarried, never been chosen by another man, did not place her in a position of high honor and esteem in her community.

Until the moment a woman marries, there is shame placed on the family. "Once the girls and boys of a family are successfully married, the risk of shame to a family is largely over. The parents can then die feeling that they have fulfilled their duties."[2]

Habiba had been married, a position of honor. She then plunged back into a position of shame when her husband died.

Wearing the public label of a widow brought an entirely different status for Habiba in her Arab culture.

"When the Moslem wife or mother loses her partner through death, she faces still another crisis . . . Older men prefer young wives and have a strong cultural aversion to marrying widows."

Because of these cultural implications, it is estimated that a fifth of all Muslim women are unmarried widows. These women will typically have little opportunity for employment. If they do not have grown sons, often, their only option is to return to their parents' home.

"There she is accepted without enthusiasm but with acquiescence and shares their already meager fare and household tasks."[2]

Before coming to Spain, that was Habiba's life in Morocco. At the death of her husband, she was forced to move back to her parents' home with her two-year-old son, unlikely to remarry.

Shame.

When she made that decision, when she boarded that boat, when she crossed that sea, when she picked those strawberries . . . it was all about honor.

It was about honor for her family and their name. It was about honor for herself, a step towards redemption, towards salvation, towards rescue from poverty. She was the way out—the way out of shame and poverty for her family.

El Dorado awaited her. She would march on the roads paved with gold, holding her head high. Honor.

Instead, shame, more shame, was heaped upon her.

If Habiba returned to Morocco, people would ask her questions about Spain—about her life of honor and wealth in that land of El Dorado. If she never returned home, however, perhaps people in her community would never know what happened—what she did, where she went, what kind of life she led. If she never returned, people might never know her secret. People might never know the shame that she had brought upon herself, upon her family, upon her name.

If Habiba never returned to Morocco, perhaps people would still believe she was providing a way out for her family—a way out of poverty. Perhaps people would imagine her in the palace of a king in that beautiful land of El Dorado.

Habiba had made a Faustian Bargain, but people didn't have to know what happened on the other side of the Mediterranean Sea, on the other side of that "deal with the devil." Habiba went to Spain to pick strawberries. Perhaps that's what people thought she was still doing. Hopefully, they would never know about the brothel, about the safe house, about the shame.

No, Habiba could never go back to her beloved land of Morocco. It would only bring more shame and dishonor to her family. She could never do that. As much as she missed her country, her culture, her parents, her only son . . . she could never go back.

It's all about honor. Oh, the things Habiba would do to bring honor to her family.

—— *ele* ——

"I have a question for you," I said to her. "There are so many things I don't know about you. I need to fill in some blanks in my mind."

I had started writing Habiba's story, but there were many missing pieces of the puzzle. I wondered if I could ever find those missing pieces and complete the story tapestry. I decided to ask Habiba some questions and to fill in some gaps each time I was with her at the safe house.

"Tell me again how they rescued you from the brothel," I said.

She began telling me the story.

I had heard it before, but I wanted to understand more. I needed to picture the scene in my mind in order to go back home and write the story accurately. I didn't want to miss anything. I wanted to be true to her story. It was sacred, and I wanted to honor it. I wanted to honor Habiba.

When Habiba got to the part about being with the men in the bar and how much or how little they would pay for sexual acts, she lowered her head.

"What could I do?" she said sadly, her eyes still turned down.

Shame. It was written all over her face, all over her body.

Shame. It was deeply ingrained in her culture, in the core of her being.

Shame. Once you're covered in it, it is heavy and painful.

Shame. I only know one way out.

As we sat on her bed at the safe house, I leaned over and gave her a hug. I then shared with her my own story, my own story of shame and pain. Although a completely different story than hers, I told her of my experience of freedom, deliverance, forgiveness, and cleansing.

Before meeting Jesus at twenty-one, I wore the same dress every day. I didn't know it, but I wore a cloak of shame. It had become familiar and comfortable. It was the only one I knew how to wear. It seemed to be the only one that fit me—perfectly.

I told Habiba my story of rescue and redemption. When Jesus burst into my life, His presence, His love, His forgiveness, His acceptance poured all over me—from my head to my toes. The filth and dirt of my life, my heart, my mind, my body, and my soul were washed away. He gave me a new gown, a beautiful white one. It was His robe of righteousness, His robe of honor. God adopted me into His family, and I became a woman of royal nobility. I became a daughter of the King.

Habiba listened carefully to my story. I told her that Jesus wanted to do the same thing for her. He wanted to take away her cloak of shame and clothe her with His robe of honor, His robe of righteousness.

"He spoke and said to those who were standing before Him, saying, 'Remove the filthy garments from him.' Again He said to him, 'See, I have taken your iniquity away from you and will clothe you with festal robes.'"
Zechariah 3:4—The Bible NIV

I prayed for Habiba that day. I prayed she would feel cleansed and holy—washed clean from all the nasty filth and dirt of the horrible things she had done and the horrible things that had been done to her. I prayed she would know that "the old had gone, and the new had come." (2 Corinthians 5:17) I prayed she would know that she was a brand-new creation in Jesus Christ. I prayed that the voice of shame, the curse of "*Ashouma*," would be erased, and that she would hear only the voice of blessing and honor. I prayed she would allow God to remove her cloak of shame and destroy it forever. I prayed she would proudly wear the beautiful robe of righteousness and honor with which God now adorned her.

"Instead of your shame, you will receive a double portion, and instead of disgrace, you will rejoice in your inheritance. And so you will inherit a double portion in your land, and everlasting joy will be yours. For I, the Lord, love justice; I hate robbery and wrongdoing . . . All who see them will acknowledge that they are a people the Lord has blessed . . . For He has clothed me with garments of salvation and arrayed me in a robe of righteousness, as a bridegroom adorns his head like a priest, and as a bride adorns herself with her jewels."

Isaiah 61:7-10—The Bible NIV

Habiba had also found the Lord, her husband, who had removed her shame as a widow.

"Do not be afraid; you will not be put to shame. Do not fear disgrace; you will not be humiliated. You will forget the shame of your youth and remember no more the reproach of your widowhood. For your

Maker is your husband—the Lord Almighty is His
name—the Holy One of Israel is your Redeemer; He is
called the God of all the earth. The Lord will call you
back as if you were a wife deserted and distressed in
spirit—a wife who married young, only to be
rejected," says your God.

Isaiah 54:4-6—The Bible NIV

Habiba may have come from a culture of honor and shame, but
her shame was now gone. Only honor remained.

When she made that decision, when she boarded that boat, when
she crossed that ocean, when she picked those strawberries . . . it was
all about honor.

Habiba came to Spain to find honor, and she had finally found it.

CHAPTER FOURTEEN

BEAUTY FROM ASHES

I t was almost lunchtime. The woman walked over to Habiba and handed her a bill. Curious, I asked Habiba what it was for.

"We get ten euros if we make jewelry on Wednesdays," she explained.

There were six women sitting around the table at the safe house that day. They had all been working since late morning, after returning to the house from their Spanish classes. It was now two p.m.—the traditional Spanish lunch hour.

The mother of the safe house director had much love and compassion for these rescued women. She wanted to help and make a difference, and that's what she did. Every Wednesday morning, she loaded up her car with her personal jewelry-making supplies and headed over to the safe house.

She wanted to provide work for these women—an activity, a way to create. By doing this, she was providing more for them than ten euros a week. She was giving them a sense of pride, dignity, and self-confidence. At the end of their three-hour craft session, the women could look back and admire their creations elegantly displayed on the table. As they looked at their own jewelry pieces, and those of the other women, they were encouraged, happy, proud.

These women had no legal right to work in Spain. Each of them carried a piece of paper in their purse, stating they had applied with the Spanish government as a refugee or victim of exploitation seeking asylum. This paper, however, did not allow them to work. Depending on the time it would take to get their permanent residence cards, these women might not be able to work legally for more than three years.

In the meantime, some women from the safe house were volunteering at a coffeehouse in a local Spanish church in the city. The church was partnering directly with the safe house to provide work opportunities for these women and to train them in much-needed job skills. A few others—including Habiba—were occasionally cleaning houses in the neighborhood. This work provided some extra cash for her to send back to her family in Morocco.

Besides lack of employment, most of the women at the safe house couldn't speak Spanish well. Some, like Habiba, could hardly speak at all. The rescued women represented several countries. Only two of the women at the house were native Spanish speakers—one from Venezuela and one from Colombia. The others stumbled along, faithfully attending Spanish classes three mornings a week at the local community center down the street. Learning a foreign language was hard and slow.

One day, after Spanish class, Habiba told me it was difficult for her to concentrate.

"I'm constantly thinking about my parents and my son back in Morocco," she said. "I can't learn Spanish right now."

My heart ached. I couldn't imagine being separated from my sons for that long. The safe house, subsidized by the Spanish government, required the women to learn the local language well. They knew they would need to speak fluently in order to get their residency papers and, eventually, to find a job to support themselves.

Not only was Habiba's mind filled with longings and worries about her family back in Morocco, but she was also traumatized. She was traumatized by her previous life chapters of horrific sex trafficking, and so were all the other women with whom she lived.

"How do you concentrate in that state of mind?" I asked myself. "The last thing they want to do is sit in the four walls of a classroom all day and try to fit a foreign language somewhere in their brain."

I, too, was a Spanish language learner. I arrived in Spain about the same time as Habiba. Learning a foreign language requires a lot of mental, physical, and emotional energy. It was hard for me, and my life and family were quite stable. If it was difficult for me to learn a foreign language in my forties, of course it was an enormous challenge for Habiba . . . and any woman like her.

It didn't matter how hard it was. The safe house required it, and so did the government. A few hours of Spanish each week would give them the basics, but eventually, these women would need to reach an advanced level of Spanish if they were going to seek employment.

On Wednesdays, however, these women had something else to look forward to. Their day wasn't full of simply Spanish lessons and lunch together.

Wednesdays were different.

On Wednesdays, after Spanish class, the director's mother would spread out her jewelry boxes on the large oak dining room table. The women, along with a few volunteers, would gather to create. While working, we talked about life—our "old life" back in our home countries and our "new life" in Spain. We would talk, we would laugh, we would smile. Soft music often played in the background. It was fun and relaxing.

Sometimes, the women would make silver or gold-plated jewelry pieces—necklaces, bracelets, and earrings. Other times, they would make keychains out of soft leather thread. My favorite jewelry pieces were the recycled ones. Beads were rolled out of magazine pages, newspapers, and colorful wrapping paper, then glued together. The women would then string them together on transparent necklace strings or attach them to silver-plated earring pieces.

I love recycling. "One man's trash is another man's treasure."

The person reading those newspaper articles or the person flipping through those magazine pages in the doctor's office probably never knew. They probably never knew that the pages they had thrown in the trash bin would one day be collected. They probably didn't fathom that one day their thrown-out trash would be another man's treasure—another woman's treasure.

Beauty from ashes . . . just like these women.

These women were rescued from the pit of darkness. These women heard a knock on the door and responded. These women fled for their lives. These women were in bondage, in slavery. Now they were free!

It delighted Habiba to receive her ten euros. The other women grinned from ear to ear as well. Habiba had been working hard for three hours. To me, ten euros didn't seem like much. However, for Habiba, it was much more than ten euros. For Habiba, her newfound pride and dignity were worth millions of euros. They had no price. Priceless . . . the ten euro bill was just a bonus.

I wondered what Habiba would do with her ten euros. Would she save it and send it to her family back in Morocco? Would she take it and spend it on some new hair supplies or a t-shirt at the local store?

Before, in their previous life chapter, earning ten euros represented something else for these women. Depending on the time spent with the man and the requested service provided, sometimes Habiba would make only ten euros on a "call." Sometimes, even less.

Dirty money.

Now, in their new lives, they could earn ten euros by making something beautiful with their hands.

Beauty from ashes.

As they sat around the table every Wednesday, making jewelry together, these women communicated a loud message.

"We will no longer earn dirty money! We are worth more than that! We respect ourselves, and we refuse to go back to a life of bondage and slavery. Yes, we can still make money, but it's not dirty money. It's well-earned, beautiful money."

Habiba was proud, proud of her work displayed on the dining room table for all eyes to see. Habiba was proud that she had made ten euros that week. Next week, she would start the process again— making beauty from ashes—and making ten more euros.

As I write this, I'm wearing a necklace from the "Beauty from Ashes" women. I don't know which woman's hands at the safe house made it. It doesn't matter.

It's a silver-plated necklace with a tree of life on it. I love it. I bought it one Wednesday, while helping the women make jewelry. It is a reminder . . . a visual reminder of these women I love, a visual reminder to pray for these hurting women, and a visual reminder that God is breathing new life into these women.

Before arriving at the safe house, these women were heaps of charred ashes on the ground, charred ashes that had been burned in the torture furnace of human trafficking. They had been thrown out like trash.

God, however, was not finished with these women. He did not leave them there. He reached down His mighty, loving arm that is not too short to save. He picked these broken women up from the pit, up from the muck and the mire. He cleansed them, restored them, and put their broken pieces back together.

Yes, "one man's trash is another man's treasure." These women were God's prized pearls, the apples of His eye, His treasures. He is the God of the impossible, and He is in the business of making beauty from ashes.

As those women gathered on Wednesdays to roll old newspaper and magazine pages into beautiful, colorful beads, they were making beauty from ashes.

They were beautiful women. They were beauty from ashes.

" . . . To bestow on them a crown of beauty instead of ashes, the oil of gladness instead of mourning, and a garment of praise instead of a spirit of despair . . ."
Isaiah 61:3—The Bible NIV

PART THREE

Her Story

CHAPTER FIFTEEN

THE TRANSLATION
BRIDGE

I answered the call and said yes. Now I was in it for good. There was no turning back.

Once you walk through the door of a shelter, meet those women, talk to them, hear their stories, see their faces, hold their hands . . . you can never leave. You can never leave them. They have already been so hurt, betrayed, abandoned, abused. How can you walk out on them?

I was committed.

During my second visit to the safe house, after deciding that I would continue with this work, I signed a contract. I signed my name on the line, swearing to secrecy, upholding the guidelines of confidentiality. But for me, signing my name on that dotted line meant even more. I declared I would walk with these women on their journey of healing. I would be there for them, listen to their trauma, carry their stories, pray for them. Most of all, it meant that I would love them.

It didn't take long for me to be known as the "Arabic translator" of the safe house.

I can still hear the director's words echoing in my mind.

"Our team has been praying for a long time that God would send us a woman—a Christian woman who speaks Arabic—to help us with the Moroccan women we rescue."

It still gives me goosebumps. It still blows my mind that this was all in God's sovereign plan. He called our family to Spain at the same moment Habiba was rescued from sex trafficking. Even though we didn't know each other, God was already behind the scenes, connecting divine dots.

This was no coincidence, no random crossing of paths. No, this was a miracle.

I was seeking my El Dorado. Habiba was seeking hers. Somehow, we would meet in the middle of that sought-after land, both searching for a new and better life in Spain.

I went to the safe house on Wednesdays, when the women made jewelry, and our conversations consisted of small talk in our broken Spanish. The rest of the week we all studied Spanish separately, and we used Wednesdays to practice with each other. Habiba and I were both at the same level—beginner.

Each week, after an hour-long drive, I would arrive at the safe house as the women returned from their Spanish lessons at the local community center. As immigrants, we were all struggling with the language and culture of our new homeland.

We would attempt to converse about everything—about our language learning, about our families back in our home, about our cultures, about what we were cooking that evening for dinner, about our clothes, hair, and nails.

It was hard to talk about anything deep or intimate while sitting at a dining room table with six women. It was especially hard with limited language ability.

Since Habiba and I were the only ones in the room who could speak Arabic, sometimes we would talk privately about other, more personal, things. We would sit together at the end of the table, whispering while making jewelry. Or sometimes, we would leave the safe house to go on a walk in the park across the street. There, we could talk heart to heart.

In the beginning, they called me in for certain appointments at the safe house to work with a young psychologist, Paola, who worked at the house several days a week. Sometimes she would send me a phone text and ask if I could do translation with her and Habiba. Thankfully, Paola spoke English perfectly, so it was only a two-way translation between English and Arabic.

I had learned quickly that translating was grueling work. As a child, I thought translation sounded glamorous and fun. I became fascinated with foreign languages as a young girl and loved the intricacy and the feeling of several languages swirling around in my brain. They challenged and intrigued me.

After deciding to become a foreign language teacher, I had even considered becoming a professional translator. I loved languages, and I enjoyed helping people jump language hurdles and understand.

It had been a long time since I thought of that glamorous fantasy when I met Habiba, and being a translation bridge was a far cry from my dream. Never could I have imagined the reality I discovered here in Spain, working as an Arabic language translator in a safe house. This was anything but exciting and fun.

Nor was it a job, a role, that I had chosen. Rather, it felt like a strong calling from deep inside my heart. I couldn't resist, couldn't push it back. I had to submit and accept the invitation from God.

Being a translation bridge is exhausting. It wears out the mind more than any other mental task I know. It's a constant jumping of language train tracks. Sometimes, I can physically feel how tired and confused my brain is. My head aches. My brain hurts.

I am not a neuroscientist, but I have been a foreign language teacher for over twenty years. I have studied the language-learning brain long enough to know what happens. Learning forms new neural pathways in the brain matter. According to psychologist Deann Ware, PhD, "Neural pathways, comprised of neurons connected by dendrites, are created in the brain. I picture these neural pathways as deep grooves or roads in the brain."[1]

Those deep grooves or roads in the brain are like train tracks.

When I am speaking my mother tongue or even a foreign language that I have mastered, I am smoothly coasting down the language track that is deeply ingrained in my brain. Simple, easy.

However, when translating between two or more languages, I have to jump train tracks constantly. It's extremely hard work. I am required to bring the brain train to a sudden halt in its track so that I can quickly jump onto a different track—a different road, a different language. Sometimes, I even have to drive my brain train down two different tracks at the same time, because I am hearing more than one language spoken around me. At times, I get stuck on the rails between two tracks and don't know which track I'm on or what language I'm hearing or speaking. Other times, I go backwards on the track or get jammed somewhere.

At those moments, I have to say, "Stop, wait, hold on. I missed something."

That happened a lot during my translation sessions with Habiba. When having conversations with the psychologist, I could jump language tracks easily between English and Arabic. Sometimes, however, I would still have to pause and ask one of them to repeat or to jump back in the story so that I could make sure I was processing everything well. However, I could usually handle the two language tracks, slowly and carefully.

It was still tiring, but it was manageable.

Everything changed the day the director called me into the safe house to do translation for her and the human rights lawyer. We would hear Habiba's entire story from start to finish—her story of trauma.

If God had not clearly called me to be there and do this, I would not have driven to the safe house that day. I would not have sat in that translation chair.

It was an enormous responsibility. Was I ready for this? Was I equipped? Was I trained? Was my Arabic good enough? What if I misunderstood or translated something incorrectly? What if I messed up Habiba's story when I told it to the director and the lawyer?

Most of all, was my heart prepared to hear her story—her sacred story of pain and suffering?

I felt heavy and sick to my stomach as I drove into the city that day.

"God, are you sure you want me to do this? Is there anyone else? Surely, there's someone else in this big city who can speak Arabic better than I can."

But no, there wasn't anyone else. There wasn't anyone else who could hear, understand, listen, and translate.

"Please be with me, God," I prayed in the car. "Please help me understand and be your translation bridge. Please equip me and give me supernatural Arabic comprehension and speaking ability today."

We met in a neutral place—a church—and sat down around the oval table. It would be a long afternoon, taking hours to walk through her story in three languages—Arabic, English, and Spanish.

I leaned over the table and looked Habiba in the eyes. "We are ready to listen. We are ready to hear your story."

───✎───

Multiple times during the conversation, I had to stop. My mind was foggy. My brain was hurting. My head was pounding. My heart was breaking.

Hearing the three languages swirling around me, hearing Habiba's traumatic story over and over—in Arabic, English, and Spanish—was heavy.

Jumping the three language tracks constantly for hours was more than I could physically, mentally, or emotionally handle. And the burden of her story felt like a ton of bricks.

I didn't want to be a translation bridge, but I had to be. I had to obey. God had called me and equipped me for this moment.

CHAPTER SIXTEEN

THE TELLING

I Came Here to Pick Strawberries

I came here to pick strawberries,
Leaving a hard life in my beloved land of Morocco,
Hopes and dreams of a better life, of a better place,
Shattered, broken—my dreams, my life, my dignity,
my heart.

I ran away from poverty, from problems,
I ran head on into poverty, into problems,
Hopes and dreams of a better life, of a better place,
Shattered, broken—my dreams, my life, my dignity,
my heart.

I struggled to cross the border into a new land,
With papers and visa for only three months,
By foot, taxi, boat, bus, I journeyed,
I arrived at my destination—weary and dreamy-eyed.

Every day, I broke my back picking strawberries in the fields,
In the heat—long hours, long days, long weeks, long months,
Every day, I broke my back side-by-side with other women,
Women with the same story of hopes and dreams of a better life, a better place.

After just a few months, I didn't want to leave,
I didn't want to return to my hard life in my beloved land of Morocco,
Hopes and dreams of a better life, of a better place,
Shattered, broken—my dreams, my life, my dignity, my heart.

A man from my country rescued me from the fields,
Rescued me and the other women from the land of strawberries,
The man promised us hopes and dreams of a better life, of a better place,
Dreamy-eyed, we followed the man into another land.

This was no land of strawberries, this land was dark, sad, scary, and evil,
A land of slavery it was, with no rescue, no freedom, no better life, no better place,
Controlled by others, terrified, locked alone in a dark

room,
Shattered, broken—my dreams, my life, my dignity,
my heart.

"Go out, go down the street, go with the men, go into
their beds,
Bring back money to me to pay for your dark room
with no lights,
Bring back money to me to pay for your scrap of food
you cannot eat,"
I have no appetite for food, no sleep, no peace, no
dream.

"Drink, smoke until you are numb and feel no more,
Drink, smoke until you forget the dark, sad, scary, evil
land,
Drink, smoke until you no longer know who you are,
Drink, smoke until you no longer want to leave the
land of slavery."

Where are my fields of strawberries now?
Where are my dreams and hopes now?
Where are the women from my land who bent down
beside me?
Where is my beloved land of Morocco?

I can never return to my fields of strawberries.
I can never return to my beloved land and family.
I can never leave this dark, sad, scary, evil land of

slavery.
I can never find a better life, a better place.

Fear grips my heart as I sit in my dark room without
lights,
Men and women enter the house, they terrify me,
They took my friend, she never returns,
Shattered, broken—my dreams, my life, my dignity,
my heart.

One day, a knock at the door, a light dawned,
Light entered the darkness of my scary land,
Two women promised me hopes and dreams of a
better life, a better place,
I took their hands, was it to rescue me or to take me to
another land of slavery?

Not knowing who they were or where I was going, I
trusted, I risked,
Any other land of slavery would be better than my
dark, sad, scary, and evil land,
Hopes and dreams of a better life, a better place, they
rescued me,
I entered a land of freedom, refuge, joy, love, and
peace.

My new land is like the land of strawberry fields,
Bright scarlet and dark green colors of life, love, and
joy,

Women from other lands sit beside me now, women
with the same story,
Restored hopes and dreams of a better life, a better
place.

I came here to pick strawberries.

⸺ℓℓ⸻

As I listened to Habiba's story and watched her cry, as I wiped
those tears that fell, I remembered. I remembered living in
Morocco—the last time I saw that many tears fall.

Our dear friends had lost their six-year-old son to meningitis. It
was sudden, unexpected. He died in his mother's arms on the way to
the hospital. They thought he had the flu.

By the time we arrived at the hospital, all the family was there.
The boy's mother, my beloved friend, screamed with agony over the
loss of her first-born son.

I'll never forget the words of the women who gathered around
her.

"Don't cry! Don't cry! Don't cry!" all the ladies shouted in
Arabic.

Crying is shameful in Arab culture—a sign of weakness and
doubt in the sovereignty of God.

"Don't cry! Don't cry! Don't cry!" all the ladies shouted.

Those words echoed in my heart and mind for days, for weeks, for
months, for years. I still hear them sometimes. They haunt me.

I watched my dear friend straighten up, tighten up, doing her
best to suppress the flood of tears that welled up in her eyes. She
tried with all her strength to hold back the wails of agony that
barreled through her body.

"Don't cry! Don't cry! Don't cry!" all the ladies shouted.

When I went to visit my friend the following week, we were alone
in her living room. I held her in my arms.

"Cry, cry, cry," I told my friend. "God grieves and cries with you.
It's okay to cry. He is the Tear Collector."

"Cry, cry, cry," I told Habiba. "God grieves and cries with you. It's okay to cry. He is the Tear Collector."

⁓

The Tear Collector

I've never seen so many tears.

I've never seen so many tears fall.

They pour from a deep well, a bottomless pit.

I've never seen so many tears.

I've never seen so many tears fall.

I reach over and brush my fingertips across your soft cheek.

It's wet.

I wipe your tears.

More tears fall.

It's a waterfall, a beautiful waterfall.

"No shame, my sister, cry, cry."

Your heart is crushed, full of pain.

Your soul is broken, shattered to pieces.

"No shame, my sister, cry, cry."

There's a bottle in His hand.

A precious bottle with your name.

He holds it gently in His hand.

A precious bottle with your name.

It says "Habiba," and it's yours.

A precious bottle with your name.

It holds your tears, each one that falls.

A precious bottle with your name.

"No shame, my sister, cry, cry."

He is the Tear Collector, the one who holds,

A precious bottle with your name.

Next to the bottle is a book.

A precious book with your name.

In it, He records each tear.

In it, He records each story.

A precious book with your name.

He sees it all, He knows it all.

The silent tears, the secret tears.

The ones that fall in the night.

The ones that no one sees.

He sees it all, He knows it all.

He won't forget, each tear, each story.

He is the Tear Collector, the one who holds,

A precious bottle with your name.

He sees each tear that falls.

He won't forget.

"No shame, my sister, cry, cry."

"You keep track of all my sorrows. You have collected all my tears in your bottle. You have recorded each one in your book."
Psalm 56:8—The Bible NIV

TODAY, I WOULD RATHER

Today, I would rather . . .

Today, I would rather sip a glass of hot, sweet mint tea with you.

Today, I would rather sit down and make small talk with you,

Today, I would rather create jewelry at the dining room table with you.

Today, I would rather work on your morning Spanish lesson with you.

Today, I would rather do a lot of things with you, my friend,

Today, I would rather spend time with you in other ways, my friend.

But, today, that's not our reality. But, today, that's not
on our agenda.

Today, we go to the private basement room,
Today, we gather with those who try to help.

Today, we sit around the table together,
Today, we talk about the pain of your journey,

Today, they ask you difficult questions,
Today, they inquire about the hard parts of your life.

Today, you have to tell your whole story,
Today, you have to remember the pages of suffering,

Today, I sit at the middle of the table,
Today, I find myself in the mixed pool of languages.

Today, I listen to them speak in Spanish, in English,
Today, I become dizzy in the linguistic dance.

Today, I listen to you speak Arabic,
Today, I become a language bridge,

Today, I absorb the onslaught of your pain and
suffering,
Today, I digest the horrible reality and truth of your
story.

Today, I process your deep and raw emotions,
Today, I transmit the message of your hard journey,

Today, I sit and watch you cry,
Today, I reach across the table and hold your hand,

Today, I wipe the falling tears on your cheeks.
Today, I weep with you, my friend.

Today, I drown in the confusing pool of words,
Today, I am a broken translation bridge,

Today, I am the only path of communication,
Today, I am the only verbal link that unites.

Today, your heart breaks as you walk the road of healing.
Today, my heart breaks as I journey with you.

Today, I would rather sip a glass of hot, sweet mint tea with you.
Today, I would rather sit down and make small talk with you,

Today, I would rather create jewelry at the dining room table with you.
Today, I would rather work on your morning Spanish lesson with you.

Today, I would rather do a lot of things with you, my friend,
Today, I would rather spend time with you in other ways, my friend.

Tomorrow, that will be our reality.
Tomorrow, that will be on our agenda.

Tomorrow, let's have a glass of hot, sweet mint tea.

CHAPTER SEVENTEEN

THE TREASURE BOX

**HABIBA ASKED ME TO TELL HER
STORY TO THE WORLD AFTER
THIS PART OF THE STORY TOOK
PLACE.**

P lease don't tell anyone my story, and please don't make me tell
my story again," Habiba pleaded with me after our meeting.

"Your story is safe with us," I told her. "We won't tell anyone. You
can trust us."

One year later, I received Habiba's permission to tell her story. I
reassured her I would change all names and locations in order to
keep her and all others safe.

Habiba's story was heavy, heart-breaking. Many of the scenes she
described brought her feelings of shame. It was as if shame cloaked
her. Her story was also scary. The horror, the fear in her eyes was real,
especially when she talked about the woman in the veil who ran the
brothel, Madame. She was terrorized, afraid that somehow her story
might leave this table, this room, and travel back down to that part
of Spain. What if they found out she was telling her story? What if
they found out she was telling people what they had done to her?

She was terrified.

The lawyer explained to Habiba that everything she shared was
confidential. As Habiba's lawyer, she was under oath, under

contract, legally bound. She could lose her job if she shared Habiba's story or information with anyone outside of the room. The safe house director and I also reassured Habiba that we would tell no one her story and the information she had shared with us. The lawyer also promised her she would report nothing to the police. If Habiba wanted to turn in her perpetrators, she would have to tell them herself.

I wasn't sure what Habiba understood about confidentiality and keeping her story safe. However, knowing that she came from an oral culture, I thought that perhaps sharing a visual image with her would be helpful.

I told her it was like a beautiful treasure box sitting on the table between us. Her story was precious and sacred . . . to her, to us, to God. I told her we would guard and protect her story, that everything she had shared would be placed in that beautiful treasure box. We would lock and seal it. No one else had the key but us. We would allow no one to open the treasure box to let out her story. When we would meet again the following week, when she was ready, we would unlock and open the lid of the treasure box to take out her story. We would continue walking with her to process and try to understand it.

Our time together that afternoon was ending, and Habiba was emotionally exhausted from sharing her story. I confess we were too. It was a lot to hear, a lot to absorb. I felt drained and overwhelmed, and I wasn't even the one telling the story. I was feeling the deep effects of Habiba's trauma.

Habiba's trauma. Habiba's story. I had not lived the story. I had only listened to it.

"Can we stop and put your story in the treasure box now?" I asked Habiba. "It's safe here. It's protected."

She nodded her head, still teary-eyed.

I went through the physical hand motions of placing her heart's story inside an imaginary box. She understood. We prayed and left the upstairs room of the church where we had gathered. When I got back to my car, I sat down and cried.

I carried Habiba's sacred story in the treasure box of my heart. It became a part of me.

For days after first hearing the traumatic details, I would often think about her story. It disturbed me, waking me in the night, haunting me, and stealing my sleep. I could hear the words of one of my favorite poets, Rupi Kaur, "It isn't blood that makes you my sister, it's how you understand my heart and carry it in your body." I truly carried Habiba's heart and story in my body.

I often had to pray and remind myself—just like Habiba—that her sacred story was locked and sealed in that beautiful treasure box. I needed to leave it there and not take it out until we would meet again.

One day, I bought two treasure boxes for Habiba and me. They were made of broken bangles from women in India, handcrafted by rescued victims of sex trafficking. The brightly-colored, mismatched, broken pieces created a beautiful treasure box. Mine sat on my nightstand.

Sometimes Habiba's story would try to seep out of the treasure box beside my bed and creep out from under the lid. With intention, I would have to close the lid tightly and seal it again.

Her sacred story was a hard one, a heartbreaking one. My heart was breaking from the burden, and I couldn't carry it any longer. That's when I began to write, when I began to write Habiba's story. I had to release it—release her pain, my pain, through the ink across the pages. That's what I'd always done, since I was a little girl, filling journal after journal with stories. Writing was my way of escape. Writing was how I processed, learned, and released.

To manage my pain, I had to get Habiba's story out of my heart and mind and onto the pages. Tears often fell onto those pages, smearing the ink. I kept those journals, those pages in safekeeping. Yes, Habiba's story needed to be protected. When the time was right, when she was ready, perhaps Habiba would be ready to open the treasure box and reveal her story. Habiba's story needs to be told. It has to be told.

Silence must speak.

CHAPTER EIGHTEEN

MY REFLECTIONS

Hating Men

As I left the church that day, after hearing the details of Habiba's story, I felt sick, sick to my stomach.

During the meeting, I experienced deep grief and sadness. It was as if I could feel her pain—physical, emotional, and mental.

I had wandered with her through that creepy house as she had gone to sit in her pitch black room. I had journeyed with her on the streets and had stood next to her, alongside the other women—like a herd of cattle. I had waited with her for the men to come and choose her, to devour her like a piece of meat. I had entered back through the door of the brothel with her after a hard day's work—taking her few euros back to Madame to pay for her room and board.

As I held her hand, wiped her tears from her face, prayed for her, I felt heavy with grief. It was as if I had absorbed her pain and sorrow as my own.

However, during my hour-long drive from the safe house back to my home that day, I began to feel something different stirring inside. I felt an anger, a rage rising in me, a disgust, an indignation fueling my thoughts and my emotions.

How could this happen? How could someone sell, traffic, and exploit these innocent, vulnerable women, taking advantage of these young girls who weren't proficient in the Spanish language, who didn't know the local cultural norms, who were far away from their homelands and families, who didn't have the financial means to care for themselves, who didn't have the power or courage to resist, fight, and say no?

It was so unjust, so unfair, so wrong. And it was illegal. Human trafficking is against the law, and it takes place right there before our very eyes, in broad daylight.

While driving, more foreign feelings began to surface in my heart. They felt dark and ugly.

One of these feelings bubbling up was hatred—powerful feelings of hatred towards men. Not just the men who had done these horribly wrong and depraved things to Habiba, but all men.

As I passed by men walking on the streets, men driving their cars next to me, men at the cash registers of my local grocery store, men everywhere, men all around me . . . made me feel sick to my stomach.

They all looked to me like beastly pigs, sex-hungry monsters, male chauvinists, disgusting gigolos.

I wanted nothing to do with the male species. It was a strong resistance and push-back that I could feel physically—inside my body, inside my soul.

But, the problem was that I was driving home. I was heading to a place where there were men. The males in my life were many—my husband and my four sons.

Hatred. Disgust. Indignation. Rage.

It was as if, in my mind, I couldn't separate the good guys from the bad guys. They were all thrown into the same basket, all lumped together in one big, ugly, deplorable heap!

Men, men, men, men...

Were they all the same? Were they all beastly pigs and sex-hungry monsters? Were they all capable of doing what those men had done to Habiba? Is that all they thought about and wanted—sex?

During the entire car ride home, I wrestled with these disturbing thoughts and emotions.

As I entered my house and greeted my husband, I swallowed those dark thoughts. I reminded myself that all men are not like those men in the bars and on the streets who pay for sexual acts with exploited women.

No, they are not all like that. My husband is not like that, he is a good man, with high moral values and ethics.

Throughout the evening, as I looked at my husband and my two oldest sons—ages twenty and twenty-two—I had to continually pray that God would help me to release my warped thoughts and feelings and see the truth of who they were.

When I lay down next to my husband in bed that night, I had to tell myself that the man I had chosen to spend the rest of my life with would not harm me, hurt me, abuse me, exploit me, take advantage of me, use me or any other woman.

Men, men, men, men . . .

No, they are not all the same.

I spoke to Habiba . . .

"I'm sorry that you never had a man, a husband, like mine. I am sorry that you never knew the love, the care, the protection, and the comfort of a real man, a loyal man, an honest man, a good man. I am sorry, Habiba. You deserved a man, a husband, like mine. You deserved to be loved, cared for, protected, and comforted by a good man. Habiba, it might be hard for you to believe this right now, but I promise you . . . there are good men in the world. There are good men out there. I met one. I know one. I have one. My husband. I hope you can meet him one day. I hope you can be introduced to a real man, a good man—at least once in your life."

~ele~

I'll Never Look at Strawberries the Same Again.

"We should probably eat those strawberries that I bought a few days ago," Vincent told me as he opened the refrigerator. "Don't want 'em to go bad."

I was in the kitchen doing the last-minute prep for dinner. I grabbed one of the wrapped plastic containers and started to tear off the clear packaging. "*Fresón Palos*" it read, stamped in white on all sides of the plastic wrapping. I quickly flipped over the container and read the words of the address, "*Palos de la Frontera, Espana.*" That's where Habiba lived and worked in the strawberry fields. That's where the women still live and work today, the very ones who picked and packaged the fruit I now held in my hands.

I love strawberries—that beautiful, bright-red, heart-shaped fruit with a leafy green hat on its head. Strawberries, one of the few fruits I'm not allergic to. I love strawberries. I love their sweet taste, their juicy center. I love everything about strawberries.

I used to love everything about strawberries. Not anymore.

I used to not react to strawberries. Not anymore.

I'll never look at strawberries the same way again.

Never.

Since I met Habiba, strawberries mean something different to me. Although beautiful, they now represent something ugly and nasty. Although sweet, they now represent something bitter and dark. Although fresh, they now represent something rotten and dead. Since I met Habiba, I'll never look at strawberries the same way again. Now, when I see a strawberry, I react. Something deep inside the pit of my stomach tightens. A mixed emotion of sadness and anger violently floods my soul. Grief overwhelms my heart. Disbelief plagues my mind.

How can a small, simple red strawberry affect me this way?

I turned over the plastic container and dumped the fresh strawberries into the white colander. The cold water from the faucet ran over them, washing them clean from dirt and debris.

"If only it were that easy to be washed clean," I thought to myself.

As I delicately picked up each strawberry in my hand, I examined its size, shape, texture, and color.

"I wonder which woman's hands picked this strawberry," I asked myself as I gently turned the fragile fruit in my hand.

Some strawberries were dark red and mushy. They were aged and bruised. I tossed them in the nearby garbage can.

"I wonder which woman's hands picked that strawberry—the one I just threw out. Which woman? Which field? Which owner?" I thought.

"Was it all worth it . . . to pick a strawberry that would one day be tossed, thrown out in the trash? Was it all worth it? All that you have gone through and suffered . . . to pick that strawberry for me?" I wondered.

Aching filled my heart, and I felt nauseous.

I'll never look at strawberries the same way again.

"Mommy, can you cut them up and add some sugar?" my seven-year-old son asked me innocently.

He didn't know what I knew about strawberries. He didn't know what I knew about the strawberry fields. He didn't know what I knew about the women who pick strawberries in the fields of Spain. He didn't know what I knew. I didn't want him to know. No, I didn't want him to know.

I cut up the strawberries in quarters, and my son happily sprinkled the cut-up pieces with a tablespoon of sugar. He stirred them. With his tiny hands, he picked up the sweet, red, juicy fruit and ate it.

"Yummy! Yummy in the tummy!" he said with a smile from ear to ear.

They tasted so sweet and good to him.

He didn't know what that woman went through to pick that strawberry for him. He didn't know what happened to that woman who picked that strawberry in the field, with her back hunched over in pain. He didn't know that woman's name. He didn't know what she looked like. He didn't know about her pain and her suffering.

He didn't know. I didn't want him to know.

But I knew. I knew her name. I knew her pain.

I'll never look at strawberries the same again.

—— *ele* ——

Morocco

Morocco—the land I left behind.
Morocco—the place I still call home.
Morocco—the country to which I can never return.

It has been ten years since we had to leave, since we had to uproot our life, our family, our work, our home...

Everything. Uprooted. Gone. Finished.

We went there to stay, to stay forever. We planted. We settled. We made it our home.

Our neighbors became family. We had more "*mamas*" and "*babas*" than any heart could hold, more sisters and brothers than a quiver could carry. People who loved us and people we loved surrounded us.

We still love them.

Our boys grew up there and loved everything about that land— the *couscous*, the *tagines*, the beach across the street from our house, the chameleons for sale in the outdoor market, the surfing lessons, the camel rides in the dunes, the friendly faces, the hot, sweet mint tea in shiny silver pots.

Their lives were there. Their friends were there. Their house was there. Their school was there. Their entire world was there.

Then, suddenly, one day, it wasn't. It wasn't there anymore. It was gone. It existed no more. It could no longer be their life, their friends, their house, their school, their world.

Gone in an instant.

One call, one decision, one word that changed our lives forever.

"Leave!"

Frantically, we packed our bags, loaded our suitcases and our dog in the van, and drove to the border to cross the Mediterranean Sea into another foreign land—Spain.

Just like Habiba.

Although, unlike Habiba, we didn't want to go. We didn't choose to leave. With deep agony, we said goodbye to the people—the family and friends we loved in that land—the language and culture that made our hearts and mouths sing, the beauty of that place that took our breath away, the land we called home.

We saw it in the rearview mirror, then we saw it no more.

Morocco—the land we left behind.
Morocco—the place we still call home.
Morocco—the country to which we can never return.

Leaving that place, our hearts broke. Our family grieved, longing for the land we loved.

Moving to France, we discovered Morocco again—people from that land now living in France. We tasted Morocco again. We smelled it again. We touched it again. We breathed it again.

But we still longed for more. We still longed to see Morocco again.

Running, grieving, longing, our feet have carried us around the world and back . . . still searching for that land of El Dorado.

We crossed the border into Spain. Could this be? Could this be it? This place of peace, this land of milk and honey, this dream? Could this be where our family could once again find happiness, find hope, find a future? Could there be streets paved with gold, a land where we could find all that we want, all that we need?

Spain got us closer to the land we love. Spain feels more like Morocco than France. Spain is only separated from the land we love by a small body of water—the Strait of Gibraltar. Maybe if we went further south, if we got closer to the shoreline, maybe then... just maybe... we could see Morocco, see our land in the far distance.

Just maybe.

Then, one day, I found you, Habiba.
I found Morocco. You are Morocco.
Then, one day, Habiba found me, Morocco found me.
I met Morocco here in this new land, this new land of Spain.
That is why I love to visit you every Monday.
That is why I love to sit and have mint tea with you each week.
That is why I love to walk and talk in Arabic with you.
Habiba, you are Morocco.
Habiba, you are the closest I can get.
Habiba, you are the sights, the sounds, the tastes, the smells, the feelings that I miss.
Habiba, you are Morocco.
I long no more.
I grieve no more.
I found you, Habiba. I found Morocco.
I love you, Morocco. I love you, Habiba.

—*ele*—

Painful Parts of Your Story

I began to fill page after page, journal after journal, processing the story God had called me to hear. Every day, every night, I wrote story after story of my journey alongside Habiba—our separate journeys to the land of El Dorado, divinely meeting each other somewhere in the middle.

As I began to write her story, I found myself skipping over chapters, chapters that I didn't want to write. They were too painful. I didn't want to remember them, didn't want to write them, didn't want to record them, didn't want to tell them, didn't want the ink to bring them into existence. If the pages of those chapters remained blank, perhaps I could convince myself that they never really happened. Those things never existed, never were.

Those stories were too painful—too painful for her, too painful for me.

Perhaps there was a reason—beyond pain—that kept me from going to those places. Perhaps there was a deeper, unconscious reason I kept avoiding the writing of those stories. Perhaps it was in the writing of those words, those stories, that I would find the greatest depth of healing—healing for my soul.

Perhaps it was time to go there, to turn that page, to pick up my pen.

CHAPTER NINETEEN

THE THREE ROADS OF IMMIGRATION

"**Y**ou have three options."

I translated the human rights lawyer's words from English into Arabic for Habiba during one of our later meetings. The lawyer explained Habiba's three options for acquiring legal residence papers in Spain.

She could wait until she had lived in Spain for three years and then hope that the government would grant her legal immigrant status. It sounded simple, but three years is a long time to wait without paperwork and no legal right to work. In the end, the government might say no and deport her back to Morocco.

Another option was for Habiba to ask for asylum and international protection in Spain because of persecution in her home country. For those seeking asylum, they usually make a decision within a year.

That option wasn't ideal either. Although Habiba had experienced difficult circumstances in Morocco with the death of her husband and raising her son alone, there was nothing in her story—no proof—that showed persecution in her homeland. Morocco is not considered a dangerous country from which citizens regularly have to flee government persecution. Like Habiba, most leave for Spain or other foreign lands because of financial hardship and poverty. They are all "dreamers," seeking El Dorado, a land flowing with milk and honey.

A last option for Habiba was to take a risk and denounce her perpetrators. According to the human rights lawyer, her story would need to be solid—"not having any holes"—clearly indicating that she was a victim of exploitation and human trafficking. In this case, she could choose to go to the police with the human rights lawyer in order to turn in her abusers. The perpetrators would then be arrested immediately, and Habiba would come under international protection. If she chose this option, Habiba would be granted paperwork and a work permit easily and quickly.

After listening to the lawyer explain the three options for residence, I attempted to translate and explain everything to Habiba. It was quite complex and difficult for her to understand.

"You have three roads you can walk down," I explained. "You have to choose which one you want to take."

I asked the lawyer for a blank piece of paper, and I quickly rough-sketched three roads. As I explained each of the options to obtain residence papers, I pointed to one of the roads.

When I got to the last road about turning in her abusers, I saw a look of horror on Habiba's face.

"I can't, I can't go to the police. If they find out, they will kill me," she said, with terror in her eyes. "I don't want to go to the police. I'm afraid."

The lawyer told her she had time to think about it. She didn't need to decide that day. This was a huge decision, and Habiba would have to be the one to make the choice.

"Don't feel any pressure. Whichever road you decide to take, you won't walk alone. We'll be with you the entire time," the lawyer reassured her.

Habiba needed residence papers and a work permit. However, if she wanted her papers quickly, she would have to be ready to take an enormous risk and step of faith. It would take great courage—great courage to turn in those who had hurt her, used her, abused her.

"Are you going to tell my story to the police?" Habiba asked the lawyer.

"No, I can't tell the police your story. You have to tell them yourself," the lawyer explained. "Everything you tell us is confidential and stays in this room."

Our meeting ended. We would have to wait and see what Habiba would decide. Which road would she choose to walk down?

"None of them denounce," the lawyer explained to me after the meeting. "They're all too afraid. It's the Mafia."

After hearing Habiba's story, I understood why she was afraid.

A few weeks later, I was called by a different safe house to translate for another Moroccan woman they had just rescued off the streets.

The lawyer and I sat in a circle with the young woman in the office.

Once again, I found myself drawing three roads on a piece of blank paper and explaining the three different options she had to obtain legal paperwork and a work permit in Spain.

When I told her she could choose to denounce her perpetrators and turn in her abusers, she immediately said, "No!"

She had the same look of horror that I had seen in Habiba's eyes.

"I can't go to the police and tell them. They'll kill me," she said in tears, "Just like they did those other girls."

I touched her arm gently to reassure her and to express my compassion. I was sorry that she had to experience something so horrific.

"She's seen death too. She's afraid," I told the human rights lawyer. It was the same story of Mafia terror that I had heard from Habiba . . . and all the other women.

The lawyer told the woman that she had time to decide which road she would walk.

I could hear the words echoing from the other safe house. "None of them denounce. They are all too afraid. It's the Mafia."

Just like Habiba, that Moroccan woman never denounced. She still awaits her residence papers, and her exploiters are still out there free, probably using and abusing more women and young girls.

A few months later, I received a text from that same human rights lawyer.

"Can you come on Friday to translate for me? We have a new Moroccan girl with us, and she's ready to denounce her perpetrators," she said. "This is really rare."

I agreed to meet the new girl and to translate for her.

"She must have so much courage and faith," I texted the lawyer.

As I walked through the door of the safe house that day, a young 27-year-old woman greeted me in the entryway. When she introduced herself, I knew she was the Moroccan woman I was there to help. She was kind and respectful and was happy that I could speak her mother tongue. Her smile lit up when I spoke to her in her Arabic dialect.

I wasn't sure if I was ready to hear another traumatic story of sex trafficking that day—another abused woman, another painful journey.

No, I wasn't sure if I was ready to hear another story of suffering at the hands of abusers. However, I was definitely ready to meet a courageous young woman who was willing to turn in her abusers. I was definitely ready to listen to the evidence that would hopefully stop one man from abusing one more woman.

I was ready.

"I'm here to listen to your story," I told her.

CHAPTER TWENTY

BROKEN WOMEN IN THE HOUSE

"Not all brokenness is compatible," someone had told me. I had never really thought much about those words—until I met Habiba—until I started spending time regularly at the safe house. I had seen brokenness before. Much of my childhood was paved with brokenness, pain, and sorrow. Our family had known grief and trauma, as a result of alcoholism. I had also lived through multiple divorces as a child and had lost my little sister. I knew what it felt like and what it looked like to be broken. But never in my life had I seen this depth of brokenness—not until the day I walked through that door.

The atmosphere in the living room was dark and heavy. There were no smiles. There was no laughter. Hearts were shattered. Souls were shattered.

I had just stepped into a world of brokenness, and I didn't know what to do.

All I could do was reach out to them with a hand of love—hug them, smile at them, serve them, love them. I couldn't change them. I couldn't make them whole. I couldn't restore them. I couldn't fix them. All I could do was listen to their stories and pray—pray that God, the Comforter, would comfort them, pray that God, the Redeemer, would redeem them, pray that God, the Healer, would heal them, pray that God, the Repairer of Broken Breaches, would repair them.

"Your people will rebuild the ancient ruins and will raise up the age-old foundations; you will be called Repairer of Broken Walls, Restorer of Streets with Dwellings." Isaiah 58:12—The Bible NIV

There was also a hardness in the hearts of these women. They had built up emotional walls for self-protection.

"I have a heart, but I can't feel," Habiba told me one day.

I wondered what that depth of brokenness would feel like. What would it be like to have a heart but not feel?

Brokenness, utter brokenness. Under the roof of this safe house lived seven broken women.

"Not all brokenness is compatible." Those words resounded in my mind.

The safe house was a melting pot of brokenness, pain, cultures, personalities, backgrounds, and languages. In this house, there were women from Nigeria, Colombia, Morocco, Russia, and Venezuela. It was a broken, cross-cultural, explosive mix.

"There are a lot of fights here," the psychologist at the house warned me. "Physical and verbal fights."

"Why is that?" I asked, in ignorance. It was one of my first days volunteering at the house.

"These women are all broken and bring a lot of pain into the house," she said. "They take it out on each other."

Pain. Brokenness. What do you do with it, when it's so overwhelming? It overflows, and you can't contain it. It seeps from your pores, and it's ugly when it comes out.

Rob Reimer, author of *Soul Care*, describes this brokenness as "infected splinters that are whacking up against each other."[1]

People's pain brushes up against the pain of others. Our pain and brokenness together cause each other even more pain.

"Not all brokenness is compatible."

On multiple occasions, Habiba was aggressive and violent with some women at the safe house. Her pain and trauma seemed to flow out of her and hurt many along the way.

Pain. Brokenness. It's ugly. It hurts.

"We have to tell you something difficult about Habiba. Last night, she had a conflict. She hit her roommate. We're trying to figure out what to do, because this is serious misconduct. The team is evaluating the situation. Can you come on Friday to the house? It's impossible to communicate with her."

When I read the psychologist's text in her broken English, four months later, I knew that this was more than a simple fight. There were going to be serious consequences for Habiba. This wasn't her first incident of anger and physical violence.

Serious Misconduct. Discipline. My heart sank.

I didn't know all the details, but there had already been other outbursts of anger from Habiba at the safe house. The smallest thing could trigger her. Her frustration, her irritability, her anger— all direct results of her trauma—were often manifested in violence and aggression toward others.

Her heart, soul, and mind were in turmoil. She couldn't contain the pain. She had to evacuate it and release it. It wasn't happening in a healthy way as her pain-filled emotions ran wildly in her destructive words and physical violence towards others. It gushed out, and it was ugly.

It hurt others, and it hurt her.

I went to the safe house on Friday. They had called a meeting with the director and another team member. I was the translator. There I was again, stuck in the middle of a mess. Once again, I would have to be the translation bridge between a hurting, broken woman and those caring for her and making decisions about her life.

We gathered in the small, private basement room and closed the door. It surprised Habiba to see me. She did not know we were meeting that day to discuss her behavior and her future.

"I was sleeping and snoring. My roommate got up, turned on the bedroom light, and started hitting me. I jumped out of bed and pushed her off me."

I listened to the comments and questions of the safe house director in Spanish. The other team member then translated them into English for me.

"You hit her and you pulled her hair braid off," I explained calmly to Habiba in Arabic.

She admitted to the fault, but felt that her roommate also deserved a punishment. The difference was this was Habiba's third offense.

"You're hurting badly," the director explained. "You need help, and we can't help you."

I translated her words into Arabic with fear and trembling. I had already witnessed first-hand Habiba's violent and dramatic reactions to difficult situations. I knew what was coming, and this shocking news had the potential to trigger her again.

The director had briefed me before the meeting. They could no longer help and care for Habiba if she would not follow the house rules. There were seven women in the house—a lot of brokenness and trauma under one roof. She would need to leave.

"We called many safe houses in the city to see if someone would take Habiba. They all said 'no,'" said the director. "They all said 'no' except for one."

When I asked the location, I couldn't believe my ears. Habiba's new safe house was only ten minutes from my house, as opposed to the one-hour drive each way into the city that I was accustomed to making. She would now be closer to me, and I was selfishly relieved and delighted. I could visit her more often.

This would not be good news for Habiba, however. She had been at this safe house for seven months. This was her home. The team of volunteers and the other rescued women were her sisters—her family. I carefully chose my words to translate the director's message to Habiba in that little room.

"You're hurting badly. You need help, and they can't help you."

Habiba's eyes welled up in tears. I listened to the next words that I needed to translate and prepared my heart to tell her the hard news.

Why did I always have to be the one to bear the bad news? Why couldn't Habiba understand Spanish, or why couldn't they speak Arabic? Why did I have to have this role, this job, this huge and heavy responsibility?

"We don't feel that we can provide what you need, so we've found another home for you."

As soon as I spoke the words in Arabic, Habiba jumped up and screamed in tears, "I don't want to go! I don't want to go! You can't make me go!"

She ran out of the room. We sat in silence, in disbelief. What were we going to do?

"If she wants to go, if she wants to walk out that door, we can't stop her. There's nothing we can do," the director told me.

One of the staff members went up to Habiba's bedroom to talk to her and calm her down. She agreed to come back to the room in the basement to talk more. We explained to her she would be in a house where there were only a few women. The director of the new house was a very kind woman who could better take care of her.

She could have a room by herself and not have to worry about trying to live with someone in a small space. A private teacher would come to the house to help her with Spanish. She could have time and space away from all the other women to work through her pain and find healing.

We presented the plan. If Habiba cooperated and was willing to follow the rules, she could return to the original safe house in a few months.

"You can pack your bags, and we'll take you to the new house tomorrow."

Despite all the advantages we described, Habiba did not like the new plan for her life.

"You don't want me! You don't love me! You're kicking me out!" she screamed.

She told us over and over that she wouldn't go to the new safe house, and then she stormed out of the room again. We all sat there in disbelief. There was nothing we could do to change her mind. All we could do was pray.

So that's what we did.

After some time of asking God for help, we walked upstairs to the living room. No one said a word. There was complete silence. The other women sat on the couches, uncomfortable and quiet. Habiba marched down the stairs of the house and went into the basement. She came up with her arms full of freshly cleaned laundry from the dryer. I met her in the hallway and hugged her.

"It's going to be okay," I told her.

"I'm leaving tomorrow morning," she said.

I knew she wasn't talking about going to the new safe house. My heart was heavy and sad.

I needed to pick up my kids from school—already running late. I walked upstairs to her bedroom. Habiba stood next to an open suitcase sitting on her desk. She folded her clothes and placed them inside, one by one. Her eyes were dark and sad.

"*Bisalaama*, Habiba," I said to her in Arabic. "Goodbye."

Was it the last time I would see my friend, my sister? I had little hope for a change of heart, a change of mind. I walked out to my car and wept.

"Why, God? Why?"

(Habiba was later diagnosed with Post-Traumatic Stress Disorder (PTSD), Bi-Polar Disorder, and Disassociative Disorder—all common among victims of sex trafficking.[2] This explained much of her violent behavior, as well as that of the other women in the safe house.)

CHAPTER TWENTY-ONE

THE STRAWBERRY FIELDS ARE CALLING

The Next Day . . .

"I'm going back," Habiba said on the phone through tears. "You're going back where?" I pleaded.

I knew she was ready to leave, ready to walk out the door. Deep down inside, I knew where she was going.

The strawberry fields were calling her back. The streets were calling her back.

Just a few weeks before, another rescued Moroccan woman from the safe house had left. She packed up her suitcase, walked out the door, and went back to the same life and work from which she had come. This woman made a choice that day to leave everything behind. It was as if she had spat in the hands of those who had saved her life. They had rescued her, clothed her, fed her, protected her, and cared for her.

They had loved her.

Perhaps all of that love and care were overwhelming for her. Perhaps she didn't know what to do with it all—how to receive it. Instead, she packed her bags and went back—back to the strawberry fields, back to the streets. Even with much love and care, it was well known that many women went back, many women chose re-victimization . . . out of fear, out of desperation, out of habit.

Now, Habiba faced the same choice. It was staring right at her, calling her, beckoning her to come. Gone was the happy and hopeful Habiba I knew during the past months. Gone were her smiles, her laughter, her jewelry making, and her newfound faith. Gone was her view of looking forward to a brighter future.

Now she was looking back, looking back at the darkness. It was inviting her to return.

"I'm going back," she told me on the phone.

"You're going back where?"

"I'm going back to the streets. Where else can I go?"

I fought back tears, and my heart hurt.

"What are you going to do back on the street, Habiba?"

"I'm going to work. I'm going to make money to send back to my son and my parents. At least I can make money. My mother is sick and needs money. I can't make money here. I can make money on the streets."

"Where are you going to live?"

"I'll find a place."

"I'm sure you will," I thought to myself, imagining her sitting in her bedroom in the brothel—the one without a light bulb. "I'm sure you will."

I didn't want to remind her. I didn't want to have to remind her from where she had come. I didn't want to remind her of the horrors of her journey from the streets to the safe house. But I didn't have a choice.

"Habiba, do you really want to go back? Do you want to go back to the house that scared you, the bedroom with no light, the drugs, the alcohol, the men? Do you really want to go back to that life? Look where you've come from? Look how far you've come?"

"What else can I do?"

"Stay in the safe place, Habiba. God has rescued you and brought you out of that dark place. You now live under His umbrella of protection. If you walk out now, you are leaving His hand of blessing, walking away from the new life God has given you. You are refusing to keep the gift that He has given you." I was in tears.

"What else can I do?"

"Stay, Habiba, stay," I begged. "Please don't go. Please don't go back to the streets. You don't have legal papers to live in Spain. Right now, you come under the legal protection of the safe house and the Spanish government. If you walk out that door, they can arrest you, put you in jail, kick you out of the country. You are illegal outside of the protection of this home."

"I'm going back. I'm leaving tomorrow morning."

I wept as I said goodbye to her and hung up. There was absolutely nothing that I could say or do to convince her to stay.

All I could do was pray.

The strawberry fields were calling. The streets were calling. The pull was strong.

WHAT WOULD YOU DO?

What would you do if you were in her shoes?
What would you do if you had left everything behind?
What would you do if your son was alone in another country?
What would you do if your mother was sick on the other side of the world?
What would you do if your father was an old and poor beggar?
What would you do if you had dreamt of the land of "El Dorado"?
What would you do if you had no money in your pocket?
What would you do if you had no job?
What would you do if you had no place to go?
What would you do if your family were hungry?
What would you do if you had no bed to sleep in?
What would you do if you had no clothes to wear?
What would you do if you had no bread to eat?
What would you do if you had no legal papers?
What would you do if you were in her shoes?
What would you do?
Would you go back to the strawberry fields?
Would you go back to the streets?
Would you go back to the mean, veiled woman?
Would you go back to the men's beds?
Would you go back to the dark room?
Would you go back to the smell of cigarettes?
Would you go back to the whiskey and gin?
Would you go back to the numbness?
Would you go back to the torture and terror?
Would you go back to the dirty money?

Would you go back to the physical pain?
Would you go back to the broken heart?
Would you go back to a life of slavery?
Would you go back to the chains around your soul?
Would you go back under their authority?
Would you go back from where you came?
Would you go back?
What would you do if you were in her shoes?
What would you do?

CHAPTER TWENTY-TWO

DARE TO TRUST AGAIN

After hanging up the phone with Habiba, all I could do was hope and pray. My words, my pleas, could not convince her. It was going to take a louder and stronger conviction than my small voice. I sent a text to my friends and family around the world asking them to pray for Habiba. I didn't tell them the details because of my unwavering commitment to confidentiality.

"My friend from the safe house is in crisis. She stands at a critical crossroads. Please pray she has the courage to make the right decision."

Many responded that they were praying. I clung to the faith of others. Mine was weak, definitely smaller than a mustard seed.

Could it still move mountains? This was an enormous mountain.

> **"Truly I tell you, if you have faith as small as a mustard seed, you can say to this mountain, 'Move from here to there,' and it will move. Nothing will be impossible for you."**
> **Matthew 17:20 — The Bible NIV**

There were moments when I had great hope. Other times, I carried only heaviness and discouragement. This was one of those moments. What if I never saw Habiba again? What if she went back to the streets, to the strawberry fields?

What if . . .

Later that afternoon, I still didn't have any news from Habiba. I texted the director of the safe house.

"How's Habiba? What's going on?"

She informed me that Habiba had finally agreed to visit the new safe house in order to meet the director for a cup of tea. Everyone hoped that if she went for a visit, if she saw the new safe house, if she met the new director, perhaps she would stay.

"You can visit and see. If you don't like it, you can leave," the director had told Habiba during our meeting the day before.

Knowing that they were visiting the new safe house right at that moment, I prayed that God would give Habiba joy and peace when she entered the new home. I asked God to give her a good relationship with the director and a desire to stay with her.

"She's agreed to stay at the new house," the director texted me later that afternoon.

I felt a tremendous burden tumble off my shoulders. Relief flooded my heart and mind.

"Oh, thank heavens!" I squealed out loud.

"Can you go to the safe house tomorrow to translate for Habiba and the new director?" she asked me.

I agreed to go. My heart was overwhelmed with joy at the miraculous answers to prayer. Only God could have changed Habiba's mind, convincing her to stay in that "safe place," to stay under His "umbrella of protection." Habiba had made the right choice, and I knew God was pleased. He would honor her right decision and would bless her in this new place. God had a plan, a plan of blessing and honor for Habiba—nothing less.

The director from the previous safe house sent me the contact information of the director of the new safe house. I plugged the address into my GPS. Driving into the city ten minutes away from my home didn't take long; however, parking was a nightmare. After impatiently turning in circles for over thirty minutes, I finally texted the director and told her I didn't know what to do. Perhaps I would need to return another day. There were simply no parking places downtown.

"I'll walk out and meet you. I'll take you to a place to park," she texted.

I didn't even know where I was. I sent her a pin of my location and waited patiently for her to arrive. I was nervous about meeting her for the first time. I had a great relationship with the director of the other house. Would it be the same in this new place? Would she welcome me at the safe house regularly to translate for Habiba and to walk alongside her? This director, this Spanish woman, was the ticket for me to continue spending time with Habiba and to continue developing our friendship.

I told her what my car looked like, and she waved from afar when she saw me. She jumped into the passenger seat and gave me two kisses on the cheek—Spanish style. We laughed and talked in the car. From the start, our relationship was comfortable and natural. I could tell that I was going to like this happy, energetic, kind, and funny woman. I will call her Andrea.

After finally finding a place to park, Andrea and I walked through the quaint cobblestone streets to the safe house, about ten minutes away. We managed to communicate in my broken Spanish and her broken English. Thankfully, we were both used to navigating language barriers, so this came naturally to both of us. Several times during the walk, Andrea pulled out her phone and asked Google Translate to help us jump the language hurdles. We chuckled together as she held her phone to my ear to have me listen to her translated message in English. Andrea explained to me the situation with Habiba.

"We have to establish trust. Without trust, I can't help her," she said. "She's very angry about what happened at the other house."

I prayed God would help us talk to Habiba together. I prayed God would heal her heart of the wounds of yesterday and give her hope and faith to move forward today in a healthy way.

"It's here," Andrea said as we approached a beautiful wooden door off the main street of downtown, right next to an old stone cathedral. From the outside, no one would ever guess that behind that door was a "safe house" for exploited women.

As I stepped through the door and walked up the marble staircase to the apartment, I prayed God would help us build a strong bond of trust with Habiba. I prayed God would help me be a language bridge and to communicate clearly and accurately.

Once again, I felt the heavy weight of responsibility.

As we entered the apartment, I greeted the other women who were sitting in the living room. It was always awkward. These women were broken and traumatized, and they didn't trust people easily. They didn't know me, and I could see the fear and hesitation in their eyes.

Andrea and I first went to her office to talk privately. She asked some questions in order to get to know me more. I asked her some questions too. We then knocked on the door of Habiba's bedroom and entered. I kissed Habiba and sat down next to her on the bed. I could feel her anger and coldness. It was clear on her face and on her body. Andrea sat on the twin bed across from us.

It was hard to know what to do or what to say. I made some small talk and asked her about her new house, her new housemates, and the food. I told her I loved this city—one of my favorites. The atmosphere changed a bit, and Habiba even cracked a smile. Andrea asked her some questions and explained some things about the safe house. I translated as best as I could.

Multiple times during the conversation, Habiba became angry and began talking aggressively about the director and women at the old safe house. She was bitter and felt like they had kicked her out. As she retold us the story, she expressed a lot of shame and embarrassment about what had happened.

Shame—one of the most powerful pieces of her Arab culture. It was devastating for her.

Sadness. Anger. Shame.

It was a painful mix of emotions.

"Can you trust me?" Andrea asked Habiba.

"I don't trust anyone," Habiba answered. "I trusted the director at the other house and look what she did to me!"

Her words were forceful, full of anger and pain. Tears streamed down her face.

"My name is Andrea. I am not the other director. I am a different person. This is a different place." Andrea explained to her.

"They kicked me out! They kicked me out!" she screamed, hitting the small wooden baby crib in the middle of the room with her fist.

Habiba wasn't a mean or violent person. It was her pain. It was her trauma. It was her brokenness that made her react in these impulsive ways. Andrea and I both knew that. We weren't afraid. Our hearts were full of empathy, compassion, and love for Habiba. I prayed God would help calm her down and give her peace.

"We don't need to talk about the other house or the women there. We don't need to talk about what happened in the past. We can just talk about today and the future. Together, we can move forward," Andrea said. "This is a new beginning for you, a new place. We want to help you and love you. We want to see you healed and made whole."

I translated Andrea's words with fear and trembling. We could feel Habiba's resistance and hardness.

"Can you trust me?" Andrea asked her again, reaching out to touch her hand. "Can you give me the gift of trust?"

Habiba was silent. So were the tears that streamed down her cheeks.

"If you aren't willing to trust me, I can't help you," Andrea said. "You don't have to stay here. You can pack your bags and go now."

Habiba remained silent. I prayed.

Suddenly, I noticed Habiba's facial expression begin to soften and her body begin to relax. She looked up at me and whispered quietly in Arabic, "I will trust her."

I held her hand as tears streamed down my cheeks. I could hardly translate. I could hardly speak.

After a few silent moments, I whispered to Andrea, "She said that she will trust you."

Her eyes lit up, and she looked at Habiba. "You will trust me?!" she asked her in Spanish.

Habiba nodded her head. There on the bed, the three of us huddled together and cried.

"This is truly a miracle," I whispered to the director. "Only God could do this!"

"Let's build a relationship of trust. Let's move forward together," Andrea said. "This is a fresh start."

We prayed, asking God to help us and to lead us.

Habiba had just made another huge decision. Standing, once again, at a major crossroads, she had chosen to trust again. With all of her pain and trauma, this decision took great courage, strength, risk, and faith. There was no doubt in my mind that God would honor and bless this decision, too. We could now move forward. We could now take the next step on the journey. Habiba had dared to trust again.

PART FOUR

Her Pain

CHAPTER TWENTY-THREE

LUMPS AND HEARTS

"We're at the ER. Please pray for Habiba!" Andrea texted me. "It doesn't sound like good news from the doctor."

I didn't understand what was going on. It was so sudden. I had just been at the safe house the day before. We had experienced a major emotional breakthrough with Habiba, and it felt like we might be making some headway. It seemed like she was willing to step out and risk trusting again. What in the world was going on?

"Habiba has been complaining about pain in a lump in her chest and armpit," Andrea texted me again. "Now she can't breathe."

I prayed throughout the night, tossing and turning. How could this be happening?

The next morning's message read, "It seems that Habiba was having a panic attack. Her heart is fine, but they scheduled an appointment in a few weeks to see the doctor about the lumps."

I went to visit Habiba the next day. She seemed listless and full of sadness. Her eyes were dark and empty.

"Do you want to go out for a cup of tea?" I asked her.

She shook her head.

"Please go out with me. I'm hungry, and I could use a little bite to eat. Don't make me eat alone." I smiled, trying to coax her.

A small grin broke out on her face, and she finally agreed to go. She took off her house slippers and put on her tennis shoes. We walked down the stairs and out onto the cobblestone streets. After wandering aimlessly for a few minutes, we found a small tapas bar and sat down in the sunshine on the terrace. Habiba didn't want to eat. I ordered a small ham and egg crêpe and a Coke. I ordered her a bottle of water, but she refused to touch it.

I explained to her what the director had told me. "You have an appointment with the doctor next week for the lump in your armpit and in your chest."

"The doctor at the emergency room told me I have nothing wrong."

"The doctor you will see this week is a specialist for women," I told her. "She will know what this is. How long have you had the lump in your armpit?"

"I don't know how long."

"One year? Two years? Five years? Ten years?" I asked.

"More, more."

"You had it in Morocco?"

"Yes. I went to see a doctor. They told me I needed to have the lump removed. I didn't have any money, so they told me to leave the hospital."

I leaned over and touched her hand resting on the table. My heart ached to do more, but I felt powerless.

"I'm so sorry, Habiba. I'm so sorry."

I went home that evening and told my husband the story.

"How can this be? How can this be?" I couldn't resist the tears that streamed down my cheeks.

———

That week, while strolling through a gift shop near the safe house, something caught my eye. It was as if they were calling me—bright, colorful hearts made of small felt balls glued together. All the separate, tiny pieces made the beautiful whole. I purchased two of them.

When I saw those rainbow hearts in the store, I thought of Habiba's heart. It had been shattered, broken into a million pieces that seemed beyond repair, beyond healing.

Those bright and colorful hearts were beautiful.

I thought of how Habiba's heart was slowly healing and being made whole again, glued back together by God's hand of love. Her heart was being repaired and mended, becoming bright and beautiful for all the world to see.

———

The next day was Habiba's first doctor's appointment after her emergency visit the week before.

I didn't know what was ahead of us on this road. I didn't know the next chapter of Habiba's story. I didn't know the next part of my own story as I walked alongside this precious woman.

We sat in the waiting room for what seemed like forever. We watched woman after woman walk by, entering and exiting the gynecologist's office.

I almost forgot the colored hearts tucked away in my purse.

"I have something special for you," I told Habiba.

She smiled and looked at me with curiosity.

I took the two rainbow hearts out of my purse and showed them to her.

"They're both the same," I told her. "One of them is for you, and one is for me. You can choose the one you want."

"*Choukran*," she said, smiling softly, as she reached for the one closest to her.

"I want you to keep this heart with you all the time to remember I love you, and I'm thinking about you and praying for you. And when I see my heart, I'll think of you and remember to pray for you."

I showed her how the colorful heart comprised many small balls of felt. All the smaller, disconnected, broken pieces made up the whole. They were glued together to make a unique design—a heart.

"These broken pieces together make something beautiful, just like you. God takes our scattered, shattered pieces, glues them together with His love, and makes us whole again. That's what He did for me. That's what He did for you."

A nurse opened the door. It was time.

"Habiba."

Andrea began explaining Habiba's symptoms to the doctor. Habiba sat silently on the chair next to us. She continuously pulled the colorful heart out of her black coat pocket, holding it in her palm, looking at it, and turning it gently between her fingers. As she touched the soft, felt balls, she remembered how much I loved her. She remembered I was thinking about her and praying for her.

That day in the gift shop, I did not know what those colorful hearts meant. I did not know how that small, inexpensive gift would deeply impact Habiba. Two colorful hearts. She held hers in her hand and remembered. I held mine in my hand and remembered.

Two colorful hearts. Mine would sit beside my bed—Habiba's heart. Hers would sit beside her bed—my heart. We would be together forever.

CHAPTER TWENTY-FOUR

WHAT IS IT?

T he doctor seemed annoyed that I was there. Andrea explained I was Habiba's Arabic translator. She explained we would need to do a three-way translation between Spanish, English, and Arabic. The doctor questioned if translation was necessary and insisted on speaking to Habiba in Spanish.

"*Hola, como te llamas?*" the doctor asked her.

"*Me llamo Habiba,*" she answered proudly.

"*Hablas español?*" the doctor continued.

"*Poco,*" Habiba replied.

That was the end of the conversation in Spanish between the gynecologist and Habiba. Although Habiba had been going to language classes several times a week at the local community center for the past few months, her Spanish was still limited. She could manage basic greetings and could understand quite a bit, but this conversation was beyond her ability.

"Tell her to get undressed," the doctor told Andrea, who then translated the words to me in English.

"She can't just go get undressed and stand there naked," I said to Andrea. "She's scared."

"Go with her. Go and help her."

I am familiar with getting undressed in doctors' offices in Europe. They never offer medical gowns. I vividly remembered having to stand completely naked in front of doctors for gynecological exams, x-rays, chiropractic care, childbirths, and more. I was a modest, conservative American, who was uncomfortable standing cold and bare in front of a doctor in France. Now, here I was, standing next to Habiba, a modest, conservative Moroccan woman of Muslim background with many traumatic experiences. She was also uncomfortable and not willing to bare it all in front of a doctor in Spain.

I could feel her pain. I could feel her shame.

The doctor was oblivious to Arab culture and the deeply ingrained element of shame and modesty in her patient. She was cold and insensitive, not seeming to care. I took Habiba to the other side of the room where the medical table was located.

"The doctor wants you to get undressed," I explained to her in Arabic.

"What?! Completely undressed? My bra and underwear too?" she asked me with horror in her eyes. "No, please, no!"

I walked over to the other side of the room where Andrea was talking with the doctor.

"She can't do this. She can't undress completely and just stand there naked. There are cultural implications in this. She is a modest, conservative woman of Muslim background. She also has a background in prostitution. We have to explain this to the doctor."

Andrea walked over with me to talk to Habiba. We tried to reassure her that she would be okay, that she was safe with this female doctor. Andrea and I proceeded to help Habiba get undressed. She was in so much pain from the large lumps under her armpit and in her neck that she screamed in agony as we helped her raise her arm and wiggle out of her shirt.

"Is it okay if I unsnap your bra?" I asked her.

I wanted to be gentle and respectful of her—her body, her womanhood, her identity, her trauma. Andrea helped Habiba use her shirt to cover her exposed chest. Suddenly, I noticed some neatly folded up medical gowns on the bottom shelf of a silver metal cart near us.

"Those are medical gowns!"

We didn't even ask the doctor, who was still busy at her desk, taking notes on the other side of the room. I quickly grabbed one of the white gowns and handed it to Habiba. She put it on, and I frantically tied the strings on her backside.

We helped to cover her nakedness. We helped to cover her shame.

"Don't worry," I said to Habiba as I hugged her. "Everything's going to be alright. The doctor is going to come and examine you.

She needs to see what the lumps are. She's going to help you. You're safe here."

The doctor came over to where the three of us were. Habiba was sitting on the edge of the medical table, trembling in fear. Andrea and I stood next to her, supportive and strong. The doctor asked us to go to the other side of the room during the physical exam. A partial wall separated us.

Alone on the other side of the room, I put my arm around Andrea's shoulder.

"Let's pray," I said to her.

We asked God to comfort Habiba and to give her peace. We asked God to give wisdom to the doctor to know what was going on. We prayed that the doctor would be kind and gentle with Habiba and make her feel safe.

As we prayed, we could hear Habiba crying out in physical pain as the doctor examined her.

"Oh, God, please help Habiba! Please be with Habiba!" we pleaded.

The doctor called us to the other side of the room when she had finished the exam. She told us we could help Habiba get dressed. I stayed with her to help while Andrea went back with the doctor and sat down at her desk. We joined them a few minutes later.

My Spanish was still quite limited after being in the country for only six months. However, knowing French helped me immensely in my understanding of this new foreign language. I was usually thankful to have the ability to understand a lot, especially at times like this. However, that day, I wished I could not understand. I wished there was not any similarity between French and Spanish. I wished I could not understand words like "metastasized."

I heard the word, and I knew.

Even if I didn't understand the language, I could clearly tell from the tone, body language, and facial expressions of the doctor and of Andrea that something was seriously wrong.

I didn't want to hear. I didn't want to know. I didn't want to understand. But I heard. I knew. I understood.

CHAPTER TWENTY-FIVE

FORGIVENESS AND SOVEREIGNTY

"They think it's metastasized, but they won't know until they do more tests," Andrea said soberly, in the hospital's hallway. "I need to make the appointments for this week. She'll be here almost every day."

Knowing it would take a while, I offered to take Habiba to get some breakfast. It was still early in the morning, and neither of us had eaten. It took us a while to meander through the hospital corridors, following the foreign signs to the cafeteria. Habiba couldn't read—it didn't matter what language—and my Spanish was limited.

We entered the large cafeteria, where we saw people eating bread and croissants and drinking coffee and orange juice. At the counter, I ordered two breakfast menus.

"This cafeteria is for hospital staff only," the lady behind the cash register told me.

I started laughing and translated for Habiba in Arabic. We both quickly glanced around the room and noticed that everyone standing in line and sitting at the tables was wearing a medical coat and a hospital badge.

"We're not doctors, and we're not nurses," I said to the lady behind the counter with a loud chuckle.

Thankfully, she laughed, too. We excused ourselves and hurried out of the room to go to the "normal" cafeteria, directly across the hall. I attempted again to order our breakfast menus at the counter. We sat down and enjoyed a freshly baked croissant, *cafe con leche*, and a tall glass of freshly squeezed orange juice. Habiba wasn't hungry, but I forced her to eat a little.

We talked a lot. She had questions—questions about her life, her hard journey, her departure from the other safe house, her sickness. I had questions, too—questions about the sovereignty of God, the mystery of His ways and timing, and the absurdity of His plans.

"Why did they have to kick me out of the house?" Habiba asked me.

This was a question, a conversation that we seemed to have every time we were together. She wanted to know why. Habiba was confused and wanted answers. I had no answers.

"I don't know all the details and the reasons they asked you to leave and to come to this new safe house. But I know this is God's plan for you."

I took the salt and pepper shakers from the table and spread them out on opposite ends of the table. Then, I took a wrapped sugar cube in my hand and told her that the sugar represented her.

"You are sweet like sugar," I said, smiling.

Habiba smiled too.

I placed the wrapped sugar cube next to the salt shaker. "You were at this house before, but it seems God wanted you at this house. He had a plan for you here."

I then moved the sugar cube next to the pepper shaker at the other far end of the table. "There were people like Andrea at this house who needed to be in your life, so God moved you."

I explained to her that the other house—the salt shaker—was far away from my house. I had to drive almost one hour to visit her. The new house—the pepper shaker—was only ten minutes from my house.

"God loves you, and He had reasons to move you. We may not understand why, but because He loves you, we can trust Him."

Habiba listened quietly, but I could see lots of emotions still stirring inside her. Mainly, she was angry—angry that they had "kicked her out."

"Why did they do that to me?"

I repeated the same words. "I don't know all the details and the reasons they asked you to leave and come to this house. But I know God has a plan for you here."

I knew I needed to talk to her about forgiveness. If she didn't forgive the people at the other safe house, the bitterness and anger in her heart would destroy her. Rather than telling her she needed to forgive them, I told her my own personal story. I shared with her my journey of forgiving my alcoholic father. I had lived with deep resentment and anger for the first two decades of my life. When I met Jesus and experienced His forgiveness in my own life, I knew I had to release my father and forgive him, too.

"I couldn't do it on my own. I asked God to give me strength. I needed God to help me forgive my father, and He did."

I then shared with her a story of being hurt by some fellow co-workers in the church.

"That was even harder. I expected Christians to act differently. It was more painful for me than what my father had done. It took me a long time to forgive them and release the hurt they had caused me. But when I did, I was finally free."

Habiba listened. She wasn't yet ready to forgive, but I believed that one day she would be.

Andrea sent me a text and told me Habiba's test appointments were scheduled. We could finally leave the hospital. I hugged Habiba, and we made our way to the hospital entrance. Andrea showed me a paper with the four appointment dates and times. It was going to be a full week.

"Can you come to all the appointments to translate?" she asked me.

"I'll clear my schedule. I'll be there."

I wasn't sure what lay ahead of us that week, but I knew I needed to be there. I would walk with Habiba on this journey until the end. This might not have been the El Dorado that either of us expected when we arrived in Spain. However, we were going to walk this road together, no matter what.

CHAPTER TWENTY-SIX

THE TATTERED TISSUE

During the next few weeks, I drove to the hospital almost every day and met Habiba at the entrance. The hospital was only nine minutes from my house. Every time I drove there, it reminded me of God's perfect and good plan—even in the midst of suffering. In His sovereignty, He knew Habiba was sick and would need our help. I had to believe that was why He moved her to the new safe house. He knew she needed Andrea. He knew she needed me.

I hoped that one day Habiba would see God's loving hand in this and believe.

"If Habiba still lived at the other house and was sick, I couldn't have helped her like this," I told Andrea one day while sitting in the waiting room for Habiba to be called in for her test.

In a later conversation, Andrea shared with me that her mother had died of metastasized cancer a few years before. It seemed obvious to me that God wanted Habiba to be with Andrea for this journey. Andrea was full of deep love and compassion. It would be especially painful for her to walk alongside Habiba during this time, but she was the best person for the job.

Although the first gynecologist who had examined Habiba suspected metastasized cancer, we didn't tell her. I struggled with keeping this information from Habiba.

"Until we have all the test results, we don't know anything for certain," Andrea told me. "Habiba is already worried and anxious."

I followed Andrea's leadership and authority and trusted that she knew best. As the director of the safe house, she was the one responsible for Habiba and her care. I needed to follow her decisions.

The first week was full of appointments for blood work, body scans, x-rays, mammograms, and biopsies. On the day of the mammogram and biopsy, Andrea wasn't available to take Habiba. She sent her to the hospital with two colleagues whom I had never met. Neither of them could speak English, so we had to manage with my broken Spanish. We all got a lot of good laughs. All of us except Habiba.

She was in intense pain from the lumps in her armpit and on her neck and shoulder. They seemed to grow by the day. She could hardly lift her arm or move her head. I held her in my arms and prayed as we waited for her to be called.

"Habiba?" they shouted loudly in the crowded waiting room.

I jumped up, along with Habiba and one of the colleagues.

"Let's tell them she needs me for translation. Maybe they'll let me go with her."

I had already explained to Habiba what the procedures were like, drawing quick sketches in my hot pink leather notebook. Sometimes just knowing what is going to happen helps relieve some of the anxiety and fear. Added to that were all the language barriers between the hospital staff and Habiba. Not knowing and not understanding caused a lot of added stress—for everyone. Habiba was clearly still nervous. Knowing what she was heading into didn't seem to help.

As we entered the room for the mammogram, the safe house worker explained that I was Habiba's personal translator. The technician smiled and agreed to let me enter. We were all pleasantly surprised. I silently thanked God and told Habiba that it was a miracle that she let me go with her.

God knew Habiba needed me—not for Arabic translation, but for love and support. After helping her undress, through pain, tears, and yelps, the technician gently and patiently helped her lift her arms to get into the necessary position for the exam. With the many tumors on one side of her body, it was excruciating. I held Habiba and prayed for her, telling her it would be over soon.

Those ten minutes felt like an eternity—to Habiba and to me. She was still crying and in much agony as she got dressed to go back into the waiting room. I helped her lift her arms to put on her shirt. She let out loud screeches with certain movements.

I sat next to her on the cracked vinyl chair in the waiting room. She couldn't seem to find a comfortable sitting position. Tears slowly streamed down her cheeks. I asked her if she wanted to lay her head on my shoulder. She tried, but the pain was too intense. I took off my soft lavender fleece jacket and rolled it up for a pillow behind her head. Again, she tried to lie back and relax, but she couldn't. We waited patiently; at least we tried to be patient.

The biopsy was next. I told Habiba that it probably wouldn't be nearly as painful as the mammogram. They would give her a shot to numb the skin and then do several punch biopsies. I did my best to explain the procedure, not fully understanding myself. I had never experienced anything like this. Everything I knew was from my internet research the night before.

Once again, we weren't sure if the doctors would agree for me to be in the room for translation. However, we weren't too shy to ask when they finally called us back. The safe house worker went with us into the dressing room and helped Habiba get into a hospital gown. At least they had gowns this time. The three of us walked into the biopsy room to talk to the nurse and the doctor. They explained I couldn't be present for the biopsy, but I could translate for Habiba beforehand regarding the procedure. Thankfully, the doctor and nurse both spoke English, so we managed to communicate together and explain what Habiba needed to know.

I then kissed her on the cheek and told her I would wait in the dressing room and pray for her. I reminded her that God was with her—she wasn't alone. The safe house worker and I stood silently in the dressing room. Once again, it felt like forever. We heard Habiba scream and cry out several times. Apparently, the biopsy was not less painful than the mammogram. I regretted having said that to Habiba. When I don't know something, it's best not to pretend that I do.

When the biopsy was over, the nurse called me in to help get Habiba up from the table, hold compresses in the areas where they had done the punch biopsies, and get the instructions for cleaning and care. I would need to explain everything to the safe house workers. Habiba was still crying and in pain. I hugged her gently and told her I was sorry she had to go through this.

We walked back into the crowded waiting room. Habiba was weeping, so I stood with her and took her in my arms. It felt like the entire world was staring at us, not knowing what to do with the pain of others. The world is uncomfortable with suffering.

I embraced Habiba's suffering when others rejected it. I leaned into her suffering when others pushed it away. I was comfortable with her suffering when others felt awkward.

We sat down again on the vinyl chairs. Habiba continued to cry. Since arriving at the hospital earlier that morning, I had noticed she had been holding a white paper tissue. When I glanced over, I saw she had shredded it into tiny pieces in her hand. It was tattered, hardly recognizable.

I grabbed my purse off the ground and rummaged through it until I found a small package of tissues. There were only two, so I took them out and placed them in her hand. I opened the empty, plastic package and told her to put her old, tattered tissue inside.

"It's like a little trash can," I said.

As soon as I heard my words, I corrected myself and whispered, "No, it's not a trash can. It's a treasure chest."

Those tiny, tattered, shredded pieces of white tissue were full of Habiba's tears. God is the tear collector, and our pain, our sadness, and our weeping are precious to Him. Habiba's tears were beautiful, and God would never waste them. He guards and keeps each tear and remembers the stories, the events, behind each one. That tattered, shredded tissue was dear to God and dear to me. I gripped it—like a treasure—and held it over my heart.

After the exams, we had to wait for Habiba's paperwork for her next appointments. She finally calmed down and laid her head on my lap, falling asleep—like a baby. I stroked her long, dark hair with one hand and clutched the package of tattered tissues in the other.

Two treasures . . . I didn't want to let go of either.

CHAPTER TWENTY-SEVEN

SARTAN!

L ess than a week after the mammogram and biopsy, the hospital contacted Andrea. Habiba had an appointment with the same gynecologist—the one who had pronounced the word "metastasized." The doctor had worked us into the schedule earlier than expected. Was that good news or bad news?

In the meantime, we had been praying for a miracle. Wasn't God bigger than cancer? Couldn't He heal Habiba of "what-seemed-like metastasized cancer." God had already healed my body and my children's bodies multiple times. Our family had seen miracles up close and personal.

I could remember laying in that ICU room in the American Hospital of Paris twenty years ago, just after the birth of our second son. I was hemorrhaging to death, and the doctors thought they were losing me. We all did. People gathered to pray. I could still remember that night—His healing touch, His powerful presence. I could still remember the doctors' awe in watching this miracle take place before their eyes.

If God could do it for me, He could do it for Habiba. But would He, or did He have another plan?

I had not been sleeping well for the past week. My nights were filled with tossing and turning, wrestling and praying, crying out to God on behalf of Habiba in the wee hours. The night before her appointment, I couldn't sleep at all. I gave up trying and finally went downstairs to the living room. Our oldest son, Timothée, was living with us at the time. He was usually up all night—a typical young adult with backwards hours. Timothée came downstairs and saw me sitting at the dining room table crying. He walked over to me.

"What am I going to tell Habiba tomorrow if she has cancer? How am I supposed to tell her that God loves her and that He has a good plan for her life? What am I going to say?"

My twenty-two-year-old son listened to me as I wrestled out loud with my faith and doubts.

"I don't understand. Why would God allow this? Habiba has already suffered so much, how can she handle any more?" I was relieved to finally have a human being listening to my heart's complaints. Timothée remained silent. No words could have comforted me.

"Do you know Habiba has had this lump in her armpit for years? She thinks at least ten. They turned her away at the hospital in Morocco, because she didn't have enough money for the operation. Do you realize?"

My questions were filled with sadness, rage, disgust. They didn't need to be answered. They just needed to be heard.

Tears streamed down my face, and I wept. My son leaned over and took me in his arms. He held me, silent. After a few moments of warm embrace, I pulled away and thanked him for being there for me, for listening. I saw tears in his eyes too. It was a moment that I would never forget.

Although comforted momentarily, I was still troubled—deeply troubled. I was also still scared. If Habiba had cancer, how would I tell her? I was the one who spoke Arabic and would have to be the bearer of bad news.

"Oh, God, please don't make me do this! Please don't let her have cancer!"

The next morning, my husband, Vincent, drove me to the hospital. He had to take our boys to school and needed the car.

"I don't even know the Arabic word for cancer," I told my husband solemnly.

I pulled my phone out of my purse to use Google Translate. This familiar phone app had become one of my best friends since we moved to Spain six months before.

"*Sartan*"* popped up on the screen. I tried to pronounce it out loud in Arabic. I then hit the small microphone icon next to the word in order to listen to its correct pronunciation by a native Arabic speaker.

"*Sartan, Sartan, Sartan, Sartan, Sartan* . . . " I listened to the word over and over, unable to hold back the flood of tears.

"What if I have to tell her? What if I have to pronounce this word?" I said to Vincent, not expecting a response.

"*Sartan.*" Before stepping out of the car, I wrote the word in Arabic on a yellow post-it note that I found in my purse. Underneath the word, I wrote the phonetic spelling, "s-ar-t-an." As I shoved the neon-colored square paper in my pocket, I spoke the word aloud to practice—just in case. The word made me cringe. I felt like I would vomit.

"What if I can't do it? What if I can't say it?" I mumbled to myself, silently asking God for courage and strength. He needed to prepare me for all that lay ahead of me that day.

Suddenly, guilt flooded my heart and mind. I had been praying all week, asking God for a miracle of healing in Habiba's body. Now, here I was, asking Google Translate how to pronounce the word "cancer" in Arabic. I felt faithless, like a hypocrite. Did I believe? Did I believe that God was bigger than cancer and powerful enough to heal Habiba's body? Did I really believe? I wrestled with my own thoughts, my own feelings, my own doubts, my own fears. They warred within my soul.

Vincent dropped me off at the door of the main hospital entrance. I didn't see Habiba and Andrea anywhere. I waited outside and prayed, tears streaming down my face. I didn't know what else to do besides pray.

"Be strong, be strong," I said to myself. "God, please help me do this. I can't do this without you."

I texted Andrea to find out where they were. Ten minutes away, running late.

I paced. I prayed. I cried.

From a distance, I saw them walking up the ramp towards the entrance. I walked towards them and greeted them with kisses. I stroked my hand across Habiba's shoulders as we walked through the hospital door.

None of us spoke. Silence, only silence.

We took the elevator up to the second floor. This time, we knew where we were going. "*Servicio de Mamas.*"*

"Did you bring your colored heart?" I leaned over and whispered in Habiba's ear.

She smiled softly and pulled it out from her black coat pocket. I smiled back and opened my purse. I showed her mine. Our hands were side-by-side, each holding a bright, colorful heart made of glued balls of felt.

It didn't take long for the nurse to call us back. I sighed deeply and prayed silently. I felt sick to my stomach. Did I have to go in?

Habiba and I sat on the chairs across from the doctor and the two interns. Andrea stood behind Habiba in a protective stance. The doctor spoke with Andrea as my hand rested on Habiba's thigh. She was wearing blue jeans and a white t-shirt. I'll never forget. I couldn't understand any of the Spanish. Honestly, I wasn't listening. All I could think about was Habiba.

"It's very bad cancer," Andrea said to me in broken English.

Broken English or not, I understood. Yes, I understood loud and clear.

My heart sank. This was real. This was really happening. It wasn't a dream. It wasn't a nightmare. Everything seemed foggy.

"What do I tell her?" I asked Andrea, shuttering. "Do I tell her?"

"Yes," Andrea said, nodding her head.

Habiba knew something was going on.

"What? What's wrong with me?"

I took a deep breath. I don't remember praying. It all happened so fast.

*Sartan—cancer

*Servicio de Mamas—Breast Department

⁓ℓℓ⁓

"*Andik sartan,*" I said, as carefully and as calmly as I could.

"*Sartan!?*" Habiba screamed. "*Sartan!? Sartan!?*"

She burst into tears, and our eyes met. The terror I saw ripped right through me. I looked away, hoping to avoid its intensity. She screamed the word over and over—like that voice on Google Translate.

"*Sartan! Sartan! Sartan!* I'm going to die! I'm going to die! I'm going to die!" she yelled hysterically.

I reached out to hug her, but she fell out of her chair and onto the tile floor at my feet. Curled up in a ball, she clutched my leg, gripping so hard I could feel pain in my calf and thigh. Tears poured from her eyes and nose, forming dark circles on my blue jeans. I leaned down to stroke her hair and held her head on my lap. She wept.

"I'm here with you. We're here with you. You're not alone."

After some time of sobbing, Habiba dragged herself up off the floor and bolted for the door.

"I'm leaving! I'm leaving! I'm leaving!" she screamed.

I ran after her and tackled her from behind. We both collapsed onto the tile floor between the examination table and the door.

"Let me go!" she yelled aggressively, pushing back my arms violently.

I clutched her tightly.

"Where are you going, Habiba? The doctors will help you here. You can't go back to the streets now."

The gynecologist rushed over to us and told us to get off the floor. The newly discovered COVID-19 Coronavirus was running rampant in Spain, and she was concerned about us touching the tiles.

I picked myself up off the floor, and Andrea and I leaned down to pick up Habiba. She was heavy with grief and could hardly move. We opened the door to go back into the waiting room. The crowd of women stared at us with concern. They had certainly heard the screams and cries coming from behind the door of the exam room. Habiba could barely walk. Andrea and I held her up strongly on either side. We walked back into the hospital corridor, not knowing what to do.

"I have to make another appointment for a test," Andrea told me. "Can you walk with her to the car?"

"I don't think I should walk with her alone in case she makes a run for it. I think we both need to be with her."

"Ok, wait here by this window."

There were no chairs to sit on, and I honestly wasn't sure if we should touch anything. The global news was all consumed with COVID-19—this unknown, mysterious virus that was taking over the world little by little. A few people passed by wearing blue surgical masks. It felt surreal. I saw a small window sill and motioned for Habiba to sit down next to me. I draped my arm around her shoulder, holding her up and trying to comfort her.

"Am I going to die?" she asked me, looking me straight in the eyes like a dagger.

I didn't know what to say. I didn't want to lie. I didn't want to tell her that everything would be okay. I didn't want to tell her something that might not be true. I didn't want to give her false hope. I didn't want her to die. I wanted to tell her everything would be okay, that she wouldn't die. But, I couldn't. I didn't know.

All I knew was that I wanted to wake up from this nightmare.

"You are in an excellent hospital here in Spain—one of the best. The doctors and nurses here want to help you. They need to find out what kind of cancer you have and how to treat it. There may be medicine that can help you."

Her tears kept falling as I held her in my arms.

"I'm going to die. My family is going to die," she kept repeating. "I'm going to die. My family is going to die."

I didn't say a word. There was nothing to say.

She calmed down for a few minutes and then began sobbing again. No longer able to sit on the windowsill, she crouched down on the white tile floor next to my feet. I stroked her hair while she firmly clutched my leg again. Everyone who passed by stared at us. Once again, they seemed uncomfortable, even unacquainted with suffering, not knowing what to do with someone else's pain. A nurse walked by with an empty wheelchair and asked me if I needed help.

"She's sad," I told him. "She's very sad."

My broken words in Spanish seemed simple. Yet, there was nothing else to say. The nurse seemed to understand, nodded his head, and continued on his way. A few minutes later, Andrea came walking towards us with the same nurse and wheelchair.

"We need to take Habiba to the emergency room to calm her down," Andrea said.

I suddenly realized Andrea could not take Habiba back to the safe house like this. She was out of control.

"Okay," I replied, and then turned to explain things to Habiba.

"Habiba, we are going to the emergency room to get some medicine for you, okay?"

She nodded, and the three of us lifted her up off the ground to place her in the wheelchair.

"*Sartan*"—I hate that word.

CHAPTER TWENTY-EIGHT

EXPOSED AND AFRAID

We dashed down the long corridors to the emergency room. Andrea and I followed the nurse, pushing Habiba in the wheelchair. It felt apocalyptic. Some people were wearing masks and gloves. Others weren't. We weren't. Our hands and faces were exposed. Upon entering the emergency room, the nurse frantically handed us masks with explicit instructions.

"Don't touch anything," he said repeatedly.

I felt scared and confused.

The nurse opened the double doors to a small room, explaining that only one person could enter with Habiba. Andrea stayed back and waited outside. She said they needed me for translation. Habiba and I followed the nurse, but Habiba refused to put on her mask. Everyone else in the room wore masks—doctors, nurses, and six patients sitting in black vinyl chairs receiving IV fluids through their arms.

A nurse ran over and yelled at Habiba, "Put on your mask! These people are sick!"

I kneeled down at Habiba's feet and told her she had to wear her mask. She had no choice. I gently put the mask on her face. I could only see her eyes, full of that all-too-familiar terror.

They transferred Habiba from the wheelchair to an oversized black chair, only two chairs down from the last woman in the row attached to an IV drip. I preferred to stand and observe from a distance, feeling nervous. Where were we?

"Go wash your hands with gel," the nurse kept telling me.

"Okay," I complied, perplexed.

"For your sake."

"Okay," I said again, not understanding the reasons behind this panic.

I followed his instructions and headed back to the nurse's station several times for more hand gel from the dispenser on the counter.

After what seemed like hours, they finally called us back to see the doctor. Thankfully, the psychiatrist could speak English, so we only needed a two-way translation between English and Arabic. He was kind and helped us walk through Habiba's story. He gave her some medicine to help her with the anxiety and sadness.

She had a long journey ahead of her.

Upon leaving the small room, Habiba and I both washed our hands with the antiseptic gel one last time. Andrea had texted to tell me she had gone to get the car. We were to wait for her at the emergency room exit. After waiting for a few minutes in the warm sunshine, Andrea finally pulled up to get Habiba. I was still waiting for Vincent.

Andrea got out of the car. She seemed stressed.

"You were just exposed to six positive Coronavirus patients in that room."

"What?!" Why didn't we know? Why didn't they tell us? Why didn't they give us a choice—a choice to go in or not? Habiba sat on a chair right next to one of the patients!"

"Go home. Take off your clothes. Wash them and shower. Don't kiss your husband or children. Wash your car and everything you touch. I have to do the same. I'm not allowed to go to the safe house for two weeks and you aren't either."

"What? We've been exposed!"

Vincent picked me up a few minutes later. I told him what had happened. I was afraid—afraid to touch anything in the car, afraid to touch him, afraid to go near my children, afraid to do anything. I had been exposed to the Coronavirus, and all I understood at that point was that this virus was killing people.

Despite our fears, Andrea, Habiba, and I had no choice but to continue to be exposed to the virus. We had to return to the hospital the next day and the next day and the next day. The following weeks were full of appointments—in that same hospital. This time, however, when we walked through the hospital doors, our hands and faces were no longer bare. We now wore gloves and masks and carried antiseptic gel in our purses.

We were like everyone else in the hospital—exposed to a deadly virus, but what could we do? The only answer we could find was to pray and ask God for protection. It was completely out of our control. Should we stay at home and not help our friend, our sister? Should we cower down in fear?

No, we refused. We resisted fear. Instead, we chose to go, to stand by Habiba's side, to wear our masks and gloves. All the while, we prayed and asked God for protection.

———ℓℓ———

I Am Afraid

Things were escalating in Spain at an alarming rate. The COVID-19 numbers were increasing each day. At first, it was by the hundreds, then by the thousands. They strongly advised us not to go out, unless absolutely necessary, and to avoid hospitals, doctors' offices, ERs . . . unless we were dying.

The past weeks had already been full of hospital visits. I had accompanied Habiba to all of her appointments and tests. These visits were in the same "Corona-infested" hospital, the same place where we had both been directly exposed to the virus the week before. It was the same place that was mentioned in all the Spanish newspapers. It was the same hospital that was "mishandling the virus," the one whose data-collecting system had gone down, the one mixing patients—those sitting in ER already diagnosed with Coronavirus and those walking through the ER doors with strokes, broken bones, and heart palpitations. I didn't want to go back there if I didn't have to.

Yet, Arabic.

I was the only one. I was the only one who could directly speak to Habiba. I was the only one who could understand her, her story, her pain. I was the only one who could be a language bridge between her and the doctors. I felt such a heavy burden and responsibility to be there, to walk alongside her, to sit next to her in the chair—facing the doctors. Yet, I didn't want to go. I didn't want to go back there if I didn't have to.

I felt guilty saying it.

Was I fearful of getting the virus? Was I no longer willing to take risks, to step into the face of danger, to sacrifice my safety, to serve and love others in need?

Where was my faith?

I could hear the words of Jesus ringing in my ears, "Why are you so afraid? Do you still have no faith?" (Mark 4:40 NIV)

Did I believe God was bigger than the Coronavirus, that He had the power to protect and shield me, that He was sovereign over my life and over the Coronavirus, that He was in control? Did I really believe, as John Piper said, "I was immortal until Christ's work in me was finished?" Did I believe God was who He said He was, that He would keep His promises? Did I still believe in God?

My faith was shaken to the core.

In talking to friends and family, I heard the same message from all of them.

"You can't go back into that hospital, risk your health and life, put you and your family in danger. Your family needs you more than your friend needs you."

When I tried to explain that there was no one else who could help Habiba understand her story, no one else who could be a language bridge . . . they just didn't understand.

I didn't want to be selfish. I wanted to be self-less. I wanted to think about others more than myself. I wanted to serve those who were hurting and dying.

Habiba was hurting and dying.

But I also wanted to serve and love my family. I wanted to care for them and protect them. By going into the hospital, I was not only putting myself on the front lines, in harm's way, but I was ultimately putting my husband and four boys on the front lines with me. If I contracted the virus, I would bring it home with me. My family could also be exposed.

I was afraid. I confess, I was afraid. I wrestled daily between fear and faith, risk and protection, doubt and belief. I didn't know what to do. My dear friend was hurting and dying, and I was afraid.

The safe house director sent me a text at the last minute.

"Can you go with us to the hospital now? I just got a call, and they want Habiba to come in for another test in forty-five minutes? It's at the hospital in the center of downtown."

I was in the middle of helping my seven-year-old son with his schoolwork. Because of COVID-19, my boys' school was closed, and they had been home doing their work online for several weeks. I couldn't drop everything and run. It would be rushed and complicated for me to get to the appointment on time. The drive to the city hospital was over an hour.

"I'm sorry. I won't be able to join you last minute," I answered. "My son needs me to help him with his schoolwork. I'll be praying. Please call me if you need me to translate over the phone."

I sighed with relief as I sent the text. I didn't have to go back to the hospital that day. I had a good excuse. I didn't have to confess my fears to them . . . not yet.

A few days later, we had another doctor's appointment on the calendar. This was the big one. It was the dreaded day, the day the oncologist would announce the results of all the tests. We would know how widespread Habiba's cancer was and if it had reached her bones.

Habiba was anxious and wanted answers. She had been wondering all these years—ten or more—she had lost count. What was that lump? What were all these new lumps? What was wrong?

Habiba wanted to know. I did not. I was afraid, afraid of hearing bad news. I was afraid of being the bearer of bad news again. Once more, I felt that heavy weight and responsibility of being the language bridge between Habiba and the doctor. The news— whatever it was—would have to travel through my ears, my mind, and my heart. It would then have to be processed quickly at each of those levels—mentally and emotionally. From there, I would have to jump neural pathways and "language tracks" in my brain and somehow—by God's grace—transfer the message from Spanish and English into Arabic.

Arabic—the only language Habiba could understand.

Why did I have to be the one? Surely in this enormous country there was someone else who could speak Arabic and take over my translation job. I had been fulfilling the role long enough, and I was tired. Wasn't there a professional, paid hospital translator who could assist Habiba for this doctor's appointment? Yet, God had called me, called me to walk alongside Habiba for this time. She needed not only my Arabic words, Habiba needed my presence, my love, my compassion. Habiba needed me.

The date of Habiba's appointment with the oncologist arrived. I had written it on my agenda weeks before. However, because of COVID-19, Spain was in total lockdown. What began with one week of quarantine turned into several weeks, then a month, until it reached 54 days. We could not leave our house except to go to the hospital, the doctor, the pharmacy, the grocery store, to work (if there was no online option), or to walk our dog around the block. Even on a dog walk, we had to stay within a perimeter of one hundred yards from our home. Police were everywhere, reinforcing the restrictions.

In order for me to circulate and to pass safely through police stops, Andrea sent me an official legal paper stating I could drive throughout the city for my work responsibilities. On the document, I was no longer simply a volunteer Arabic translator pulled in off the streets to help. I was now an official part of the safe house team, the Arabic translator. I was Habiba's translator.

As a translator—such a huge role—I had to somehow be her ears, her mouth. I had to listen, speak, think, understand, interpret, and process information in multiple languages simultaneously. At the hospital, I now had to take complex medical information and condense it into simple, bite-size words that Habiba could understand and chew on.

It was complicated, and it was draining . . . mentally draining.

In addition to the mental fatigue of normal, everyday translation situations, Habiba's story added an emotional exhaustion I had never experienced before. I had to hear her story, her devastating story, in multiple languages, multiple times. Often, I couldn't find the time, space, or mental and emotional energy to process her story until later that day when I got home. Sometimes, it wasn't until I could sit down to write her story in my journal, or take a walk the next morning to be alone, or talk to God about it.

Sometimes, I buried Habiba's story in my heart, hid it away in the "treasure box" . . . not wanting to pull it out again and think about it. It was too painful.

I dreaded this appointment with the oncologist. I was scared— scared of walking into that Coronavirus-infested hospital again, scared of hearing Habiba's diagnosis, prognosis, impending death. We already knew she had breast cancer. We already knew she had tumors in other places throughout her body. From my perspective, things did not look good.

Going to the appointment was an all-day commitment. There would be waiting . . . waiting in the lobby for Habiba and Andrea to arrive, waiting in the doctor's office, waiting with the doctor, waiting to hear the news, waiting . . . My husband planned to stay home with the kids that day. The younger ones were doing their school work online. The big kids could take care of themselves. Everything was prepared.

Just before walking out the door, I received a text from Andrea.

"Today's doctor's appointment has been cancelled. Habiba is being transferred to another hospital."

A flood of relief washed over me. I felt freed—freed from the responsibility, burden, fear, danger, and risk. I didn't have to go. I didn't have to go into that high-risk, infested hospital. I didn't have to hear bad news today. I didn't have to translate and be the bearer of bad news.

I also felt guilty to be relieved.

Was this transfer to a new hospital good news? Maybe the results were excellent, and there was no urgency for Habiba to be seen by a doctor? Or was this change bad news? Was her case so extreme and serious they couldn't properly care for her at the first hospital? Perhaps she needed a specialist.

Or perhaps it was only out of precaution. The hospital where we had been going for all of her appointments and exams was the one receiving all the negative publicity. Perhaps they had simply reached maximum capacity with Coronavirus patients. Perhaps they needed the entire hospital to care for those in crisis. Perhaps they wanted to protect Habiba and not expose her again unnecessarily to those who were known to be infected with the virus. We did not know the reasons, but we had no choice. We had to wait . . . wait more.

I knew Habiba was disappointed. She was anxious and eager to find out what was going on inside her body. Understandably, she wanted to know. I did not, and I felt guilty. Habiba was upset, even angry, when I called her later that day to tell her about the cancelled appointment. She wanted to see the doctor that day. She wanted to get her results. She wanted to know.

Days and weeks went by. Still no call from the new hospital about an appointment. Andrea called regularly to schedule an appointment with the oncologist. Each time, they turned her away with no information. In the meantime, the statistics of new cases and deaths from the Coronavirus continued to climb in Spain. Day after day, fear increased in the country. Day after day, fear escalated in my own heart and mind.

A few days later, just after eleven a.m., I received a text from Andrea.

"I just got a call from the hospital. They have an appointment slot to see Habiba, but we have to be at the hospital before noon. Can you come?"

My heart was beating fast. What was I going to do? I was still in pajamas. I looked at my watch, then quickly plugged in the hospital's name into my phone's GPS. The drive would take me over an hour. There was no way that I could make it.

I quickly texted back. "I'm so sorry. There's no way I can be there before noon. Go on without me. Don't miss the appointment. You may not get another one for weeks. Call me when you're with the doctor, and I'll translate."

"Okay. We'll call you."

Relief, again. Freedom, again.

Maybe it was God's protection of my heart. Perhaps hearing bad news through a telephone screen would be easier. Perhaps the screen would be a buffer between the painful words and my broken heart. Perhaps seeing Habiba's face through the glass and telling her the news would be easier. Perhaps she wouldn't be able to see the tears in my eyes, the moisture on my cheeks, the tattered tissue in my hand. Perhaps she wouldn't hear my heart beating out of my chest, my rapid breathing, my heavy sighing. Perhaps she wouldn't notice that I was sweating in panic, shaking and trembling with fear. Perhaps she wouldn't feel my soul bleeding and shattering into pieces.

Perhaps she wouldn't notice. Perhaps she wouldn't notice through a screen.

I was so relieved. I was so thankful. I felt so guilty.

I was afraid—afraid to walk into another hospital in our Corona-infested city, afraid to hear news that Habiba was dying, afraid to be the one to tell her what was wrong.

I was afraid.

CHAPTER TWENTY-NINE

THE SENTENCE AND TRANSLATION ETHICS

"I'm sorry I can't be there with you," I told Habiba through the phone screen.

Tears streamed down my face, tears through a screen. Habiba cried too. She was in extreme physical pain in her neck and shoulders. The tumors seemed to grow daily. Andrea sat next to her in the waiting room. Time seemed long and heavy.

"Are you coming to be with me?" Habiba kept asking me through the screen. "Are you coming to be with me?"

My heart was broken as I slowly shook my head. I was sorry I couldn't be by Habiba's side that morning, to hold her hand, to stroke her hair, to look at her face-to-face as we met with the doctor. At the same time, I felt that same twinge of relief. I felt selfish that I was relieved. I felt guilty that I was relieved. My friend was dying, and I wasn't there with her. I could only cry with her—through a screen.

Deep down inside, I knew it was the best decision—for me, for my family. Yet, it seemed like a lame excuse, especially when Habiba looked at me with those eyes, those beautiful, dark brown eyes pleading with me to come.

"I'm sorry I can't be there with you," I repeated. "I'm sorry I can't be there with you."

Inside, though, I was saying, "Honestly, I'm not sure if I want to be there anymore with you. I'm not sure if I can continue to walk by your side through this."

I prayed with her on the phone. Then, the doctor called her name, "Habiba." It was time for the verdict. I hung up reluctantly and then waited for Andrea's call. Strangely, the call never came. I tried to keep myself busy—especially my mind. It was racing with worry and fear. What did the doctor say? Was it good news, bad news? I knew that today was the day for either a spoken word of hopeful healing or a sentence of imminent death.

I glued my phone to my side. Why wasn't it ringing? Andrea planned to call me to translate during the doctor's appointment. I was tempted to call, but I didn't want to disturb her. It was odd. I knew that the doctor had called Habiba into her office while we were still talking on the phone together. Hours had now passed, and Andrea had still not called me.

I could not stop watching the clock. Every minute was an eternity. By two p.m., I felt like I might lose my mind with worry. I texted Andrea and apologized for bothering her. No answer. At four p.m., anxiety flooded my mind, and I could no longer contain myself. I picked up the phone and called Andrea.

She answered right away with her video camera turned on. She was in a hospital room. There was movement behind her—a nurse. Then, I saw Habiba in the background, wearing a hospital gown, getting an IV placed in her arm.

"They admitted Habiba to the hospital," Andrea said.

My heart shuttered. Was she dying? The verdict, the sentence, must be so bad that Habiba had to be hospitalized for treatment. Or perhaps it was too late for treatment. Perhaps she was being admitted for her last dying days.

"They are putting her on morphine for the pain."

She was dying. Clearly, she was dying. It reminded me of Hospice Care at the end of someone's life. They give the suffering patient pain killers and try to make them comfortable so they don't have to struggle during their last days.

"They will keep her here for two weeks."

I listened carefully, trying to remain calm inside. My heart was pounding out of my chest. I was in shock. My friend was dying. Habiba was dying.

I greeted Habiba in Arabic through the phone screen, and Andrea pointed the phone camera towards her.

"*Salaam, r'ti, la bas?*" "Peace, my sister, how are you?"

With a weak voice, Habiba responded in traditional Arabic fashion, "*La bas.*"

Yet she was clearly not fine.

"What did the doctor say?" I said in English, trying to get Andrea's attention again.

Andrea placed her face near the phone screen and walked into the hospital corridor to speak to me privately.

"Habiba has metastasized cancer everywhere. It's in her lungs, her chest bone, her breasts, her lymph nodes. It's bad."

"How long does she have?"

"We don't know. Maybe one year, maybe two."

Tears flooded my eyes and slowly made their way in a small trickle down my cheeks.

"How could this be? How was this possible?" I screamed inside my head. "At least Habiba has a few years. I guess it could have been a few months, a few weeks, a few days . . . "

"They'll start chemotherapy this week to see how she responds. She's on morphine for intense pain," Andrea explained.

I quickly did some research on my phone while talking to Andrea. Not knowing where Habiba's cancer had originated, the information on lung cancer was the most disconcerting. It was not curable, only treatable by chemotherapy, giving the opportunity for an extension of quality of life. The statistics were grim, and the mortality rate was extremely high.

Without a miracle of healing from God, we were going to lose Habiba.

Translation Ethics

"What do you want me to say to Habiba? Do I tell her?" I asked Andrea anxiously.

"She already knows she has bad cancer. If we tell her all the details, it's going to cause more worry and anxiety for her she doesn't need right now. She's already on anxiety medicine for panic attacks. It will only make things worse," Andrea explained.

I nodded my head in agreement, but inside I was shaking my head in disbelief. Once again, I submitted to Andrea's leadership as the director of the safe house. She was responsible for Habiba and her care. My role was as a translator.

But what about my role as a friend, as a sister?

Courage escaped me, but I wanted to yell through the screen, "We have to tell Habiba she's dying! We have to tell Habiba she has cancer all over her body! We have to tell Habiba there's no cure for her cancer, outside of a miracle from God! We have to tell Habiba she only has one year to live! We have to tell Habiba everything!"

All I could think about was Habiba's family on the other side of the Mediterranean Sea. Habiba had a right to know about her health, about her cancer, about her life . . . and so did they. What if Habiba wanted to return to Morocco to be with her family—her parents, her son—during her last year of life? What if she wanted to have them care for her during her dying days? Habiba needed to know right now she had a death sentence over her. If not, she couldn't make those decisions.

I felt a wrestling deep within. We knew things about Habiba she didn't know. That didn't seem right. It didn't seem fair. It felt like we were withholding information from her about her health, her body, her life. Wasn't there something ethically and morally wrong with that?

It didn't feel right. It felt wrong, and I was struggling. It was a question of translation ethics.

There was a language barrier between Habiba and the doctor, and that was why she couldn't understand, why she couldn't know the extent of her diagnosis. That was not fair. Andrea and I knew. Andrea and I were fortunate enough to go to school. We were educated and spoke several languages. Habiba was not educated and not fortunate. We clearly had advantages in life that Habiba did not have. If Habiba knew what we knew, she might make different decisions.

I didn't sleep for nights. The wrestling in my soul continued. I tossed and turned my body in my bed like I tossed and turned my choices and responsibilities. Questions flooded my mind. Should I tell Habiba the truth or should I let her die in peace?

I had no answers.

CHAPTER THIRTY

A TRIP TO MOROCCO

Later that night, after they settled Habiba in her hospital room, I called her. She was still weak and tired from the pain. The morphine was finally kicking in and working its magic. Andrea had arranged for a worker from the safe house to stay with Habiba every day at the hospital. However, at night, she would be alone in her hospital room.

"Can you tell Andrea that I want someone with me at night, too?" Habiba asked me.

I sent a text to Andrea to make the request.

"There aren't enough workers. We have to have someone on duty at the house with the other women, too," Andrea explained. "Someone can be with her during the day, but not at night."

I translated the message to Habiba in Arabic. She understood, although she was clearly disappointed.

"I'm scared. I'm afraid that if I need to get up to go to the restroom or something in the night, no one will be there to help me."

I showed her how to push the "call nurse" button on the console next to her bed. It reassured her to know that a nurse would, at least should, come quickly.

"God is with you at night," I told her. "That's most important. Jesus is the light with you at night. He'll help you."

Habiba nodded.

"Call my family," she said. "Please call my family."

"Your family in Morocco? You want me to call your mom?"

"No, my family in Spain."

I was surprised, not knowing that Habiba had family on Spanish soil.

"Call them and tell them I'm sick and in the hospital. They need to call me."

I asked her to text me the name and number of her family members. It was her cousin, her aunt's son. Her request surprised me, but I understood what was going on. Habiba was sick, and she wanted to talk to her family. She wanted to connect to her roots, her country, her culture. Her parents and her son were too far away, on the other side of the sea. However, her long-distance family and cousins in Spain seemed closer. They were geographically nearby— at least on the same foreign soil.

I felt rather uncomfortable calling a perfect stranger on the phone, introducing myself, and explaining that Habiba was sick and in the hospital. My awkwardness and my lack of comfort did not matter, and it would not hinder me. This was about Habiba, not about me. I would do anything for my dear friend, my sister.

I called her cousin and introduced myself in Arabic. My call surprised and confused him. After explaining Habiba's medical situation, I asked him to please call her at the hospital. I gave him her phone number, and we parted ways and said goodbye in typical Arabic fashion. An hour later, I sent an audio message to Habiba and asked her if she had spoken with her cousin. She had. I was relieved.

The next morning, I called to see how her first night at the hospital was. She seemed okay. They were heading to her first chemotherapy treatment to see how her body would respond. For now, their focus was still on reducing her pain with morphine.

"Keep pushing on that little button when you have pain," I told her, explaining that the magic button would release a dose of morphine into her body. It didn't take her long to understand the situation and to control her own medication.

Throughout the night, I wrestled with my thoughts. All I could think about was Habiba's family back in Morocco. Did they know? What if I had to make a trip to Morocco one day?

"I think I need to get to know Habiba's family now," I told Andrea in a text that morning.

If something happened to Habiba, I would need to know how to contact them. I didn't want to be meeting them for the first time through a phone screen when I was breaking hard news to them about their daughter, about their mother.

Habiba didn't ask me questions, thank goodness. She didn't ask me why I wanted to contact her family. She didn't seem to connect it with her cancer or her hospitalization. If she wondered, she didn't say anything. Rather, she willingly gave me the contact name and number for her mother.

I hung up the phone and immediately sent an audio message to her mother in Morocco. I introduced myself and told her how much I loved her country and her culture. I shared with her that Morocco had been my home for seven years, that my children were raised there. I then expressed my love for Habiba and reassured her I would take care of her precious daughter in her absence.

Her mother sent me an audio message in response, almost immediately. She expressed her gratitude for my love and care for her daughter. She invited me to their home in their small village in the south of Morocco, promising me sweet mint tea and my favorite Moroccan meals—lamb and prune *tagine*, couscous, *s'fa m'dfouna*, *rafissa, bataboute*, and *m'simmon* pastries. Her family wanted to pay me back for all that I was doing to help their daughter. They wanted to somehow return to me the time, the money, the love that I had sacrificed.

I needed nothing in return. The unending supply of strength, love, compassion, and mercy flowed freely from God through me to Habiba. There was no sacrifice. They didn't know that it was an honor to journey alongside their daughter. They didn't know how I was blessed to call her my friend, my sister. They didn't understand that it was a calling from God, that I was simply obeying what God had asked me to do.

I smiled as I listened to "*Mama's*" invitation, but inside, my heart sank.

"I would love to come visit you one day," I replied.

Deep inside my heart, I was expressing something more ... "I may have to come and visit you one day, and Habiba might not be with me."

———ele———

"What if I have to make a trip to Morocco one day?" I asked my husband in the car, several weeks later. I couldn't stop thinking about it.

I didn't have to explain my question, and I wasn't looking for a response. My husband knew exactly what I was talking about. I wasn't referring to a vacation in Morocco. I wasn't referring to a fun, relaxing, touristic trip back to the land that I love—the place I called "home" for seven years. Rather, I pictured myself carrying a suitcase full of Habiba's belongings—clothes, jewelry, shoes, toiletries, and other personal items that she had accumulated during her life in Spain. I would meet her family for the first time, kissing them, crying with them . . . perhaps mourning together the loss of their mother, daughter, sister, niece, cousin, neighbor, and friend.

Like with Habiba, my messages in Arabic to her mother were in audio form. Neither of them could read and write, so written texts were out of the question.

Mama and I began exchanging audio messages every day. I think that somehow it made her feel closer to her daughter on the other side of the Mediterranean Sea—her precious daughter whom she might never hold in her arms again, her sweet daughter who left their land two years ago in search of El Dorado and financial provision for her family, her beloved daughter who had become enslaved in a sex trafficking Mafia, her dear daughter who was now diagnosed with a lethal cancer that was invading her entire body.

Our back-and-forth conversations each day must have brought her comfort. She seemed to enjoy hearing my voice and my news—both good and bad—from the person who was walking alongside her daughter, caring for her, loving her . . . during all those days, weeks, and months when she couldn't.

She couldn't, because she was stuck on the other side of the sea. Mama could never come to Spain, and Habiba could never return to Morocco.

—————

The Dreaded Medical Question

"The doctor asked me if I had family here in Spain," Habiba told me on the phone. "He asked me if he could talk to them. I don't understand."

My heart sank as I looked at her confused face through the screen.

It was Saturday evening. I had called her to check in. Other than a few audio texts, I had not connected with Habiba during the week. Our family was in the middle of a move, and life felt overwhelming.

Although it was 6:00 p.m., Habiba had been sleeping. She wasn't feeling well that day, nauseated and exhausted. She didn't know why.

"The doctor changed my medication on Thursday. Maybe that's why I don't feel well."

I reassured her we would call the doctor on Monday morning if she wasn't better.

Habiba had spent the entire day at the hospital on Thursday, during which she had an appointment with a new oncologist, as well as chemotherapy, all afternoon. It was a long day. The hospital had become her second home.

"What did the doctor say?" I asked her hesitantly.

Honestly, I wasn't sure if I really wanted to know what the doctor had to say. Sometimes, it is best to be ignorant and uninformed. Sometimes, it is best not to know . . . not to know the truth.

I knew that the purpose of the doctor's visit that day was to get the results of her most recent body scan. They were looking to see if the chemotherapy was doing its job. Everyone—except Habiba—knew that the chemotherapy was not a cure. Rather, it was a treatment. Metastasized cancer in the lungs and bones was incurable. It could be treated to extend the quality of her life, but it couldn't heal her completely. Nothing could heal Habiba—nothing outside of a miracle.

"The doctor asked me if I knew I was sick. I told him, 'yes.' He asked me if I knew I had cancer. I told him, 'yes.' That's all he said."

"Did he tell you if the treatment is working? If it's helping?"

"Surely the doctor said more than that," I thought to myself. "Surely, he said more."

"He said the medicine is working."

"Great," I answered under my breath.

"The doctor asked me if I had family here in Spain. He asked me if he could talk to them. I don't understand why."

My heart sank as I listened.

"I told him I have no close family in Spain, no one."

I felt sick to my stomach. It was a sad reality. She knew it. I knew it. We were her family now—the safe house director and workers, the other rescued women living with her at the house, and me. We were her family in Spain.

"I told the doctor my family was in Morocco."

"Did he tell you why he wants to talk to them?"

Before asking, I knew why. I knew that the doctor wanted to bring her family in on the conversation—tell them the truth. The truth was that Habiba was dying, and she still didn't know it.

"No, the doctor didn't tell me why."

"Who was with you during the doctor's visit? Was Andrea with you?"

"No, Anita was with me."

Anita spoke English, Spanish, and Arabic. The doctor was obviously trying to communicate more than just words. There was meaning, deeper meaning, behind his questions and inquiries.

I sat on the other side of the telephone screen with my own questions. Did Habiba know she was dying? Did Habiba know her diagnosis—her cancer—was terminal? Did Habiba know she had little time to live?

I was confused too. I was at a loss. What was I supposed to do? What was I supposed to say?

"I'll call Andrea and try to get more information about what the doctor said," I reassured Habiba. "If I have news, I'll send you an audio text to let you know what I find out."

I didn't want to find out anything. I didn't want to know. I never asked Andrea. Habiba never talked to me about it again.

Maybe she didn't want to know either.

CHAPTER THIRTY-ONE

DEAR HABIBA

*D*ear Habiba,

I need to talk to you. I need to tell you something. It's very important.

I've been carrying a secret . . . a deep, dark secret in my heart.

This secret haunts me day after day, night after night. This secret is too heavy for me to carry. It's too much for me to bear, too much for me to handle.

I can't carry it anymore.

I need to talk to you. I need to tell you something. It's very important.

I'm sorry. I'm sorry that I've been carrying this secret for so long.

It's wrong, and I've been wrestling. There is a battle raging inside my mind and my heart.

I can't carry it anymore.

I need to talk to you. I need to tell you something. It's very important.

Habiba, please listen to me.

I'm sorry. I'm sorry that I've been carrying this secret for so long.

Do you remember that day, that day you had an appointment with the doctor? The new one at the new hospital? Do you remember?

I was supposed to be there. I was supposed to come with you that day, with you and Andrea, to talk to the doctor. I'd been with you for all of your doctors' appointments. I'd always been by your side, to hold your hand, to stroke your back, to wipe your tears. I'd always been there to listen, to understand, to translate between you and the doctors.

I'd always been there.

That day, I felt the weight of the world upon my shoulders. I was needed in multiple places, in multiple roles. My family needed me. You needed me.

I wanted to go with you, but I needed to stay. I wanted to be with you, but I felt sick to my stomach.

I didn't want to go. I didn't want to hear the doctors' words. I didn't want to know. I didn't want to tell you.

So, I didn't. I didn't go. I didn't hear. I didn't know. I didn't tell.

I'm sorry. I'm sorry, because I felt relieved that day. I felt the burden lifted off my shoulders.

I didn't go. I didn't hear. I didn't know. I didn't tell.

I'm sorry.

Do you remember that day? That day that they admitted you to the hospital—right after your appointment with the doctor?

Do you remember that day?

Before you went to see the doctor, you called me from the waiting room. I told you I was sorry that I couldn't be there with you. But inside, I was relieved that I wasn't there. I wasn't responsible to hear, to know, to tell.

Looking at you through a screen, we talked. You were in so much pain—physically. You could hardly talk. You couldn't smile, even when I tried to make you laugh.

There was nothing I could do through the screen to comfort you, to take away your pain, to give you peace. There was nothing I could do that day except pray for you. So, that's what I did.

I prayed.

I asked God to be with you when I couldn't. I asked God to comfort you when I couldn't. I asked God to hold your hand, to stroke your back, to wipe your tears when I couldn't.

Just after I finished praying, the doctor called you into her office. Andrea had planned to call me during the appointment so I could translate.

I never got the call.

I was scared. I was worried. I was relieved.

I still didn't know. I didn't hear. I didn't tell.

I didn't have to tell you. I couldn't tell you, because I didn't know.

"Habiba has metastasized cancer everywhere. It's in her lungs, her chest bone, her breasts, her lymph nodes. It's bad."

I didn't want to hear more. I didn't want to know. I didn't want to tell.

"She doesn't have much time, one year, maybe two. They are trying to comfort her and extend her life," Andrea said.

I didn't want to hear more. I didn't want to know. I didn't want to tell.

"Please don't tell me anymore!" I screamed inside. "I don't want to know the diagnosis. I don't want to hear what's wrong with Habiba! If I know, I have to tell her! If I know, it's my responsibility to carry it. If I know, I have to translate the message to her. If I know, I have to be the bearer of bad news. If I know . . ."

"What do you want me to say to Habiba? Do I tell her?" I asked Andrea anxiously. "Do I tell her what the doctor said? Do I tell her she is dying? Do I tell her she doesn't have long to live?"

"They don't have all the results from the other hospital. Let's wait until we have all the scan results before we tell her everything," Andrea explained. "Just tell her she has cancer in her lungs and in her bones. That's why she has so much pain. Explain to her that they are giving her medicine to fight the cancer."

When I saw your beautiful face on the screen that day, I didn't see you in the same way.

This time, I saw you through different eyes, different knowledge.

Now, I know.

I preferred not to know. I preferred being ignorant. I preferred not to hear.

With tears in my eyes, I sat staring at you through the phone screen. I couldn't speak. I felt sick to my stomach.

I told you what Andrea told me to say . . .

But we didn't tell you everything.

I'm sorry.

I need to talk to you. I need to tell you something. It's very important.

I've been carrying a secret . . . a deep, dark secret in my heart.

This secret haunts me day after day, night after night. This secret is too heavy for me to carry. It's too much for me to bear, too much for me to handle.

I can't carry it anymore.

I need to talk to you. I need to tell you something. It's very important.

I'm sorry. I'm sorry that I've been carrying this secret for so long.

It's wrong, and I've been wrestling. There is a battle raging inside my mind and my heart.

I can't carry it anymore.

I need to talk to you. I need to tell you something. It's very important.

Habiba, please listen to me.

I need to tell you something.

I need to tell you something. You're dying.

I love you, always and forever, my sister.

—M

I never gave my letter to Habiba. Writing the words on paper gave me some relief. One day in my bedroom, I read them out loud. Perhaps she heard them. I'll never know.

CHAPTER THIRTY-TWO

I'M TIRED

I'm tired.

I feel guilty.

I'm tired.

I feel guilty.

I don't want to talk. I don't want to talk to you. I'm too tired to talk to you today.

Every day, I try to talk to you.

Usually, in the evenings, I call you on WhatsApp. We chat for thirty minutes, covering everything from the local weather to what's cooking for dinner at the safe house to how you like your new wig.

Other times throughout the day, I send audio messages, reminding you of my thoughts, my prayers, my care, my love.

I also try to communicate regularly—almost daily—with your mother back in Morocco. She relies heavily on me to share your latest news. She is especially relieved to know there is someone who can speak Arabic with her daughter.

But, some days, I'm simply tired. I'm too tired to talk, too tired to look at you through a screen, too tired to encourage you, too tired to make you smile, too tired to make you laugh.

I'm too tired to keep praying, too tired to keep believing, too tired to expect healing, too tired to be strong for you.

If I keep these feelings inside, no one knows they are there. I wrestle with them on my own, in the darkness, in the silence.

If I tell someone how I feel, how I honestly feel . . . then, guilt floods me.

How can I be too tired to reach out, to serve, to help, to care for you, my dear, broken friend who is dying of cancer?

Shouldn't I have limitless energy and strength to give out, to sacrifice? What's wrong with me?

———ele———

I received an article from a friend in Spain. It was timely. I was empty, depleted, drained of life, energy, and hope. It felt like the life and breath inside of me had been sucked out.

> *"Those of us who minister commonly experience compassion for others as a part of our calling. The awareness of the suffering of the world coupled with a wish to relieve it produces compassion—the reflection of the love of God. In times of crises, this response can become fatigued."* [1]

The experts describe four phases of "compassion fatigue," and I had been experiencing them all. When I first started working at the safe house, I was in the *Zealot Phase*—"full of energy, committed, involved, and available." I remembered feeling passion and excitement as I went to the safe house each week to serve Habiba and the other women, even when things were hard.

Next came the *Irritability Phase*. The name said it all. When I read the article and the description of that stage, I recognized myself during the past months. This stage typically includes "cut corners, cynicism, loss of concentration, begin pulling away . . . " Little by little, I had been pulling away from Habiba. The COVID-19 restrictions in Spain had created the needed space and distance between us. I felt relief and release to be less present.

That distance naturally led me to the *Withdrawal Phase* —"irritated, defensive, loss of hope, neglect of self and others, isolation." That's where I was.

Tired. Withdrawn. I didn't know if I had anything left in me to give to Habiba—or to anyone else—even my own family.

The next stage was the *Zombie Phase*—"no humor, patience, condemnation of others as incompetent or ignorant, dislike life and other people, disdain the people we serve." I did not want to head down that road.

"Compassion fatigue is always a possibility for those who care for others and is common in a crisis such as we are experiencing. If we do not care for ourselves physically, emotionally, and spiritually, there will not be enough left to care for others."[1]

Self-care—perhaps that was the answer.

4 Stages and Symptoms of Compassion Fatigue: (Mescia, 2004)

Dear Habiba,

It's not your fault. You haven't done anything wrong.

I just have nothing left inside of me, nothing left to give you. My cup is empty. My well has run dry.

Please wait. Please be patient. Please hold on while I go and sit on the shoreline of the rivers of living water.

Please wait. Please be patient. Please hold on while I drink and fill my empty cup from the rivers of living water.

Please wait. Please be patient. Please hold on while I get refreshed, restored, and strengthened by the rivers of living water.

Please wait. Please be patient. Please hold on.

I'm coming. I'm coming back to you. I'm coming back to you, Habiba.

I love you, forever and always, my sister.

—M

I MISS YOU

Dear Habiba,
I miss you.
I miss you terribly.
I miss visiting you at the safe house.
I miss sitting next to you.
I miss talking to you about your land.
I miss speaking your heart language.
I miss holding your hand.
I miss wiping your tears.
I miss seeing your sweet smile.
I miss giving you kisses.
I miss seeing you face-to face.
Instead . . .
I talk to you through a screen.
I perceive your face through the glass.
I misjudge your feelings and emotions from afar.
I hear your quiet voice from a distance.
I sit alone in my house; you sit alone in yours.
I sometimes misunderstand your language.
I smile and wave to greet you.
I hold my phone, not your hand.
I cry, and you cry—each with our own tissue.
I miss you.

CHAPTER THIRTY-THREE

LAMENT FOR HABIBA

"Has the suffering you've faced, seen, or even just heard about, begun to tear at the fabric of your faith? Has your heart of faith been wounded?"

I read those words in a friend's writing about lament, as she encouraged me to give myself freedom to cry out and complain to God.

I immediately answered, "Yes! The fabric of my faith feels tattered and torn!"

As far as complaints, I had more than a few. I knew it was about to get real, get ugly.

I sat down with pen and paper and poured out my heart in prayer. There was nowhere else to turn. I was afraid my faith was waning. Perhaps I was simply exhausted, confused, lost. Perhaps I was searching for meaning, purpose in the mess, in the chaos. Perhaps I could no longer see God in the darkness, no longer find Him.

Dear God,

How, how, Lord, could You allow so much suffering in the life of one person? I just don't understand. I don't understand Your ways, Your thoughts, Your plans.

It's at times like this that I struggle with holding on to the truth and promise that You are a good and loving God. Everything I'm seeing right now in the life of Habiba doesn't seem to show that.

This woman left her hard and broken life in Morocco in search of a better life—in search of hope, in search of freedom, in search of provision, in search of peace, in search of joy.

Before she even left the soil of her homeland, she was miserable. Her life was shattered. Her heart was broken. Her family was desperate. She was poor and destitute.

She left it all, risked it all, to come here—to this foreign land. Her choice seemed innocent—picking strawberries in the fields of Spain for three months, making some money, and returning to her home and family.

Instead, she was lured, trapped, and forced into a dark and evil world of the Mafia and sex trafficking. She was stolen, purchased, used, and abused by many. More suffering, more pain, more hardship.

How, how, Lord, could You allow so much suffering in the life of one person? I just don't understand. I don't understand Your ways, Your thoughts, Your plans.

Finally, after several long months of selling her body to the night— physical pain, battering, abuse, torture, and death threats—You provided a way of escape for her. When that knock came at the door that day, You opened the way for her rescue.

Habiba grabbed the hand of Your children that You sent to her and ran away to a place of freedom, joy, and peace. You lifted her up from the miry clay and set her feet on solid ground. You provided for her every need and showed her what it meant to be cared for, protected, and loved.

You became for her a refuge, a strong tower, a solid rock, a hiding place.

Just weeks later, in Your sovereignty, You would lead and direct my steps to Habiba—this woman You were seeking and pursuing. Through Your love poured out through me, through a language bridge You built, You allowed me to share Your love with her in her heart language— Arabic. Your sovereign hand that led and guided our paths to cross is beyond my human understanding.

Her newfound life with You gave her joy, hope, peace, and freedom like she had never known. It was beautiful to watch her transformation.

You began to restore her life, to make beauty from ashes, and show us You are a God who redeems. You brought her out of her hard, broken life in her homeland to a place where she could have the freedom to find You and choose You.

"Hallelujah," we all said, rejoicing!

But then . . . only a few months later, a new crisis, this time failing health and a death sentence. A lump dating back decades in her homeland. A lump that could not be removed in her homeland because she was poor, without the means to pay for needed medical care.

Life is so unfair.

How, how, Lord, could You allow so much suffering in the life of one person? I just don't understand. I don't understand Your ways, Your thoughts, Your plans.

How, Lord, can I continue to tell her You are a God of love? How, Lord, can I continue to tell her You will meet all of her needs and the needs of her poor family back in Morocco? How, Lord, can I continue to tell her You are a God with a sovereign plan? How, Lord, can I continue to tell her You are a God who has the power to heal? How, Lord, can I continue to tell her You are a God who delights in miracles? How, Lord, can I continue to tell her You hear our prayers?

Not only does a sudden death sentence come from a cancer that has invaded Habiba's entire physical body, but this death sentence comes at a moment when the world has been turned upside down. She now battles this voracious enemy in her body while the world is hushed and silent. She battles alone—far from her family across the Mediterranean Sea and far from any of those here who can walk physically by her side.

The Coronavirus separates us physically. I can't hold her hand. I can't hug her. I can't wipe the tears from her face. I can't walk by her side. I am thankful for a screen, technology that can bridge the gap. But, it's not the same. No, it's not the same.

How, how, Lord, could You allow so much suffering in the life of one person? I just don't understand. I don't understand Your ways, Your thoughts, Your plans.

Sometimes, I don't know if I still believe. My faith is weak, Father. The fabric of my faith is tattered and torn. Please help me to believe.

I cry out, "Father, I believe, but help my unbelief!"
Mark 9:24—The Bible NIV

I believe! Yes, I still believe! Even if I can't understand, even if I don't know, even if I don't see what You are doing. I declare that I still believe!

I know You are good and loving. I have seen Your faithful hand in my life and the life of my family for many years. I declare You are good and loving to Habiba!

I know You are Jehovah-Rapha, a mighty, powerful, healing God. I have witnessed Your miraculous healing hand reach down from the heavens and touch my sick body and the sick bodies of my children. I have experienced You saving my life! I declare You can heal Habiba's sick body and miraculously remove this cancer if that is Your sovereign will!

"But I will restore you to health and heal your wounds,"
declares the LORD.
Jeremiah 30:17—The Bible NIV

I know You are a God who never leaves us nor abandons us. I have felt and known Your presence with me in the darkest and loneliest times. I declare You are with Habiba, by her side, manifesting Your presence to her in the darkest and loneliest hours of her days and nights!

"Never will I leave you; never will I forsake you."
Hebrews 13:5—The Bible NIV

I know You are Jehovah-Jirah, our Great Provider. Our family has seen You provide for our needs in small and big ways throughout all these years. I declare You are providing everything that Habiba needs —physically, emotionally, spiritually, mentally, and financially! Now that she has You in her life, she lacks nothing!

"And my God will supply all your needs according to the riches of his glory in Christ Jesus."
Philippians 4:19—The Bible NIV

I declare my faith and trust in You, and I stand in the gap on behalf of Habiba to declare her faith and trust in You! Father, please have mercy. Please reach down and reveal Your great love to her today. Father, please reach down from on high with Your powerful healing hand and touch her body from the top of her head to the soles of her feet—cleansing, removing this cancer, battling on behalf of Your daughter, rescuing her from illness and death. Please have mercy, Father!

" . . . the sun of righteousness shall rise with healing in its wings."
Malachi 4:2—The Bible NIV

Please provide in every way for her needs and for the needs of her son and her parents back in Morocco. They are hungry and need food. Please provide for them. Please give Habiba peace as she intercedes on their behalf and trusts You to be their Provider.

"The poor will eat and be satisfied . . ."
Psalm 22:26—The Bible NIV

"He gives justice to the oppressed and food to the hungry."
Psalm 146:7—The Bible NIV

I believe, Father, that even as I am writing these words, You are hearing my cries. You are hearing my prayers and my petitions. Even if I can't see Your hand at work, I believe You are hearing and *answering my cries for help. I believe! Father, I believe, help my unbelief. Please increase my faith to trust in You through this trial.*

Father, I do not know how this story will end. I do not know how the last chapter of Habiba's story will be written. I do not know. You alone know, for You are the author and finisher of our faith and our story.

> *"Let us fix our eyes on Jesus, the author and finisher of our faith."*
> *Hebrews 12:2—The Bible NIV*

I declare You are a God who redeems and restores. You restore what the swarms of locusts have stolen throughout all these years of her life.

> *"I will restore to you the years that the swarming locust has eaten."*
> *Joel 2:25—The Bible NIV*

I believe You are working out all things for the good of those who are called according to Your purposes and plans. I believe You are at work.

> *"We know that in all things God works for the good of those who love him, who have been called according to his purpose."*
> *Romans 8:28—The Bible NIV*

No matter how this story ends, I promise, Father, to declare Your story and Your words in Habiba's life—as well as mine through her story. I promise to write the chapters and the story as I see them unfold in her life. I promise to tell the world what You've done, how You've redeemed her life and her story. I promise to give You all the glory for what You have done! I promise to point people to the One who rescued

*me and who rescued Habiba. I promise to tell Your story to the world!
I promise to tell Habiba's story to the world!*

*Father, please open doors for Your name and Your fame to be
proclaimed through her life. May her story, her journey, her
brokenness, her pain, her hardship . . . not be wasted. May it not be
thrown out with the other tragic stories like hers. Rather, may it be
recorded. May it be collected. May it be written. May it be shared.
May it be declared. May it be told. May it be proclaimed. May it be
redeemed. And, may You, alone, receive all honor and glory for
Habiba's story. I give it to You, and I trust You to write the last
chapters.*

—*M*

_____

My hand did not stop writing and lift from the paper until I had no
more words, until I was emptied of pain, emptied of questions. I laid
my pen down on my desk and read the black scribbles. I spoke my
words out loud—my humble words. Did I speak them to myself? To
God? To whoever might be present?

As I listened to my own words, the silent cries of my heart poured
out in wet ink on the white-lined pages of my journal, I saw it. I saw
my faith as weak as it was. I saw the fingerprints of God. I was on a
journey of faith. Habiba was the catalyst, taking me deep into a
place of questioning, wrestling, and searching for God in the
mystery, in the darkness, in the unknown. The mystery remained,
but I was beginning to see God again.

_____

"Is healing possible this side of heaven?" I asked myself as I sat
outside on my back porch. I was suddenly reminded of what heaven
looks like. I hadn't thought of it for a while. The reminder was
much-needed.

I was always mesmerized by the streets of pure gold—like glass—
the pearly gates, the foundation made of precious stones. This time,
however, the physical beauty of the place was not what struck me.
Rather, it was the emotional beauty of that space—the healing
beauty of heaven.

"He will wipe every tear from their eyes. There will be no more death or mourning or crying or pain, for the old order of things has passed away." He who was seated on the throne said, "I am making everything new!"
Revelation 21:4—The Bible NIV

Oh, what a glorious day that will be, when all things are made new. When there will be no more sadness, no more weeping, no more brokenness, no more trauma. It's hard to imagine what that will be like. What would a world without pain and death be like? What would it feel like to live in a place without sadness and tears? It was especially hard for me to imagine when I was surrounded by such pain and brokenness. I lived in the world of sadness and death.

In our years of living and working overseas, I have seen a lot of brokenness and heartache. Many sick people, poor people, and needy people have been sovereignly placed on our paths. I have felt extreme emotional pain as I have journeyed with the poor through hardship, through death.

However, what I am experiencing with Habiba is different. I have never seen or felt such brokenness, trauma, and pain as in these women rescued from sex trafficking. It is incomprehensible. It is unimaginable. It is unfathomable. It is a brokenness that is perhaps irreparable . . . this side of heaven.

It is a brokenness of the soul. The hearts, bodies, and souls of these women have been used, abused . . . and shattered. Shattered into a million little pieces, so shattered that the pieces can hardly be picked up . . . let alone be put back together.

I have never been a victim of sexual slavery. I can't even imagine the pain—physical, emotional, mental, spiritual. I have only heard the stories of some of these women and seen the broken pieces of their hearts and souls piled up on the floor. I have only seen the empty shell of one woman who stares at me with an absence, a void in her eyes.

"I can't feel anymore," Habiba told me.

Numbness, total numbness . . . body, soul, mind, heart. Numbness.

God's grace. God's protection. God's mercy.

Numbness.

That's what happens when a person can no longer physically, emotionally, mentally, or spiritually endure the amount of pain inflicted.

Numbness.

Something happens to the souls of these women. Repetitively forced to have physical intercourse with man after man after man after man after man . . . day after day after day after day after day . . .

Numbness.

Physically ripped apart, emotionally crushed, mentally abused, spiritually bound. Strongholds, chains tie them to each one of these men in this act, intended to be sacred and divine.

Broken souls.

As I have walked alongside these women, I have prayed on their behalf. I have read promises to them from God's Word. I have fought spiritual battles in the darkness surrounding them. I have bound their wounds—physical and emotional. I have wiped the tears flowing down their cheeks. I have pleaded with God for healing of their bodies and souls. I have tried to be the hands and feet of Jesus—this side of heaven.

But, I do wonder. Is complete healing and restoration even possible this side of heaven? I honestly don't know. When I first heard Habiba's diagnosis, a horrible thought came to my mind. I actually spoke it aloud to my husband, who sat next to me in the car. He was driving me to the hospital to be with Habiba for more tests.

"Maybe it's better that God takes Habiba home now. She won't have to suffer, no more pain and sorrow. I don't know if she can have complete healing this side of heaven."

I have never been a victim of sex trafficking, so I don't fully know or understand that kind of pain of the broken soul. I have never been to heaven to know what that will be like—no more death, mourning, crying, or pain.

But, I do wonder . . . is healing possible this side of heaven? Is healing possible this side of heaven for Habiba? I honestly don't know.

For now, I continue to journey alongside her and be the hands and feet of Jesus in her life. For now, I continue to pray for healing and restoration of her mind, body, and soul. For now, I continue to imagine what that day will be like, when Habiba and I will stand together in heaven—no more pain, no more mourning, no more sorrow, no more death.

El Dorado . . . it is coming, it is drawing near. For now, I wait.

CHAPTER THIRTY-FOUR

I'M JEALOUS!

I think I'm jealous, and I'm embarrassed to admit it. Jealous? How is it possible that I'm jealous . . . jealous of you, jealous of someone else walking alongside you? I'm feeling possessive, like you belong to me. Is this what happens in caregiving? I don't know, this is all new to me.

———*ele*———

It started when I read a text from Andrea.

"I wanted to let you know I called Yousef * when we were at the hospital," Andrea told me. "He speaks Spanish and Arabic, so it was easier for translation. I wanted you to know."

I read the text twice to digest the words.

"My English is very bad," Andrea said. "When I need a quick translation, it's easier for me to have someone who speaks Spanish and Arabic, so that I don't have to translate from Spanish to English first."

My heart sank. I understood the situation. A three-way translation was difficult for everyone. We had been doing this for Habiba for the past nine months. The translations had to go in both directions. It took a lot of time, patience, and energy. Multiple translations, in multiple languages, also left more room for error in the message's content.

It reminded me of that game we used to play in France. They call it "Téléphone Arabe," or "Arabic Telephone." Everyone sits in a circle. The first person comes up with a sentence, or a message, to share. It is then whispered into the ear of the person sitting next to you. The message slowly travels to each person, one-by-one, around the circle until it is finally whispered into the ear of the original messenger.

I have yet to see that game played during which the original message remains accurate and complete. Usually, the content is largely distorted by the time it reaches the original messenger. It always leads to a lot of surprises and laughs for everyone involved.

Translation. It's scary. It's an enormous responsibility.

I had been feeling this same responsibility in my translation sessions with Habiba. I had been feeling sandwiched in the middle translation position, receiving messages in broken English from the safe house directors, psychiatrists, and human rights lawyers. They either tried to translate into English themselves, or they asked a colleague to translate for them. I always had to lean in close, listen intently, and focus intensively to decipher the message. Sometimes, I felt like I had to put the broken puzzle pieces together and hoped I could make sense of it. For nine months, we had been walking this three-way translation bridge, hoping that we were communicating clearly and accurately to Habiba.

She was the focus. She was the most important. She was the priority. She was the reason. It was all about Habiba. It was not about me. It was not about anyone else.

My heart sank when I read Andrea's text. I felt like I was being replaced. I felt like I was being replaced by another translator— another translator who could speak Spanish and Arabic, not English and Arabic. My Spanish was improving after nine months of language study. However, I was far from being fluent. As much as it surprised me, I knew that having a translator who spoke Spanish was the best solution. It was better for everyone involved.

Andrea was under intense pressure at the safe house. She was regularly walking head on into danger on the streets with police escorts to rescue traumatized women and children. Often, she was dealing with conflict resolution and reconciliation between the broken, incompatible women living in the house. Recently, she had to expel a woman from the house for misconduct.

She was always looking for new staff, because most couldn't last long-term. There was a lot of turnover. Many couldn't handle the trauma, the brokenness, and the hard work inside the safe house. Andrea was also now dealing with the unexpected stress of the COVID-19 pandemic that ran rampant in her city, in her country.

Spain had been hit hard. Several colleagues in the house had been infected, adding multiple layers of challenge. Now, one woman at the safe house—Habiba—had been diagnosed with metastasized cancer and needed chemotherapy treatment weekly at the city hospital. These long days of chemotherapy often lasted fifteen hours.

Stress, stress, stress.

On top of all of this, Andrea was married with two little girls. How could she balance it all?

"I'm tired," Andrea texted. "It's so hard for me to speak English. I just can't find the words. It's so much easier for me to just speak Spanish. I don't have the energy to do it."

When I read her words, I felt terrible. I was feeling jealous, but what were the best interests of everyone involved? Andrea was weary. She needed someone who understood and spoke both Spanish and Arabic. That was what she needed.

Habiba also needed someone who could translate correctly—at all times. She needed to be informed accurately about her illness, her treatment, her diagnosis, her situation. Yousef, the North African pastor, was a native-Arabic speaker. He could speak fluently. He shared Habiba's heart language.

On the other hand, I was not a native-Arabic speaker. At times, I stumbled through my translation and needed to search for unfamiliar medical terms on Google Translate. I loved Habiba's heart language, Moroccan Arabic, and spoke it well. However, I was not fluent. I was not a native speaker, and I never would be. Habiba needed an excellent translator. It was in her best interest to have a North African, not a French-American woman.

I was being selfish and feeling jealous, replaced, and booted out. Was I still needed?

"You're still the one closest to Habiba," Andrea tried to reassure me, without knowing how I felt. "You're the only one she really wants to talk to. You know her better than anyone else. Your care and service to her are so important—to her, to me."

My heart felt better, although I had to confess I was still feeling jealous and possessive of Habiba. She was my dear friend, my sister. I had been walking by her side for over nine months. I wanted to continue to journey with her. I didn't want to be replaced by someone else. It didn't matter who it was. I had been her personal translator. I didn't want to give up that role, that position, that honor.

I finally released it and felt better, trying to stay focused on everyone else's best interests and needs, not my own. What did Habiba need? What did Andrea need?

The more I thought about it, the more I realized this was a nice, much-needed break for me. I didn't have to carry that responsibility for medical translation. I didn't have to be the bearer of bad news from the doctors. I had worn that hat too many times, and it was horribly painful and uncomfortable. It was a tremendous responsibility that had been weighing me down since the lump was first examined by the doctors.

My husband had heard me complain of compassion fatigue. I had grown weary in caring for Habiba, in calling her daily, in going to the hospital for medical tests and visits, in translating. I needed to just let this go and focus on what was most important—Habiba.

I felt better until later that night.

It was 1 a.m. I should have been in bed, not looking at my phone. I should have known better than to read texts before going to bed. They could either hype me up with excitement or discourage me with bad news.

This one shocked and saddened me.

Andrea had contacted me a few days before, asking me to talk with the new psychiatrist, who was working with the women. She asked me if I could translate for Habiba that Wednesday at 5 p.m.

I gladly accepted and even considered going into the city to meet with them face-to-face at the safe house. It had been way too long since I had seen Habiba. Perhaps I could even arrive early before our appointment to take Habiba on a much-needed walk in the neighborhood. We had all been in COVID-19 lockdown for almost three months. We all needed fresh air and exercise—especially Habiba.

In my agenda, I wrote the appointment time with Habiba and the psychiatrist. It was set. That's why I was surprised when I read the text.

"On Wednesday, the psychiatrist will call you at 5 p.m. so you can talk to her about Habiba, since you know her better than anyone. Then at 5:30 p.m., Anita will come to the house. She speaks Spanish,

English, and Arabic. My idea is that she'll help with Habiba's visits to the hospital."

"What?!" I thought to myself. "She'll help with Habiba's visits to the hospital? That's my job! I'm her translator!"

I could not believe it. Those horrible feelings of jealousy crept in again until I suddenly felt like I was drowning. I had been to all of Habiba's doctor and hospital visits. I wanted to be the one walking with her. During that night, I could not shut off my brain. Thoughts of Habiba and Andrea's text swirled around in my mind.

The next morning, I went outside and sat on my back patio—Bible, journal, and pen in hand. I needed to stop trying to be in control. I needed to stop hanging on to Habiba. I needed to give this situation to God—give Habiba to God. She didn't belong to me. She belonged to Him. I couldn't take care of her, only He could.

Maybe that was the problem. Maybe I had been trying too hard. Maybe I had been running on my own strength, my own energy. Maybe I was hanging on too tightly.

Maybe the real healing would come to her if I let go of her, if I released her, if I gave her to God.

So, that's what I did.

I wrote these words . . .

"Habiba, I'm letting you go. I'll still be here for you. I'll still walk with you. But, I have placed you safely in the hands of our loving Father. Only He can help you, care for you, serve you, heal you, walk with you. Habiba, I love you, and I'm letting you go."

CHAPTER THIRTY-FIVE

A SWEET REUNION

It had been over three months since Habiba and I had seen each other face-to-face. The last time was at the Coronavirus-infested hospital for her tests, just before we learned about the cancer raging throughout her body.

The last time I saw Habiba, I didn't know she was dying. The last time she saw me, she didn't know she was dying. She still didn't know.

In the months COVID-19 had been ravaging the world, it brought chaos and disruption to every area of our lives—including my work and friendship with Habiba at the safe house.

Spain had been hit hard from the onset, with numbers skyrocketing quickly. It did not take long for the country to be ranked second in the world in the number of cases and deaths, just behind Italy. The pandemic brought everything to a sudden standstill—school, public transportation, outdoor markets, soccer, and driving back and forth between *provincias* (regions).

At the birth of COVID-19 in Spain, we were living in one region, and the safe house was in an adjacent region. With the state of alarm and the restrictions, we could not cross regional borders. We would be heavily fined. Andrea had given me a signed contract as the house translator, along with a letter from the organization explaining my work among trafficked women. With that letter and contract, normally, I would have had no problem crossing the *provincia* border to visit Habiba. If the police stopped me, they would have let me go.

However, my personal situation had changed, and I wondered if going to the safe house was best for me and my family. I suddenly found myself in the middle of homeschooling my two youngest sons full-time. My two oldest sons were now living with us, one home from his university because of the pandemic. I had a lot of unexpected responsibilities as a mother suddenly thrown on my plate.

We were also in the middle of a major move, stuck between two borders—France and Spain. Our belongings were in a storage unit in France, and we couldn't get to them. European borders had been closed for over three months.

Besides my new roles in my home, I wasn't sure if visiting Habiba was wise. Her health was extremely fragile, and cancer already compromised her immune system. If I were a carrier of COVID-19, unknowingly, I might pass it on to her. With cancer in her lungs, contracting the virus could be deadly. Habiba might not have long to live, and I didn't want to make things worse.

If I were honest, I had to confess that I was also scared for myself and my family. Habiba was going to the hospital every week for chemotherapy. She was being exposed to all kinds of germs, along with the deadly Coronavirus. She might be a carrier. In addition, the safe house was regularly receiving new women and children off the streets. Who knew to whom and to what they had been exposed.

I didn't want to take any risks—for Habiba, for my husband, for my kids, for me.

Instead, I spoke with Habiba several days a week through WhatsApp video calls. That was great, but I longed for more. I could tell she needed more, as she continually asked me to come and visit.

After all those months of separation, I set a date to go to the safe house. I was eager and nervous about going there and seeing Habiba. Through the phone screen, I had watched her physically decline over the course of the past twelve weeks. She had lost all of her long, dark, flowing hair, along with her eyelashes and eyebrows. She had lost weight. She hardly looked like the same woman I had met nine months before.

As I drove to the house, my stomach was in knots. I wasn't sure how things would feel after three months of not seeing each other face-to-face. I wasn't sure how I would react when I saw Habiba in her failing health, wearing a veil upon her bald head. I wasn't sure how she would feel about seeing me. I wasn't sure what I would say at first, what I would do.

I prayed. I asked God to give me peace, strength, and courage. I prayed that I would be a wave of joy for Habiba as I walked through her bedroom door. I asked God to make our reunion sweet.

He did.

When we saw each other, I kissed her and held her for a long time. I didn't want to let her go. Although I was wearing a mask, there were no barriers, no obstacles between us. It was pure joy, pure unity, pure love.

We caught up with everything about her life—her mother's cooking that she missed, her son's recent bike accident during which he broke his front tooth, her unstable sleeping patterns, her lack of appetite, her next medical appointments. We certainly didn't lack for topics of conversation. Habiba kept telling me how happy she was. I'm sure my visit contributed to her jovial state of mind. It had been a long time—way too long.

I asked Habiba more questions about her story, hoping to fill in some gaps in my mind about the chronology and order of events in her life. During all those long conversations with the director of the previous safe house and the human rights lawyer, I had never taken notes. I stored everything in my mind—the trauma, the pain, the suffering. I hoped that my aging, foggy memory could keep an accurate record of the events. There were holes, missing pieces in the puzzle of her story. Little by little, I would need to walk back through her entire journey and make sure that my storytelling was full of truth and integrity.

I still had not told Habiba that I was writing a book about her. I had not yet told her I wanted to share her story with the world as a bridge, to bring awareness of a global issue that had infiltrated and corrupted Spain. I needed courage to tell her, and I hoped I would know when the right time would be.

───✿───

Come and Visit!

During that visit at the safe house, I suggested we call Habiba's family in Morocco and say hello. I had been exchanging audio messages with her mother every day, but we had never seen each other face-to-face. Through the screen, I caught glimpses of their modest home. It was small and simple, made of cement. It reminded me of the traditional homes where most of my Moroccan friends lived. I was always in the village *douar**, visiting them when we lived in Morocco.

Her mother invited me again to their home, promising me my favorite Moroccan treats and sweet mint tea.

"My mouth is watering! I'm starving!" I told her through the screen.

Habiba laughed. I loved seeing and hearing her laugh. It made me smile and feel happy. We also talked to Habiba's son, Zacharia, who showed us his busted front tooth.

"How old are you?" I asked him.

"Twenty one."

"Wow, I have four boys, and the two oldest are twenty-two and twenty. They grew up in Morocco and have it in their blood forever."

"Bring them when you come to visit, 'my aunt.' "I'll make you couscous."

Calling me "aunt" in Arabic meant that his mother was my sister. We were officially family, and they had adopted me. The idea filled me with joy. Of course, his family did not know that Habiba and I were sisters in more than one way. They didn't know that Habiba had decided to follow Jesus. We were now spiritual sisters.

"I will come one day," I told them, not knowing exactly what that meant or what that would entail.

"Only come if you bring my mother," Zacharia said through the screen, laughing.

I smiled and chuckled uncomfortably. In response to her son's request to bring his mother back home to him, tears welled up in my eyes. I knew that one day I would return to Morocco and take a trip down south to visit Habiba's family. I wondered, "Will I have Habiba with me?"

After I hung up the call with her mother and son, I felt a need to ask her the dreaded, yet obvious, question. It took me a while to muster up the courage.

"Do you want to return to Morocco to be with your family?"

"No, I can never return to Morocco. Never. You're my family now.

"Don't you miss your family?"

"Yes, but I can never go back home. Never. I will die if I return to Morocco."

"Death" in Arabic symbolized physical death, but there was more meaning behind her words.

Habiba described the lack of good healthcare in her country. She had no money, which meant that she would have no medical care. Without chemotherapy and modern technology, she would have no means to fight her ferocious cancer. Death for Habiba in her homeland also meant shame. Habiba had left Morocco two years ago in pursuit of honor for herself and her family. She boarded that boat hoping to find financial gain and provision on the other side of the Mediterranean Sea. Her impoverished family in the village planned to receive money monthly from Habiba in Europe—money that would bless them and provide for all of their needs.

The El Dorado that Habiba had dreamed of was only a mirage. It wasn't real.

Rather, other than a few months of picking strawberries in the fields of Spain, Habiba had encountered nothing but hardship and trauma. Sex trafficking, the Mafia, alcohol, drugs, fear, sadness, anger, and now cancer had overtaken her. Her pursuit of honor—for herself and her family—had come to a dead end. The shattered pieces of her dreams were now buried deep in her soul.

Habiba could never return to Morocco. Even if the Spanish government, or the safe house, or my family helped her purchase an airline ticket to be with her family, she could never return. Even if Habiba's health deteriorated in the coming days, weeks, and months . . . even if she wanted to die in her homeland, in the comfort of her own home, surrounded by her only son and her aging parents . . . she couldn't.

Shame.

That was all Habiba knew in those days. That was all Habiba felt when she saw her family, when they talked through the phone screen from opposite sides of the sea.

Shame.

A poor woman. A widow. A prostitute. A husbandless mother. A cancer patient.

Above all of that, now a Christian . . . a follower of Jesus . . . a *cafard* * . . . an infidel.

Shame.

No, Habiba could never return to Morocco. Morocco was no longer her home. Spain was her home. Habiba's mother, father, sisters, and only son desired to see her again on the soil of their land; however, there was little chance of that.

God would have to find another way to restore Habiba's honor and the honor of her family.

cafard—roach (Arabic name for infidel, those who do not follow Islam)
douar—shantytown

CHAPTER THIRTY-SIX

STARING CANCER IN THE FACE

For the past six months, I'd been staring at the ravages of cancer in the face.

It was ugly; it was tired; it was bald; it was sick; it was mysterious; it was aggressive; it was sad; it was angry; it was weak; it was violent; it was confused; it was desperate; it was painful.

For the past six months, I'd been staring cancer in the face—in the face of Habiba.

Sometimes, I honestly didn't want to look. I didn't want to see her. I didn't want to look into her eyes. I didn't want to visit her. Sometimes, I wanted to walk away. I wanted to fight it. I wanted to back off. I wanted to confront it. I wanted to avoid it.

I hated cancer. I hated watching cancer eat away at my friend's body. I hated watching it suck the life and breath out of her. I hated staring cancer in the face.

HATED.

I was beginning to get used to seeing the face of cancer regularly. It was becoming more and more familiar. I recognized its look, its smell, its sound, its taste.

CANCER.

I hated it the closer it got to me, the more familiar it became. I didn't want to go near it. I didn't want to touch it. It scared me. I certainly didn't want it to ever come near my home, my family, my children.

NEVER.

Even though I stared cancer in the face every time I visited Habiba or chatted with her through my phone screen, it still seemed far away and foreign. I wanted to keep it that way—at a distance, at least a good arm's length away.

DISTANT.

But something happened. Something suddenly blindsided my family. Out of the blue one day, I found myself staring cancer in the face. However, it wasn't the face of Habiba this time. It was the face of my fourteen-year-old son.

Several years earlier, David* had injured his thigh playing soccer. Months later, he noticed a large lump. We thought it was scar tissue. We ignored it . . . for almost two years. One night, David came to me and showed me the lump. It had definitely gotten larger, and it felt like there were now two lumps.

"Maybe it's from lifting weights," I reassured him.

I finally took him to see a pediatrician, who ordered an ultrasound.

"It will be good to know what it is," the doctor stated.

The next day, we just happened to have an appointment with a cardiovascular specialist at the children's hospital for a follow-up appointment for David. An echocardiogram was already scheduled.

"Maybe the doctor can take a quick look at his thigh," I told my husband.

The doctor asked if there had been any changes or news since we had seen him a year ago. I mentioned the lump in David's thigh—the only changes we had visibly noticed.

"Let's take a look," he said kindly.

Upon examining him, he immediately said that it was a herniated muscle.

"Great!" I thought to myself. "That doesn't sound too serious."

As the specialist proceeded to do the ultrasound, he said, "No, it's not a herniated muscle. These masses are located in the interior of his thigh muscle. I don't know what they are. They're bizarre. I've never seen anything like them."

"Masses?" That didn't sound reassuring.

After he completed the echocardiogram, he called his friend who worked in radiology.

"I have a patient here who I see regularly. He has two large masses in the interior of his right thigh. It's bizarre. They aren't vascular. Can you take a look today or tomorrow?" he asked over the phone.

That especially didn't sound reassuring. I could feel my body tensing and my heart racing as I sat at the desk across from the doctor on the phone. The following day, we went to see the radiologist. We waited for over thirty minutes in the waiting room. I tried to occupy my worried mind with texts and emails. Distraction . . . I needed it. So did David. The radiologist finally called us back.

"This is from a sports injury?" he asked, as David took off his jogging pants and laid down on the exam table next to the ultrasound machine. "This is very common—probably a herniated muscle."

I explained to the doctor that there had not been any recent injuries, only the one from two years earlier. At first, the doctor couldn't find the lumps.

"That's strange," I explained. "The doctor looked at them yesterday and described them as two large masses in the interior of his thigh muscle."

"Two masses?" he said.

My heart relaxed for a minute. We had been praying. Perhaps the "masses" had disappeared.

"The doctor could only see them when he contracted his muscle," I said.

The radiologist continued to look, asking David to contract and relax his thigh muscle repetitively.

"It's not a herniated muscle," he said, "They're cysts."

That word sent a shudder through my body.

"A cyst?" I questioned. "Why would they only show up when he contracts his muscle?"

"They're also there when his muscles relax," the doctor said, as he continued to move the ultrasound wand across the gel on David's upper thigh. "You need to do an MRI and find out what these cysts are. I can't tell what they are. He'll also need a biopsy."

Heat rushed through my body, and I could hear my heart pounding in my head. I tried to stay calm in front of David. I had questions—lots of questions.

"Could they be scar tissue from the injury two years ago?" I asked, groping for a glimmer of hope and reassurance from the doctor.

"They wouldn't look like this," he said solemnly.

He measured them both, approximately five centimeters.

"Do you see cysts in the interior of muscles often?" I asked, still reaching for something that could calm the fears and worries that invaded my heart and mind.

"No, this is rare. You need to find a children's research hospital for tests."

We were all wearing our blue medical face masks. It was hard to read facial expressions and body language. However, I could see the doctor's eyes and could feel the concern. There was a loud message that was clearly unspoken. There was something wrong—seriously wrong. I could feel it. I could hear it. I could see it. I could smell it.

David and I walked silently back to the waiting room. The images and written report would be ready in thirty minutes. We would have to wait. It was not a herniated muscle—like everyone assumed.

"David has two cysts—rare—five centimeters each. We need to find a children's research hospital for an MRI and biopsy. I'm shaking," I texted Vincent.

David and I sat down in the waiting room. We weren't sitting side-by-side, as the COVID-19 regulations required social distancing of at least six feet. The black, cushioned leather chair between us was marked off with black and yellow security tape.

"Well," David said.

I could hear the concern in his voice.

"Well, we didn't expect that, did we?" I replied. "We'll take care of this as soon as we can and find out what's going on."

The secretary called David's name, and we picked up the white file full of images and words. I scanned them quickly.

"Cysts, MRI, atypical, biopsy . . ." Certain words jumped off at me from the page, violently slamming me in the heart. Those words quickly zapped my joy and peace. Fear, worries, and heaviness took over the deepest part of this mother's heart and soul.

⌒ℓℓℓ⌒

I began frantically doing research on my phone. I looked up "cysts, thigh, muscle." Each time, no matter what I typed, the internet directed me to "soft tissue masses." My eyes speedily read medical reports and journals for the next hour.

"Benign, malignant, Sarcoma, teenagers, legs, growth, spread, cancer, MRI, biopsy, surgery, radiation, chemotherapy . . . " All these words scared me.

I kept typing in different searches, hoping to find something more reassuring . . . "cysts forming in thigh from sports injury," "5 cm cysts in adolescent's thigh muscle." Soft-tissue masses could be benign, but they could also be malignant.

SARCOMA.

For young people, Sarcoma often starts in the legs and arms. The masses often aren't noticed and examined until they have grown significantly. The ones of most concern are the ones five centimeters or more. Those that are painless are of more concern. My heart pounded as my eyes scanned the screen. Everything was matching.

"We need to make an appointment for an MRI first thing in the morning," I told Vincent. "There's concern."

I tried to pray and contain my thoughts—take them captive, dwell on something positive, distract my racing mind, calm my worried heart. Nothing worked. It suddenly became all-consuming. Thoughts and questions plagued my mind. "What if David has cancer? What if he dies? What if we lose our son?"

I didn't want to ask those questions out loud. I didn't want to say the word. I didn't want to confess my fears and worries to anyone . . . only God.

The next day, all I could do was pray. I talked to God and cried out to him throughout the day—while doing dishes, folding laundry, taking a shower, swimming and playing with my seven-year-old son, eating, sleeping.

"God have mercy!" was all that I could mutter. "God have mercy!"

I spent hours on the phone calling private and public hospitals, trying to explain my son's medical situation in my broken Spanish. The massive language and cultural barriers only increased my anxiety. Sleeping became nearly impossible. My mind full of fears would not shut off. I prayed and released them to God continually, but they still invaded my calm and peace. I was tired, weary, and stressed.

The earliest appointment was two weeks away—two weeks of dreadful waiting. The next day, I received a call. There was an opening for an MRI two days later. In forty-eight hours, I would know.

"So, I have muscular cysts?" David asked me out of the blue in the car.

"Yes," I said. "We'll find out what they are on Wednesday."

"How did I get them, and how will I get rid of them?" he asked, his voice trembling.

"I don't know," I replied. "Are you worried?"

"Well, yes," he said. "Will they have to surgically remove them?"

"I don't know," I replied.

"Will they have to cut off my leg?" he asked.

I had read about limb amputation for advanced cases of Sarcoma. What was I supposed to tell my son? I wanted to tell him that everything would be okay, that this was nothing, that he would not have to have surgery or have his leg amputated. I wanted to reassure him, but I didn't know. So, I couldn't.

"We'll know more on Wednesday," I told him again. "We don't know what is going on, but God does. Until then, whenever you have worries or fears about this, you can do what I do. I just say, 'God, I trust you.'"

Lately, that was all I could mutter. "God, I trust you." It's like I had to declare it out loud to convince myself and remind myself that God is good, loving, and faithful.

"God has been so faithful in your life and has always taken care of you. He will do the same now," I told David. "Remember all that God has done in your life. Don't forget."

I told him story after story of God's faithfulness, protection, and miraculous healing in his life . . . in his physical body.

"I almost lost you at three months of pregnancy. A dog attacked me when I was seven months pregnant. You were born with a hole in your heart that miraculously closed in three months—not two years, like the doctors first said. You almost died of whooping cough in Morocco when you were four months old. You had three nodules on your thyroid that needed to be biopsied—they disappeared within a week's time. God is certainly bigger than these two cysts in your thigh!"

My prayer during the next few days became, "God, do it again! We will tell people the story. We will thank you and praise you in public. Do it again, Lord, for David!"

Those forty-eight hours of waiting felt like an eternity.

— ✍ —

Wednesday arrived. We were silent in the car for much of the drive. As we neared the hospital, I asked if we could all pray together. I had been praying every night with David when I went into his bedroom to tell him goodnight. I always prayed with him—ever since he was little, but my prayers were more intense during those past days. We called upon God—asking for peace in our hearts and minds, wisdom and insight for the doctors, protection during the exam, and most of all . . . healing, miraculous healing of these cysts.

"Please don't let my son have cancer," I prayed silently.

Because of the COVID-19 restrictions, only one parent could accompany David. I went with him while Vincent waited in the main lobby. Someone came to take David and me to a private waiting room. I could stay there until the end of the MRI, they told me. They brought in a young Spanish woman who spoke fluent English. She translated the paperwork and questions for me as I gave authorization for my son to have the MRI and contrast dye. I signed. They took David into another room for the MRI.

"I love you," I told him as he walked away.

I could see the door from where I was sitting through the glass window. I had the perfect vantage point, the perfect place to pray. That's what I did. I prayed, and I read my Bible. It comforted me. I texted my mother and friends—keeping them up-to-date and reminding them to pray. I listened to worship music. I cried. I begged. I wrestled with my faith and with God's mysterious, sovereign ways.

DISTRACTIONS. WAITING. UNKNOWN.

It was a long hour.

I kept wondering if this might be the best side to be on—the waiting, the unknown. Right at that moment, I knew nothing. I didn't know if David had cancer. Perhaps in a few hours, I would know. I would know something. I would know if David had cancer.

FEAR gripped me.

David walked out, and my heart was relieved and free. I hugged him and asked him how it went. He was fine, relieved, too, that the test was over.

"You can come back in forty-five minutes to pick up the results," the young woman said to us in broken English.

"Forty-five minutes?" That wasn't long to wait.

Did we really want to know?

"Let's go grab lunch," I suggested, realizing that David had been fasting all day. It was now nearly 4 p.m.

I wasn't sure if I could eat. There was a huge knot in the pit of my stomach. David chose McDonalds, the closest place. We ate. We laughed. We joked.

DISTRACTIONS.

I looked at my watch. 4:30. The results were in. The sentence was delivered. The reports were written.

"Let's go," I said.

Parking was complicated there, so Vincent dropped me at the door to go inside and pick up the results. David waited with his father in the car.

I walked in, passing a woman with no hair and a scarf.

CANCER. CHEMO. HABIBA.

I was once again staring cancer in the face. It was everywhere I turned.

I entered the radiology center, and they asked me to take a seat and wait.

"I can't wait any longer!" I screamed silently.

The kind, young Spanish woman who spoke English walked towards me, carrying the large white envelope.

"The CD, images, and written report are all in there," she said.

"Thank you," I replied. But was I really thankful? I didn't know.

"Should I open it here?" I thought to myself. "That way, I'm prepared when I go to the car to tell them the news."

That seemed unfair, so I decided to not open the envelope until I was seated in the car with Vincent and David. I walked quickly to the car, my heart racing.

We opened the envelope. My eyes jumped down to "conclusion." I quickly scanned the words for "Sarcoma," "cancer," "biopsy," "malignant."

I saw "*grado**1" and wondered if that meant "stage 1."

"Use Google Translate, the camera function," David said from the back seat of the car.

I used my phone as a camera and watched the English words magically appear on my screen.

"Muscular, rupture, tear, edema . . . "

"It's muscular!" I screamed. "They aren't cysts! They aren't cysts!"

Thanksgiving and relief filled the car.

"Thank you, God! Thank you, God!" I repeated. It was time to celebrate God's goodness. I was no longer staring cancer in the face . . . in the face of our son.

The following day, I had plans to see Habiba at the safe house. They needed me to take her to the hospital for her chemotherapy session. Why, in God's sovereignty, did my son not have cancer, but Habiba did? Why didn't God heal Habiba and give her clean results? The next day, when I would pick up Habiba at the safe house, I would, once again, stare cancer in the face.

I hate staring cancer in the face.

HATE.

grado—degree

PART FIVE

Her Life

CHAPTER THIRTY-SEVEN

SOMETHING TO HOLD ON TO

H abiba had nothing.

She owned little other than the clothes on her back and in her suitcase. Most of her clothes had been given to her from safe house donations or through gifts at her first birthday party. She had nothing material, but she had an abundance of hope, friendship, and smiles during our daily phone calls. I gave her "quarantine smiles" during the COVID-19 pandemic. Habiba needed them, and so did I. She looked forward to our phone calls each day.

Honestly, sometimes I dreaded them.

My family responsibilities exhausted me—homeschooling and trying to survive total lockdown. However, once I saw Habiba grin and heard her laugh through the screen, I was energized and happy that I had taken the time to call.

"You and my mother are the only ones I want to talk to," she said.

That made me happy to hear. Just weeks before, I was feeling replaced and wondered if I was still needed. I was. Habiba needed me. Habiba wanted me.

I told Habiba not to pick up the phone if she was tired or sleeping. I would leave a message. Habiba and I had to exchange audio messages, not texts. She was illiterate, so it was the only option. I could send her prayers in my voice message, which allowed her to listen to my words over and over if she wanted to.

Some days, I would joke and make faces at Habiba through the screen, trying to get her to grin. Sometimes we laughed so hard we couldn't talk for a few minutes. I loved taking screenshots of those "quarantine smiles."

Other days, Habiba would try on her new wigs or new headscarves for me and play dress up through the phone screen. I would give her my opinion on which ones I liked best.

Every day, however, when we talked, Habiba would hold up her colored heart to show me through the screen. I, in turn, would show her mine. They were constant reminders for both of us, of our love for one another. It also helped me to remember to pray for her whenever I saw it lying on my bedside table.

One day, Habiba directed the phone to show me a little teddy bear sitting on her nightstand next to her colored heart.

"It's from Elena."

I knew Elena from the first safe house. She was an energetic and boisterous girl, full of joy and excitement. It was obvious she loved Habiba dearly. On the day of her departure from the safe house, Elena gave her a teddy bear.

"That's 'Elena Bear'?" I asked.

She nodded and held the bear tightly in her arms.

I had made the mistake of thinking Habiba had little in the way of material possessions. Actually, she had all she needed, including reminders of people who loved her. She had her clothes, her shoes, some jewelry she had made, her telephone, her favorite almond oil to soften her skin, Elena Bear, and her colored heart. She also had her daily needs for food and lodging met by the government-run safe house.

However, there was something more that Habiba wanted.

One day, after lockdown ended, Habiba made a vegetable *tagine* for me during one of my visits. After lunch, she pulled me aside privately in the courtyard of the apartment and whispered softly. I wasn't sure why. We were speaking in Arabic, and none of the other women in the safe house could understand.

"I want to talk to the lawyer on Friday," she whispered to me, gazing into my eyes.

"Why do you want to talk to the lawyer?"

"I want my papers. I want to know when I'll get my papers."

It seemed like a strange request for a woman who was dying of cancer. Why did it matter if and when she got her residence papers to stay and work legally in Spain? She had a roof over her head, and they paid for her food and lodging. She was in a good and safe place, protected by the government as an asylum-seeker.

"The lawyer's coming on Friday. Can you come and talk to her with me? I want my papers."

I reassured her I would do my best to come back on Friday to translate.

"Do you want to know where you are in the process of getting your papers?" I asked her.

She nodded her head.

"I understand," I told her, even though I didn't, really. "You have a right to know about your situation."

If Habiba didn't know all the details about her cancer, she could at least know all the details about her paperwork.

I explained to Habiba that Andrea and the lawyer were working on getting her medical residence papers. The Spanish government would likely grant her legal residence and protection because of her medical situation. Andrea had already told me Habiba should receive her papers quickly.

What Habiba didn't know is that, with her medical residence, she would not have the right to work. That was going to be another disappointment for her. Habiba felt daily pressure from her family back in Morocco to send them money. She needed to work. She wanted to work.

However, she was too sick to work. She was also dying, but she still didn't know that.

Other thoughts and questions crossed my mind. Did Habiba really think she could work, even with her serious medical situation and weekly chemo sessions? Did she want to leave the safe house and return to the strawberry fields, where she could work to send money back to her family? Did she want to have legal papers so she could return to Morocco to see her family before she died, then be able to re-enter Spain legally?

I didn't have answers to those questions.

Unfortunately, I wasn't able to return to the safe house that Friday to meet with Habiba and the lawyer. When I saw her the next time, I took her out for a *crêpe* and a drink.

"The lawyer's coming back to the house next week. I want to talk to her about my papers," she said again, adamant and strong.

I realized her paperwork was vital to her, and I wanted to understand why.

"Why do you want your papers right now? Do you want to work?"

"I can't work right now. I'm sick with cancer and have to go to the hospital for treatment."

"Then, what difference will it make to have your papers? What will it change?"

"It'll change everything."

"Like what? What exactly will it change?"

"It'll change everything for me. I'll have a good situation, be able to stay in Spain, maybe even buy a house one day."

"Other than the house, you already have all of that. You have a good situation here. You can stay in Spain with no problems."

"It will change everything for me."

I listened and reflected on her words. It suddenly occurred to me what she meant.

Habiba had left her country two years ago to come to Spain to work. Originally, she had only planned to stay for three months on her short-term visa. She had left the strawberry fields, because someone promised her a better life, stable work, and legal papers. She had gone through so much, sacrificed so much, to see that promise fulfilled—legal papers.

"You just want to have those papers in your hands, right? You want to hold them and know that you've accomplished your dream?"

"Yes, having my residence papers will change everything for me."

In my eyes, Habiba had nothing, but with her papers, her colored heart, and her Elena Bear, she would have everything that mattered.

———————

The following week, Habiba could finally meet with the lawyer. I wasn't available to go to the safe house that day to translate, but I quickly learned what had happened.

"Habiba is really upset and crying," Andrea texted me. "She's very angry with us, because she can't have her papers right now. COVID has slowed everything down. We have no idea how long it will take."

"Even with her medical situation?" I asked.

"Yes, even with her medical situation. She's going to have to be patient."

I understood Habiba's desire to hold those legal residence papers in her hand, but I still felt like there was something I was missing.

"Do you know why Habiba wants her papers so badly?" I texted Andrea, wondering if perhaps she had information I didn't have.

"I think she wants to bring her family from Morocco," she texted back.

I struggled to put the puzzle pieces together in my mind. Habiba had always told me she could never return to Morocco, and she didn't want to. However, hearing Andrea's words made me wonder if getting her family to Europe was a part of Habiba's original El Dorado dream. If she could get her paperwork and get her family across the Mediterranean Sea to join her here before she died, then she would have accomplished her mission.

Would Habiba one day see her dream come true—her dream to provide for her family? Would Habiba's Faustian Bargain all be worth it? Would the sacrifices she had made, all she had given up, all the pain and suffering she had endured, all be worth it in the final chapter of her story?

None of us knew how this story would end.

CHAPTER THIRTY-EIGHT

HER FAMILY IS STARVING

We were smack in the middle of the COVID-19 pandemic. It was May 16, 2020.

The number of Coronavirus cases had continued to increase around the world by the hour, by the day, by the week. In many countries and cities around the world, this virus was killing hundreds of thousands.

It was also causing another global sickness to intensify and spread. POVERTY. Some people in the world were dying of the Coronavirus, but many people elsewhere were dying of hunger.

Hunger has always been a global challenge. In this world, there are the rich, and there are the poor. There are the "haves," and there are the "have-nots." It is nothing new under the sun. However, the COVID—19 pandemic had intensified poverty, and therefore hunger spread like wildfire.

Countries that had always battled poverty and hunger now faced it on an even greater scale.

Morocco was a perfect example. During our seven years living there, we witnessed and experienced the extreme poverty of that land.

We remember the handicapped beggars sitting on the dirt floors in the marketplaces, the mud-faced kids who stood at the stoplights, waiting to approach paused cars, children hoping to sell one box of Kleenex to drivers and people passing by.

We remember those who looked through trash bins for scraps in wealthy neighborhoods, those who sold everything they had—all their furniture—in order to buy a lamb for *l'Aid l'K'bir,* the Muslim's annual celebration. There was great shame heaped upon you and your family if you couldn't afford to buy a lamb to sacrifice.

Morocco was steeped in shame.

We remember watching our friends be turned away from a local hospital with their dying daughter, because they couldn't afford to pay for the expensive health care needed for her failing kidneys.

We remembered poverty in Morocco . . . and so did Habiba.

The front pages of newspapers and the primetime news reports all screamed daunting statistics of Coronavirus cases and deaths. But there were other stories that should have been on the front pages and in the news headlines. But they weren't.

Stories of poverty, of shame, of plagues beside this killer virus.

For example, East Africa was facing one of its most alarming manifestations of locusts in history.

According to National Geographic, "With their seemingly bottomless appetites, locusts can cause devastating agricultural losses. An adult desert locust can munch through its own bodyweight, about 0.07 ounces, of vegetation every day. Swarms can swell to 70 billion insects—enough to blanket New York City more than once—and can destroy 300 million pounds of crops in a single day. Even a more modest gathering of 40 million desert locusts can eat as much in a day as 35,000 people."[1]

Where there was no money for food, there was also no food to be had.

Yet no one was telling these stories, and no one was listening. When I asked my friends and family if they had heard about the devastating locusts sweeping throughout East Africa, no one had even heard about them. No one.

" . . . With attention almost totally consumed by the COVID-19 pandemic, locusts have tumbled down the priority list. The locusts and the Coronavirus seem to be converging toward a catastrophe . . ."[2]

No one was paying attention but Habiba. She filled in my gaps of ignorance every time I visited her. She stared poverty in the face daily. She remembered walking into a Moroccan hospital with an enormous lump in her armpit, and a doctor telling her she needed to have it removed. Habiba remembered the hospital kicking her out, because she didn't have money to pay for the operation.

Habiba remembered poverty, hunger, shame.

However, as horrible as it was, the poverty I had seen and Habiba had experienced when we lived in Morocco was nothing compared to the poverty facing Morocco in 2020.

Morocco was one of the first nations to close its borders and to stop all travel in and out of its territory. The entire country went into lockdown because of the COVID-19 crisis. Although the numbers of cases and deaths were not extreme, the country had serious restrictions of confinement and curfew in order to keep the virus at bay.

Typically, there were multiple boats sailing daily between Spain and the African continent, but those sea excursions came to a sudden halt. We were shocked by the drastic measures they took.

Morocco wanted to protect its people, its resources, its industries. That sounded good. However, the effects of those drastic quarantine measures were devastating for the Moroccan people—especially poor families, like Habiba's.

Habiba's family lived in rural Morocco, where living was more difficult. Habiba's family was extremely poor, most likely among those three million in the rural areas of Morocco who lived on less than $4/day.[3]

Talking to her mother several times a week, Habiba received regular news about their sad reality. When I asked her how her family was doing, she tried hard not to complain. However, we both knew that their lives were greatly affected by the global pandemic.

Morocco had shut down the local open-air markets and closed the small corner *hanoute* stores. There was no food to be found, and even if there was, Habiba's family had no money with which to buy it.

Habiba told me that non-profit, humanitarian organizations in Morocco—local and foreign—were working around the clock to deliver basic staple food items to everyone across the country. For a moment, it seemed likely that her family would receive what they needed. A few days later, however, Habiba told me a different story. She told me how difficult things were getting. They had no work, no food, no money.

"What about the humanitarian organizations? Aren't they still delivering food?" I asked her, alarmed by this news.

"The only ones receiving the food now are the wealthy people in Morocco. It's being controlled by them. It's not reaching the poor," she explained.

I understood right away. We had seen this happen time and time again while living in North Africa.

The wealthy, who were also lacking work, income, and food, were the initial recipients of the food baskets from the generous aid organizations. They would receive the gifts for distribution, but they would never pass on the blessings. Rather, they would hoard it for themselves.

The poorest of the poor weren't seeing any of the donated food items as the chasm between the rich and the poor, the haves and the have-nots, grew wider and wider.

"My mother asked me to send them some money to eat. They're starving," Habiba told me on the phone.

"Do you have money to send them?" I asked her.

"Yes, I have some money that the safe house gives me for personal items—soap, shampoo, clothes. I haven't spent mine. I'll send it to my parents for food," she said.

My heart sank.

"How will you send it?" I asked her. "Do you need to go to a bank?"

"I'm not sure," she answered. "I'll ask the women who work here to take me on Monday. I'll find a way."

Habiba was stuck here on the other side of the Mediterranean Sea while her family starved. Her entire purpose in coming to pick strawberries in the fields of Spain was to make money to send to her family in North Africa. Lured into sex trafficking, she was even tempted to make "dirty money" to provide for her family's needs.

Now, almost one year later, Habiba sat in a safe house, saving her personal soap and shampoo money, still desperately trying to provide for her needy family back in her homeland.

Poverty. It's what compelled her to leave her family, compelled her to work in the most inhumane circumstances. All this time later, poverty still continued to compel her to make sacrifices.

Yes, Coronavirus was a devastating, deadly, global pandemic that was sweeping across the world. It was major, and we needed to hear about it in the newspapers and on the evening television reports.

However, it was easy to forget to tell, to listen, to read the other stories from around world. There were other devastations taking place, and growing poverty was one of them.

People around you may have been dying of the Coronavirus, but people around me were dying of hunger. Hunger. Poverty.

We had to remember ... lest we forget.

CHAPTER THIRTY-NINE

FRENCH FRIES AND ICE CREAM

"What was it you wanted at the grocery store the other day?" I asked Habiba when I went back to visit her. My friend, Cecilia, had come along that day.

"*Lado*," she said.

She could tell by my facial expression that I did not know what she was talking about.

"You don't know what '*lado*' is?" she said with surprise.

"Is that the word in Arabic?" I asked her.

"No, in Spanish," she replied.

Cecilia spoke good Spanish. She looked at me, puzzled, obviously as clueless as I was.

Habiba repeated several times.

"Oh, *helado**!" I exclaimed.

"Yes!" Habiba said with a big smile and laughter.

Habiba wanted ice cream.

"Well, let's get this girl some ice cream!" I said as I turned to Cecilia, sitting on the bed beside me.

"But you have to eat some lunch first," we told her.

She agreed, got dressed, changed her headscarf, put on her sandals, and coated her arms and legs with scented almond oil. We were finally ready to go.

"*Helado! Helado! Helado!*" Cecilia and I said joyfully as we walked out of Habiba's bedroom.

We stepped slowly down the staircase to the entrance of the apartment complex. It was the first time I was going out with Habiba since we had been at the hospital for all those tests three months before.

Her physical health had rapidly declined during those twelve weeks. How can someone's health fail so quickly? She slowly took one step at a time, gripping the stair railing. The pain in her legs was intense. I hated to see her suffer, but her doctor told us she needed to walk every day.

We opened the heavy wooden entrance door and stepped out onto the cobblestone street. The sun was blinding, and we all covered our eyes.

I'm not sure when Habiba had last seen the light of day, perhaps when someone had taken her to the grocery store last week or to the hospital for chemotherapy.

We were working on a weekly schedule for her. The plan was that a volunteer would come to the house every day to get Habiba up and out of bed, take her to the hospital, take her on a short walk, or do an activity with her. She needed to get up and move. If not, her health was going to deteriorate even faster.

Today, we were going to get her ice cream.

"How do you feel?" I asked her as we walked. "We'll go at your pace, but you need to tell us if you want to stop and rest on a bench somewhere. We'll listen to you."

She nodded, and we walked slowly for about fifteen minutes before arriving at our favorite tapas bar.

Because of the COVID-19 restrictions, we could only sit outside. We sat under a large umbrella. Habiba didn't want to be in the sun, and neither did I.

I went with her to look at the tapas selection behind the glass counter.

"I don't want any of that," she said, turning up her nose.

I understood she had little appetite. With chemotherapy, she had lost much of her sense of taste. She also felt bloated and nauseous most of the time.

"Do you want a cheeseburger?" I asked her, pointing to the picture menu.

She saw a colorful photo of french fries and said, "I want *patatas fritas**!"

I laughed and told her a story about french fries, my favorite food in the world. Growing up, that's all I wanted to eat—McDonald's french fries. I ate so many as a child that my cholesterol spiked. The doctor told me and my mother, "No more french fries!" They were still my favorite food.

Habiba smiled and laughed at my story. We ordered french fries for both of us and sat down with our friend at the table.

They served us lunch, and Habiba ate her french fries slowly with her hands. She was happy and so were we.

"After lunch, we'll walk down the street to the ice cream shop," I said.

Cecilia chuckled and started telling Habiba another story.

"My daughter likes to dip her french fries in her ice cream," she explained.

Habiba had a look of horror on her face.

"Do you want to try it?" she asked.

Habiba shook her head in disgust.

"Now, that would be a fun cultural experience!" I said.

We laughed together, then stopped talking to eat some more.

"I'm afraid to die," Habiba said. "At night, I sometimes lie in bed and wonder if I'm going to die."

It felt like my heart stopped beating. I felt sick to my stomach.

I turned to Cecilia and translated her somber words from Arabic into English.

"Ask her if she's afraid of death or if she's afraid of dying and leaving her family behind," Cecilia said.

I translated her question.

"I'm afraid of leaving my family, my parents, my son. They're so far away," she answered.

I asked her the same question that I had asked her the week before.

"Do you want to go back to be with your family?"

Her answer was the same, "No, I can never go back to Morocco."

She told us that a woman she knew back in Morocco had just died of brain cancer.

"I have bad cancer," she said. "I have cancer all over my body, in my bones, everywhere."

When she spoke these words, I wondered if she knew. If she knew she had bad, metastasized cancer throughout her body, perhaps she knew that she only had a short time to live—outside of a miracle.

"Who told you this?" I asked her.

She explained that during her last doctor visit, the doctor had told her she had "bad cancer." Perhaps she knew now. Perhaps she knew she was dying. I was afraid to ask.

We talked about her fears and about how God could give her peace and strength to walk through this trial. We also reassured her she was not alone. She was in a good place, surrounded by people who loved her.

Tears streamed down my face. I told Habiba that Cecilia and I had prayed while walking from our car to the safe house that day. We had asked God to fill our hearts with His love for Habiba, that she would feel it pouring out of us. Habiba cried and reached over to hug me. She wiped my tears off my cheeks—just like I had wiped her tears so many times.

"I feel God's love in my heart for you. It's strong, Habiba. He loves you so much," I told her.

She could feel it. I knew she could feel it.

We changed topics and went back to talking about french fries and ice cream. Habiba suddenly noticed a black hair on her plate of fries.

"I can't eat them anymore," she said.

We laughed and told her that the hair was probably clean and would only add more taste and nutrients to the potatoes. Habiba didn't agree and said that she had lost her appetite. Cecilia and I removed the uninvited hair and then ate her plate of french fries for her.

"Now, if it were a cockroach on the french fries, I couldn't eat them," Cecilia said. "But a hair is nothing."

"What about a fly?" Habiba asked. "Would you eat it?"

We nodded our heads, and then she told us she wouldn't eat it.

"What?!" I said. "If your mother made a delicious *tagine* with beef, prunes, and grilled almonds, you wouldn't eat it if a fly landed on it?!"

She shook her head. I shook mine in disbelief. We laughed, we joked, we smiled. It felt good. We paid the bill and got up to walk to the ice cream shop. The famous "*lado*" was just around the corner. We were heading to the best ice cream shop in town.

The wide selection of flavors was overwhelming. It took us a while to decide—which flavors, how many scoops, cone or cup. We all walked out with two scoops in our hands. We took a selfie to commemorate the moment and walked back to the safe house, savoring our yummy treats. As we approached the entrance, Habiba and I were still eating our ice cream.

"We can't go back to the house," Habiba said. "We can't eat in front of the other women. They don't have ice cream."

She was thoughtful and respectful. We found a bench where we could sit, in the courtyard of a beautiful stone church. We were all happy. It felt good.

A few minutes later, after finishing our ice cream, we entered the apartment building and trudged up the stairs. The safe house director greeted us. She smiled when she saw us. She knew it had been a great visit. I asked Habiba if I could pray for her, and we huddled together in the entryway with our arms wrapped around each other. We prayed that Jesus, the Prince of Peace, would invade Habiba's heart and deliver her from all her fears—all her fears of death.

We kissed each other and said "I love you" in Arabic multiple times. "*Aziz alia.*" Habiba thanked us over and over for a beautiful day. We parted ways, our hearts overflowing with joy and gratitude. Cecilia and I danced back to our cars, overwhelmed by happiness.

"God is good! God is good!" we said.

*helado—ice cream
*patatas fritas—french fries

MINT TEA

Moroccan mint tea, I long for it.

My Moroccan mint tea glasses sit empty in my kitchen cupboard —hoping to be filled once again with the hot, brown liquid, bright-green, fresh mint leaves, and heaping spoonsful of sugar.

My mouth waters.

My Moroccan mint tea glasses sit empty in my kitchen cupboard —the glasses given to me by my dear Algerian friend at our going away party. My family was about to cross the border from our home in France to our new home in Spain.

My Moroccan mint tea glasses sit empty in my kitchen cupboard —next to my favorite silver Moroccan tea pot—rarely used during this first year in this foreign land.

Moroccan mint tea, I long for it.

However, I don't want to drink it alone. I long to drink mint tea with you, my sister.

You look like Morocco. You smell like Morocco. You sound like Morocco. You are Morocco.

Habiba, I would love to sit down under a palm tree in your land and sip hot, sweet mint tea with you—alongside freshly baked *m'simmon* pastries, smothered and dripping with melted butter and honey.

But we have never enjoyed Moroccan mint tea together, my sister. In our nine months of knowing each other, we have never had a glass of mint tea together. It's so strange, because in Morocco, that's what friends do. Friends drink mint tea together.

Yet, we never have.

Rather, I sit with you in rooms full of strangers—human rights lawyers, safe house directors, and doctors.

I long to drink a glass of mint tea with you, my sister.

Rather, I listen to your stories of horror, trauma, pain, and suffering—your stories of abuse and sex trafficking.

I long to drink a glass of mint tea with you, my sister.

Rather, I walk into the hospital with you week after week, listening to doctors talk of your illness—your metastasized cancer—that is quickly sucking the last bit of life and breath out of your body.

I long to drink a glass of mint tea with you, my sister.

Rather, we wear medical masks, wash our hands repetitively, keep our distance from one another.

I long to drink a glass of mint tea with you, my sister.

You are my friend, and that's what friends do in Morocco. They drink mint tea together. I have waited long enough—staring at my empty mint tea glasses in my kitchen cupboard.

Next week, when I visit you at the safe house, before taking you to the hospital for one more chemo treatment, before we put on our suffocating medical masks, before we walk out the safe house door... I will bring some fresh mint from the local market, bring my favorite silver Moroccan tea pot, and bring my empty mint tea glasses from my kitchen cupboard.

Before one more day goes by, I will sit down and have a glass of Moroccan mint tea with you, my sister.

CHAPTER FORTY

TAGINE, BEETS, AND A TEA PARTY

I parked my car in the dusty, dirt parking lot. My favorite metal thermos full of ice water was tucked tightly inside my purse. It splashed with every step. Every week, the same spot, the same walk, the same heat, the same view, the same thoughts, the same questions. It's the same prayer, week after week, on the same 5-minute walk from my car to the safe house.

"God, prepare me. Help me make a difference today in Habiba's life."

I wished I could do more.

I wished I could pray my little heart out until this aggressive cancer was gone—long gone. I wished I could speak a word of encouragement to Habiba that would instantly take away all her pain, suffering, sadness, and grief.

I wished I could make it all go away.

Rather, I visit. I sit. I hug. I chat. I laugh. I hold. I touch. I smile.

"Am I making a difference?" I asked myself regularly.

Then, I heard Habiba laugh out loud and saw her cover her mouth timidly.

"Yes, somehow, I think I'm making a difference," I whispered to myself.

———

It was Monday—the day of my weekly one-hour session with Habiba and the safe house psychologist, Jessica*. Thankfully, Jessica spoke English fluently. During the sessions, I carefully, yet casually, translated her questions from English to Arabic and then translated Habiba's answers back into English.

Sitting next to Habiba on her bed, across from the only other person in the room, I realized once again that I was the bridge of this conversation. Somehow, I needed to translate and communicate words, thoughts, and emotions. If I weren't there, present in that bedroom, the language and cultural barriers between them would be too long and too high to jump.

After our meeting, I hurried to the local pharmacy to buy some cream for a fever blister on Habiba's bottom lip. I returned to the safe house, hot and sweaty from walking only a short distance under the blazing Spanish sun. Habiba was standing in the kitchen, stirring a pot of vegetables on the stove.

"Can you stay and have lunch with me?" she asked. "I made a *tagine*."

I discreetly glanced at the clock hanging over the kitchen door. It was 1:30 p.m. I needed to leave in an hour to return home.

"Yes, I'd love to stay and have lunch with you."

Habiba smiled, delighted to share her Moroccan delicacy of stewed carrots, peas, potatoes, and beef. It had been simmering all morning, its spices now perfectly blended and absorbed into the tender morsels.

After setting the table in the dining room, we sat down next to some of the other women at the table. Two young children ages two and three sat beside us, along with a new fourteen-year-old girl from Nigeria.

Habiba proudly served me a heaping plateful of her Moroccan dish and a tall glass of dark purple "juice."

"What's this?" I asked, curiously.

"*Barba*," she said in Arabic. "The doctor told me I need to eat a lot of them."

"*Barba* . . . I know that word in Arabic, but I can't remember what it means," I said to her, laughing.

I took a small sip of the cold beverage, unable to recognize its distinct flavor.

"Do you like it?" she asked.

"It's different," I said smiling, not wanted to offend her by my dislike of her special drink.

I devoured the delicious *tagine* and forced myself to empty my glass of the strange purple smoothie. I thanked Habiba for her kindness and generosity, and quickly said goodbye.

When I arrived at my car, I looked up the meaning of "*barba*" on Google Translate.

"Beets," it said.

"Ah, that was beet juice! It certainly wasn't my favorite drink, but I'm sure it was good for me," I said out loud, chuckling as I drove home.

———ele———

During my visit the following week, Habiba was waiting for me at the safe house full of smiles.

"She got up early this morning and has been baking bread all day," Andrea told me. "She's so happy!"

After meeting in her bedroom with the psychologist, I asked Habiba if I could taste her bread.

"Yes, come," she said, leading me into the kitchen.

Someone had recently donated a small oven to the safe house, and Habiba was the first one to use it.

That morning, she had been mixing, kneading, and baking traditional, round Moroccan bread, *r'hobes*. Next to the oven was a dish cloth covering three warm, round loaves. She unwrapped them and handed one to me.

"Take it home for your family," she said. "Eat it with some butter."

I could hear the joy and pride in her voice. She had created something beautiful and delicious, and she wanted to share it with me.

"*Choukran*, my sister," I said to her in Arabic.

"Can you and Cecilia come and visit me on Friday?" she asked. "I will make *m'simmons* and mint tea for you."

I couldn't wait to call Cecilia and invite her. She loved Morocco as much as I did and had spent nine years there before coming to Spain. We were going to have a Moroccan tea party.

———ele———

Cecilia, her fourteen-year-old daughter, and I arrived at the safe house on Friday morning. We walked into the kitchen to discover that Habiba had once again been awake since early morning. A pile of fresh, warm, and flaky *m'simmon* pastries were piled high on a white and blue China plate. Loose, dark Chinese gunpowder tea leaves brewed with fresh mint in a silver pan on the stove. The aroma wafted through the air when I opened the front door.

"It's time for our Moroccan tea party!" I shouted when I greeted Habiba in the kitchen. I could not contain my excitement.

Habiba grinned widely and kissed me on the cheeks.

Once again, she set the table and proudly served us *m'simmons*, fresh Moroccan bread, almond cake, and tall glasses of hot mint tea. As Habiba watched us eat and enjoy homemade treats from her homeland, she beamed with joy.

As I watched Habiba's delight, the question that constantly resonated in my heart and mind was answered. Was I making a difference?

"Yes, somehow, I think I'm making a difference," I heard my own thoughts whisper back.

I could not heal Habiba's cancer. I could not make her pain and suffering go away. However, as I visited, sat, hugged, chatted, laughed, held, touched, and smiled . . . as I was present with her week after week . . . I could contribute to her happiness. God was making a difference in Habiba's life and reaching her through my love and service. That's what kept me going day after day, week after week, month after month.

I was making a difference in the life of this one woman, and it was all worth it. Habiba was making a difference in my life, too, and it was all worth it.

MONDAYS

I love Mondays. I hate Mondays. I look forward to Mondays. I dread Mondays. I feel joy and excitement on Mondays. I feel pain and sadness on Mondays.

Mondays.

Every Monday, around 11 a.m., I circle the same crowded parking lot, mixed with mud and gravel, for five to ten minutes, searching for an empty space. The lot is nestled in the center of the old town, right next to the majestic Archbishop's Palace dating back to the 13th century.

Its elaborate Arabesque arches create the perfect blend of two cultures, a beautiful marriage between two lands that I love—Spain and Morocco.

The storks peck loudly as they construct their enormous nests in the tall, narrow steeples. People come and go to work, to school, crossing town in the early morning hours, while cool water gushes from the plaza's central fountain. As I step onto the cobblestone streets, I pinch myself. Is this real? Is it a dream? It's my life. It's Monday. It's beautiful.

I listen to the Spanish crowds gathered in the tapas bars along the sidewalks, drinking their strong, black coffee, or sipping a cold *cerveza*. Small plates of *tapas* adorn the table. Community gathering, fun, freedom, happiness.

I didn't come here for *tapas* and beer. I didn't come here for fun. No, that's not why I've come. That's not why I'm here. I walk down the cobblestone streets, breathing deeply, struggling to focus my mind.

I can't wait to be with my Moroccan friend today—to speak Arabic, to drink sweet mint tea, to be immersed in her culture that I love. I fear being with my Moroccan friend today—to see her teary eyes again, to hear more stories of pain and trauma, to see her hairless head and weakened frame from the metastasized cancer that now ravages her entire body.

When I walk up to the door, those on the streets—men, women, children—have no idea. I pass by them. They don't know me. They don't know what I do. They don't know where I'm going. They don't know what lies hidden behind that door.

I ring the bell and wait. Upstairs, they push the button to buzz me in.

I leave the beautiful, fun, free, happy land of Spain, and I enter the dark corridor and turn on the light. I walk up the stairs. I breathe deeply, preparing myself for what lies ahead.

"Please, God, help me. Give me strength, courage, love, joy, and peace."

I realize I may be the only wave of joy in my friend's life this week.

Mondays.

The door of the safe house is ajar. I walk through and enter another land—a dark, broken land of women in slavery. Rescued off the streets, their world of pain and suffering still traps them, still haunts them.

Mondays.

I go to listen, to sit, to drink tea, to talk, to pray, to comfort, to encourage, to be present.

She waits for me at the door, dressed and ready to go. I kiss her through my face mask, on both sides of her cheeks, Moroccan style.

"*Yala*! Let's go!" I tell her . . . on Monday . . . every Monday.

We go to the same *tapas* bar for lunch and sit at the same table in the sun. The same server takes our order—orange Fanta, eggs, and french fries are Habiba's favorites. The safe house psychologist joins us. I translate into Arabic. Every Monday.

We hope that our time together comforts her and helps relieve some of her pain, her trauma. We then go to some of her favorite places—the church across the street, the best ice cream parlor in town, the local market that reminds her of her homeland. Habiba points out that the fresh fruit and vegetables are much cheaper than the local supermarket.

After a full day on our feet, we make our way back to the safe house, passing the Moroccan merchant where Habiba buys her favorite spices and fresh mint for tea.

At the safe house door, I look around us. Still, no one knows who I am. No one knows who she is. No one knows who walked among them today. Hidden, discreet. A woman who once roamed the streets to sell her body to the night, now walks rescued, freed, redeemed.

Does anyone care?

Inside, she takes me into the kitchen, where she makes a pot of hot, sweet, Moroccan tea with her fresh mint. She pours me a glass. She pours herself a glass. We chat in Arabic. She tells me stories. I tell her stories. We laugh, we cry, until it's time for me to go. I need to pick up my children from school.

I kiss her goodbye at the door—on both cheeks—Moroccan style.

"*B'salaama*, my sister. Goodbye, I'll see you next Monday."

Mondays.

CHAPTER FORTY-ONE

HER FATE IN BLURRED IMAGES

It was time to stop hiding, time to know. No more wondering or guessing. It was time for truth, clarity, and honesty.

Habiba had gone to the hospital for another full body scan, to determine if the chemotherapy was working. She had an appointment with her oncologist to hear the results.

We all prayed, full of hope and belief. But, the waiting was agonizing.

———

As I sat down on that gray and gloomy Spanish day, I heard these words echo in my heart and mind.

"Write! Write! Write for Habiba!"

That is what I did. I wrote for you, my dear sister. I wrote these words.

———

Father, what are You writing? What words are You pouring out on the paper? What sentences? What chapter? What story?

How will this book end?

Father, what are You writing?

If You are the author and finisher of our faith, then You are the one writing Habiba's story. I am not.

You are the one who holds the quill in your hand. You are the one who holds the scroll.

You, Father, are the author and finisher of Habiba's story.

I sit and wait, watching the flame of the candle flutter—gently, silently.

Father, what are You writing? May I see?

Habiba sits in a room with a doctor, a doctor who may pronounce her fate, but not determine her fate. The doctor is not writing her story. No, You, You alone, write Habiba's story.

You, You alone, have the last say, the last word, the last sentence. You, You alone, hold the keys of life and death. You, You alone, give breath and life, pulse and heartbeat. You, You alone, are the creator of the body and the One with the power to heal, to cleanse, to restore, to redeem.

You, You alone, are the author and finisher of Habiba's story.

I sit and wait, watching the flame of the candle flutter—gently, silently.

May You show me Your words? May I know Your sentence? May You tell me Your plan? May You reveal the story You are writing— now, yes, even now?

Right now, I don't know. There is something comforting about being on this side of "knowing." Right now, I don't know. Soon, at any moment—a call, a text, a few words will jolt me to the other side of the bridge of the unknown. It won't be a slow, steady walk across the creaky, wooden planks. No, it will be a sudden leap to the other side.

What lies on the other side of this bridge of the unknown? Are there dancing and tears of joy? Are there weeping and tears of sorrow?

What lies beyond? What awaits us in the distance? What stands to greet us on the other side of the bridge?

Here in this place, in the middle of this unknown, there is only one thing. There is only You.

You are the one who holds all authority, power, and sovereignty in the palm of Your hand. You are the only one to determine our fate. You are the only one to pave our life journey. You, You alone.

I sit and wait, watching the flame of the candle flutter—gently, silently.

Father, what are You writing? May I see?

Is Habiba prepared for the knowing? Am I prepared for the knowing?

"Be still and know that I am God," I hear You whisper, as the flame of the candle flutters.

Help me rest in Your river of love and peace, Father. Help me be carried by the soft, rhythmic current of Your cool, calming waters— Your presence underneath the bridge, the bridge of the unknown.

What lies beyond? What awaits us in the distance? What stands to greet us on the other side of the bridge?

No matter what lies beyond the bridge of the unknown, You are the author and finisher of Habiba's story. You hold the quill and scroll. In death, in life, in You, there will be dancing and tears of joy on the other side of the bridge of this life. El Dorado—it awaits us all. I sit and wait, watching the flame of the candle flutter—gently, silently.

—————

"The images are blurred," the doctor told her. "You must have moved during the scan."

Shocked, Habiba replied, "I didn't move."

"I can't see the images. They aren't clear," the doctor continued. "You'll have to do another body scan."

When we heard the news, I felt a twinge of relief. We could remain on this side of the bridge of unknown. Somehow, it felt safer here. It felt happier here. It felt more peaceful.

We continued to pray, hope, believe, wait.

The following month, Habiba went for another full-body scan. A few weeks later, she had another appointment with the same doctor.

"The images are still blurred," the doctor told her. "You must have moved during the scan."

Shocked, Habiba replied, "I didn't move."

"I can't see the images. They aren't clear," the doctor continued. "You'll have to do another body scan."

How could this happen twice?

Blurred images. It gives us more time to pray, more time to hope, more time to believe, more time to wait . . . to wait on this side of the bridge of the unknown.

CHAPTER FORTY-TWO

FLAMENCO AND THE BACKWARDS WARRIOR

Flamenco

"The safe house might have to close," Andrea texted me. "What?!" I wrote back in a state of shock. "What do you mean?"

"There's been an honest mistake made on our paperwork requesting government funding this year," Andrea explained. "Our lawyers are in conversation with the government, but we have little hope of them overturning the decision."

My heart sank. My mind immediately went to Habiba. I didn't think about the house. I didn't think about the staff. I didn't think about the other ladies. I didn't even think about the children. I only thought about Habiba.

What would happen to her, a woman who was sick and dying? Where would she live, in another safe house, another city? She was in no shape to move, to start over, to be alone. What if she was too far away for me to see her?

My heart raced with fear and anxiety at the idea of days without seeing her. What if it were months or longer? The thought of Habiba dealing with her illness alone made me sick to my stomach. I was aware of my loss as well. I was afraid.

"Can you help spread the word among your friends, family, contacts, and networks?" Andrea asked. "We have to raise 120,000 euros in the next two months in order to keep our safe house open."

I had faith, but my faith shrunk when I heard those words.

Fundraising was a part of our work among refugees and immigrants. I knew what it entailed to solicit people. I also knew that raising 120,000 euros in a few months was no simple task. Actually, it seemed like an impossibility—outside of a miracle! It sounded like the major mountain of cancer in Habiba's body that needed to be moved.

"How, God, could this be happening?" I shouted out loud to whoever might be listening.

A few weeks later, Andrea organized a flamenco concert to raise money for the safe house. Being an incredible flamenco singer herself, Andrea would be a part of the evening's entertainment.

Even with the tight restrictions of the COVID-19 pandemic in Spain, Andrea found a small venue that could hold fifty people and still respect the social distancing guidelines. An incredibly talented flamenco guitarist, vocalist, percussionist, and dancer took the stage to give us all a taste of authentic Spanish culture.

Before and after the concert, the women from the safe house proudly, yet timidly, displayed their arts and crafts on folding tables in the foyer. Habiba had made over fifty key chains, uniquely designed animals, each sewn and filled by her hands of love with soft, white stuffing.

The other women laid out their sewn tote bags and framed artwork of pointillism for those who wanted to admire and hopefully take treasures home with them. They all needed money. None of them had residence papers. None of them had the right to work. The few euros Habiba would earn that evening would go to her son, Zacharia, on the other side of the Mediterranean.

The beautiful flamenco concert brought in 500 euros, but we were still far from the needed 120,000. We continued to pray, continued to hope, continued to believe, continued to wait.

Whether it was Habiba's test results or the safe house's financial need, I felt like all I did was pray and wait. It felt like one thing after another was hitting us. I wanted to scream, "Relent, Lord, relent!"

Once again, all I could think about was Habiba. What would happen to her if she had to change homes, change cities, change hospitals, change doctors? Already, she had been kicked out of one safe house because of disciplinary issues. At the house with Andrea, she had also had multiple incidents. At one point, Andrea told us if there was another major incident, then Habiba would have to leave the house.

How could Habiba possibly adjust to another major change with a new house, new women, new roommates, and a new director?

I reached out to as many people as I could—sending emails, texts, and asking people to spread the "GoFundMe" page that Andrea had created for the house. A few hundred euros trickled into the fund from time to time, but we were still far from the needed 120,000 euros. We needed a miracle.

"Pray! We have a meeting right now with the lawyers and government officials, asking them to overturn the decision because of an honest mistake of numbers on the funding paperwork," Andrea texted me.

The panic in her words was loud and clear.

"The meeting was tense, but it ended well," Andrea wrote. "They are reconsidering. For now, we need funding, and we have to continue to wait and pray."

That's what I did. Waited and prayed.

Several months later, Andrea informed me that the government had overturned their decision. The mistake on the paperwork was covered with grace and compassion. Habiba would not have to be moved into another safe house in the middle of her pain and sickness. I could continue visiting her every week.

Finally, one answer to prayer.

The Backwards Warrior

While brushing my teeth, I noticed my pink pearl earrings sitting in the ceramic dish next to my bathroom sink. I smiled and carefully put them on, thinking about Habiba and praying for her.

I don't typically like pink. I don't typically wear pink, but now I do—every Monday.

An online store, *Trades of Hope*, had hosted a sales campaign for breast cancer awareness. Female artisans around the world, rescued from human trafficking, were hand-making unique pieces of jewelry. Income from their products helped them to become financially independent and to stay off the streets.

When I saw their gorgeous products, all pink, I couldn't resist. Fair-trade items, made by the hands of survivors to raise awareness for breast cancer, would be perfect for Habiba and me.

I got the pink pearl earrings for myself and the "Warrior" bracelet for Habiba. Prominently displayed in the middle of the shiny pink beads was the word "WARRIOR" in gold. It was beautiful and would be a constant reminder to Habiba that she was a fighter, battling breast cancer . . . and every other cancer that had invaded her body. Habiba was one of the strongest women I knew. She had been through so much and was a model for me—a model of a courageous warrior.

It was Monday, and I wore my earrings. I rubbed them between my fingers as I waited outside for Habiba and Jessica to arrive. They were running a few minutes late. We sat down at the *tapas* bar next to the safe house, the same one we go to every week. The server came over to greet us.

"Regular Coke for you, Diet Coke for you, and Orange Fanta for you," she said, smiling as she went around the table, making eye contact with each one of us. Looking at Habiba, she said, *"Huevos rotos con jamón** for all of you. But, no ham for you, and eggs over hard."

Same *tapas* bar, same server, same day of the week, same order.

We all chuckled.

As we waited for our food to arrive, I noticed the pink shiny beads on Habiba's wrist.

"You're wearing your special bracelet," I said to her, as I leaned over to touch it. "I'm wearing my special pink pearl earrings too."

She fingered her bracelet and flashed me a proud smile.

The week before, I had given Habiba the small, beautifully wrapped gift. She loved presents. They seemed to speak straight to her heart. She loved the gift and immediately put it on her wrist, promising to wear it and remember.

"Each time you go to the hospital for chemo, look at that bracelet on your wrist," I told her. "Remember that God has made you a strong and courageous warrior to fight your cancer. God's fighting for you too."

I then showed her my pink pearl earrings. "I'll wear my earrings every Monday when I come to visit you. And whenever I see them or wear them, I'll remember to pray for you."

Like the colored hearts made of felt, these pieces of pink jewelry would bind us together forever.

My heart flooded with joy when I saw the bracelet on Habiba's wrist that day at the *tapas* bar. She had remembered to wear it.

"Show it to Jessica," I encouraged her.

Habiba lifted her shirtsleeve and proudly showed her shiny pink bracelet. I explained to Jessica the meaning behind the color pink and the hands that had made the jewelry.

"*El pecho,*" Habiba kept saying to Jessica.

"*El pecho?*" I asked. "What does that mean?"

They tried to explain it to me, laughing hysterically.

"I don't know that word," I said to them. "Tell me!"

Habiba grabbed her breast and said, "*El pecho,*" "*B'sula.*"

"Oh, *b'sula!!!*" I screamed. "Yes, pink is for breast cancer awareness!"

Together, we looked at the bracelet on Habiba's wrist, and I pointed to the word spelled out in tiny gold beads. Much to my surprise, it didn't say "WARRIOR." The letters were upside down and backwards. I smiled and explained to Jessica that it was supposed to say "WARRIOR."

"She put the bracelet on backwards," I told her. "Today, she's a backwards warrior."

It didn't take me long to have a paradigm shift.

"No, actually, it's not backwards. Habiba can't read, so she doesn't know what it says or how it's spelled," I told Jessica. "She isn't a backwards warrior, after all. She's just perfect."

"Yes," I thought to myself. "She's just perfect."

huevos rotos con jamon—eggs, potatoes, ham

CHAPTER FORTY-THREE

WAIT FOR ME!

"Wait for me. In two years, we'll go together," Habiba said. Tears welled up in my eyes and slowly trickled down my cheeks. I couldn't hold them back. Quickly turning away, my eyes reached out to Cecilia for help.

I was choked up and couldn't translate. Nothing came out but tears.

Cecilia and I had gone over to the safe house together that day. For lunch, Habiba had served us fried eggs and french fries—her favorite—followed by some sweet mint tea served in tiny Moroccan glasses.

We were gathered at the dining room table, along with the other women and children who lived at the house.

Sitting down at the far end of the table, Habiba and I spoke Arabic together. I had been translating for Cecilia.

Just before lunch, Habiba and I had an appointment with the human rights lawyer at the house. She was still working on filing Habiba's medical residence papers. It was a long and complex process, but we were making baby steps of progress. The pandemic had slowed everything down in Spain, from getting responses from the embassy, to making an appointment for fingerprinting at the police station, to getting paperwork from Habiba's home country, to getting medical exams.

Habiba's case was especially complicated. The Moroccan Embassy in Spain required a document from the police in her hometown in Morocco. Her mother had tried several times to retrieve it, to no avail. The lawyer had sent emails and made phone calls to the Moroccan Embassy. No answer. Finally, the lawyer went to the embassy in person and got something accomplished. The embassy agreed to obtain Habiba's police report.

Things moved quickly at that point. The embassy called a few weeks later to tell us they had Habiba's police report. They just needed her fingerprints. Habiba was treated like royalty. Cecilia drove her into the city, and the embassy representative came to the vehicle to get her fingerprints. Habiba didn't even have to open the car door.

All the paperwork was finally assembled, and it was time to meet with the lawyer. The last step before they could submit Habiba's request for a medical residence was her signature on the documents. I explained everything to Habiba in Arabic. She grinned from ear to ear. Her dream was finally coming true. In her hand, she would soon hold a little part of her El Dorado.

Habiba's medical residence papers would allow her to stay in Spain legally. She could finally hold an official resident card in her hands. What she didn't know was that medical residence did not give her the right to work. The government assumes that the person is too sick to work. That was certainly Habiba's case. With her aggressive cancer, she didn't have any energy or time to devote to something other than her health and her treatment.

I purposefully didn't translate the details about the work restrictions. I didn't want to rain on Habiba's parade. She was overflowing with joy that day. We celebrated in the office, and I took pictures to commemorate the big moment—"the signing."

Just before leaving the room, the lawyer explained to Habiba that it would take approximately three months to receive her medical visa. She would then be free to travel in and out of the country.

"Wow! Do you want to go to Morocco?" I asked her again, wondering if perhaps she had changed her mind since I'd broached the topic months earlier.

"No," she said firmly. "Spain is my home, and you are my family. I can never go back to Morocco."

"What if I went with you?" I asked. "Would you go?"

"No," she said, shaking her head, with her eyes lowered. "I can't go."

I dropped the subject, and we left the office to join Cecilia in the dining room.

Over lunch, I shared with Cecilia the wonderful news about Habiba's paperwork finally being signed and submitted. I showed her the picture of Habiba signing the documents, and we rejoiced together.

"Habiba can travel in and out of Spain once she has her medical residence papers. She can even go to Morocco to see her family," I translated back and forth between Arabic and English.

I realized I was pushing the subject. Cecilia and I had both lived for many years in Morocco, and we had already discussed the possibility of going together on a trip and taking Habiba to see her family. Perhaps with Cecilia, Habiba would process her feelings more. Deep down inside, I hoped Habiba would change her mind.

"Do you want to go see your family?" Cecilia asked Habiba.

"I can't go to Morocco. I would need money to go—a plane ticket, gifts for my family, nice clothes to wear."

"So, your mother, father, and Zachariah know what has happened here in Spain, but not everyone knows?" I asked. "Do some people think you have a glorious life here in Spain, a good job, and lots of money?"

"Yes."

She was describing her Moroccan tradition perfectly. When someone travels to visit family from a "rich country," where they live, they are culturally obliged to come bearing gifts. They are expected to carry suitcases bulging with presents—perfume, clothes, food. They cannot arrive empty-handed. That would be shameful.

Cecilia and I looked at each other and gently nodded. We both understood. Having lived in that country and culture for many years, we knew. It was the first time it made sense why Habiba kept shutting me down whenever I extended the invitation for her to visit her family in Morocco.

By that time, we had finished eating our eggs and french fries. We were drinking Habiba's sweet mint tea.

"Once I have my papers, I can work and save money to go to Morocco to visit my family," Habiba said.

I felt nauseous.

In English, I explained to Cecilia what the lawyer had told me in the office. Habiba could not work with her medical residence papers. The only exception was if someone hired her with an official contract, then the government would make an exception and allow her to work.

"In two years, I can work, save money, buy presents, and even buy a house," Habiba added, still dreaming of her El Dorado.

"A house?!" I thought to myself. "I can't even buy a house in Spain!"

Habiba's dream was a mirage. Most likely, there would be no work. Certainly, there would be no house.

"Wait for me. In two years, we'll go together," Habiba said.

"Where?" I asked.

"Morocco! Wait for me. In two years, we'll go together!"

Tears welled up in my eyes and slowly trickled down my cheeks. I couldn't hold them back. Quickly turning away, my eyes reached out to Cecilia for help.

I was choked up and couldn't translate. Nothing came out but tears.

When I could finally speak, I looked at Cecilia and translated Habiba's words.

I then turned back towards Habiba and looked into her eyes.

"I don't know if you'll be here in two years," I muttered under my breath.

~ell~

A few months later, Habiba had another appointment with the oncologist. Andrea encouraged her to ask as many questions as she wanted. We all agreed that Habiba had a right to know about her health, about her body. She needed to know.

"The doctor told me I have a very bad cancer," she explained to me and Jessica during her counseling session at the *tapas* bar. "The chemo treatment isn't healing my cancer and making it go away. It's only stopping it from spreading."

"How do you feel about this news?" Jessica asked Habiba. I translated.

"It's hard," she answered stoically.

There was no emotion in her voice, no facial expression. I remembered her words months before, "I have a heart, but I can't feel."

"Do you want to continue chemo if it's not making your cancer go away?" I asked her.

"I'll follow the doctor's advice, and right now, it's continuing chemo. That's what I'll do."

"You're a strong woman," Jessica said. "Full of peace in the midst of the storm."

Jessica left us at the *tapas* bar, and Habiba and I walked down the street to find a café and some treats.

We sat at a small table in the sun. Habiba had a giant glass of fresh-squeezed orange juice—her favorite—while eating her *pain o chocolat*.

It had been a few weeks since I had asked her about going to Morocco to see her family. I felt relentless and stubborn, and I wasn't sure why. She had already told me no many times. I guess I didn't want her to have any regrets. I knew time was running out, and I felt guilty every time I spoke with her mother on the phone. Although I didn't know how little time she had left, I could encourage her to see her family once more.

With fear and trembling, I asked Habiba again. "Have you thought anymore about visiting your family in Morocco?"

I explained she would receive her medical residence papers soon. It was nearing the three-month mark. When she had her papers in hand, she could move freely and easily across borders.

"Don't you want to see your parents and your son?" I asked her.

"I can't go right now. How about next summer 2022, during *l'Aïd*?" she said, already dreaming of being with her family for the annual celebration and feasting on the traditional sacrificed lamb. "Right now, I need to work and save money for presents. And, what I really want is a small house in my village. I want to buy my own house in Morocco where I can stay whenever I visit my family."

I shuddered. It felt like someone had stabbed me in the heart.

"Let's go in summer 2022," she repeated. "Let's go in summer 2022."

"Would she even live to see the summer of 2022?" I thought to myself. I felt doubtful and fearful. "Why don't I have the courage to tell her she is dying and that she probably doesn't have another year to wait to see her family?"

We sat in silence at the café. I had no words.

CHAPTER FORTY-FOUR

MENOPAUSE, ORANGE JUICE, GRAY HAIR, AND BALD HEADS

"I'd like to paint a portrait of Habiba," my friend, Kami*, told me one day while our families were out having a picnic together. "It could help promote your book, Habiba's story that you're writing." Upon hearing this idea, I was thrilled. Kami was an artist who painted breathtaking portraits of people, so real, so perfect, that one was convinced he was admiring a beautiful photograph. Habiba loves art, and she would be more than happy to be the subject of Kami's painting.

"It could be a gift to her, or perhaps a gift to her family one day," Kami said, knowing that Habiba's prognosis was not good.

I suddenly had flashes of me carrying suitcases of Habiba's clothing and belongings to her family in Morocco. Along with the overweight suitcases, I had a vivid image of me delicately cradling a large, beautifully painted portrait of Habiba underneath the pit of my arms for safekeeping.

"I need to meet her first and study her a bit," Kami said. "She may need to come to my studio a few times for me to paint her."

As soon as I heard Kami's idea, I shared the news with Habiba. She was ecstatic.

The next Monday, after my regular session with Habiba and Jessica, Cecilia and Kami joined us at the *tapas* bar. Andrea walked over from the safe house to meet Kami, following the strict security guidelines. Any volunteer in contact with the trafficked victims must sign a contract and give their personal information. It didn't take long for Kami to fill out the paperwork and be officially "approved." I then took them to my favorite coffeehouse in town, where I often go to write in the mornings. It was quiet and empty inside, just right for a heart-to-heart conversation.

We laughed, and we chatted about life, our lives as women. Cecilia and Kami were both going through menopause. They shared their woes, and I translated to Habiba in Arabic. She laughed with us, but stood firm in her belief that healthy women have their menstrual cycles for their entire lives. In her mind, there is no such thing as changing hormones and aging bodies. After trying hard to convince her that a woman's hormones and body naturally change with age, we all finally gave up. For Habiba, menopause did not exist. Cecilia and Kami begged to differ.

"We're old and have gray hair," Kami said.

Cecilia and I pointed out our gray hair, too.

"Even you have gray hair," I told Habiba, smiling.

"I do?" she asked with surprise, touching the stubble on her bald head underneath her stocking cap.

"Yes, you do," I said, laughing. "You're old like us."

She removed her stocking cap, and I took a close-up picture with my phone to show her the gray hairs. She was shocked.

"We're all old with gray hair!"

In the meantime, Habiba ordered an enormous glass of fresh-squeezed orange juice, while the rest of us ordered the typical *café con leche*. Habiba and I walked over to the glass display case. After drooling over the variety of cinnamon rolls, croissants, *pains au chocolat*, and every other yummy treat, I let her choose. Habiba picked out a chocolate-covered croissant for us to share. Perfect!

While we waited for our drinks and croissant to arrive, our women's conversation continued.

"Did you know that Kami once shaved her head to support a friend with cancer?" Cecilia asked me.

"No, really?" I asked, in shock.

Kami quickly scrolled through photos on her phone to reveal her shaved head.

"Wow! You look amazing without hair. What a beautiful way to honor your friend," I said. I was moved and impressed by my friend's courageous gesture of love and affection.

"Would I ever have the guts to do that?" I thought to myself.

We showed the picture to Habiba who was deeply touched to discover that Kami had shaved her head to connect with her friend with cancer.

"Maybe you should do that too!" Cecilia said to me. "To honor Habiba!"

My eyes popped out of my head, and I gave a horrified look to Cecilia, a meager attempt to quiet her outlandish suggestions.

I translated out of moral duty.

Habiba smiled and looked at me, as if to say, "How about it?!"

"You're going to get me into a lot of trouble," I teased Cecilia and Kami, laughing. "A lot of trouble. I'm going to kill you, gals!"

Habiba's giant glass of orange juice arrived, along with our tiny cups of *cafe con leche.*

She tasted her juice and said, "Oh, it's not good! The oranges are bitter."

Cecilia handed her a few packets of granulated sugar to add. That seemed to help a bit, but she was clearly disappointed.

Habiba was from Morocco, the land of oranges. In her country, this fruit was bright and big and sweet, especially in the *Place Jemaa el-Fna* in Marrakech. She visibly began reminiscing about her homeland and the cheap, fresh-squeezed orange juice that you could buy in the large public square.

Cecilia, having lived in Morocco for nine years, quickly scanned photos on her phone and pulled up the one for which she was searching. She pointed her phone towards Habiba to show her a picture of her children standing next to the local "orange juice guy" with his pyramids of bright-colored oranges perfectly displayed for all to see.

"Yes! That's Marrakech!" Habiba said with joy. "The orange juice is so good and so cheap, not like here."

We all chuckled and dreamed together for a moment of sweet, fresh-squeezed orange juice in Morocco. Maybe one day, we would taste it again.

Our chocolate covered croissant arrived, and I split it down the middle with a knife. Habiba and I looked at each other tenderly. I did not want this moment to end. It felt like life was good, life was normal . . . for just a moment.

"Yummy!" I said, as we both bit into our little treat, giggling.

CHAPTER FORTY-FIVE

MOMMY, WHAT'S A SAFE HOUSE?

Habiba's forty-third birthday was approaching. She couldn't wait. Being open and direct, she told us exactly what she wanted—lots of food, lots of cake, lots of people, and lots of presents. Her expectations were high! After all, she wanted and needed to make up for those forty-one years she never celebrated her birthday.

This year, her birthday fell on a weekend, so I asked my son, Pierre*, if he wanted to go with me to the safe house. A simple invitation to Habiba's birthday party turned into a life-changing moment for my eight-year-old son and me. Our conversation would eventually turn into a children's picture book, written from the perspective of my child.

—ele—

Every Monday, my mother goes to the city to work at a safe house.

"I like it there," she said. "I talk to the women and children, drink tea with them, take them to the market, and help them make jewelry. They are my friends."

"Mommy, what's a safe house?"

"It's a place that protects men, women, and children who have been hurt. A safe house welcomes people off the dark streets—like a lighthouse."

I felt sad and scared. "Who has hurt them?"

"There are people in the world who buy and sell men, women, and children and make them do bad things."

My mother took a price sticker off the bottom of my new water bottle and stuck it on my back.

"Some people think men, women, and children are for sale. They think they can buy and own a person like they can buy and own a water bottle," my mother explained. "But, people aren't for sale. All people were created to be free."

I still felt sad and scared. "What kinds of bad things do they have to do?"

"Men, women, and children who are slaves have to do hard work they don't want to do. If they don't make money and do the work their bosses want them to do, they can be hurt."

"So, those are the people you help at the safe house? Women and children who were hurt as slaves?"

"That's right. The safe house is a place where women and children are protected. They get food, clothes, and a nice place to live. They don't have to do hard work anymore. Most of all, they don't have to be afraid, and they are loved."

I felt better knowing these people were now free, protected, and loved.

"How long do the women and children live at the safe house?"

"Usually one or two years. They need to learn to work and live on their own. It takes time for them to feel better and to heal their broken hearts."

Sometimes, during my mother's video calls, I said hello to her friend at the safe house. Habiba was from North Africa and was friendly.

She made a chocolate cake and chicken and vegetable couscous for my big brother's birthday. That was nice of her.

One day, my mother invited me to the safe house to celebrate Habiba's birthday.

"She would love for you to come."

I was scared and didn't know if I wanted to go.

"Mommy, what does the safe house look like?"

"It's a big house, with a living room, a kitchen, two bathrooms, and four bedrooms. It looks like our house."

"What are the people like?"

"They look, talk, and act like us. There are three women and three children from all over the world—Morocco, Nigeria, and Colombia. There are also women, like Mommy, who work there every day."

I was nervous. But, as soon as I met the ladies at the safe house, I discovered they were friendly—like my mother.

And the kids were just like me. I wasn't sad and afraid anymore.

That afternoon, I played, danced, sang, laughed, and ate birthday cake with Habiba and the others.

Everyone was smiling and cheerful. They were one big, happy family who loved each other and found freedom in this lighthouse.

As we walked out the door that day, I asked, "Mommy, when can I go back to the safe house to see my new friends? I want to help those women and children too."

BROKEN PIECES OF YOUR STORY

What if I never get to hear the rest of your story?
What If I never get to fill in all the blanks?
What if I never get to know what happened?
What if I never get to find the other pieces?
What if you are never well enough to talk again?
What if you are too weak to tell the end?
What if you are too sick to sit with me?
What if you are too sad to tell me more?
What if there are always gaps between the chapters?
What if I never know the details?
What if I never know all the names?
What if I never know where you were?
What if I only know the bits of broken pieces?
What if I never know the whole story?
What if the puzzle pieces don't match?
What if the writing isn't complete?
What if I never know?
What if I never hear?
What if the world never knows?
What if the world never hears?
If I never know your whole story . . .
If I never hear your whole story . . .
If I never tell your whole story . . .
If the world never knows your whole story . . .
If the world never hears your whole story . . .
If the world never reads your whole story . . .
May the broken pieces of your story be enough.

CHAPTER FORTY-SIX

THE EL DORADO REVELATION

The rain pitter-pattered on the roof of my car. I sat in the quiet on that Sunday afternoon, reflecting as I looked out through the dark clouds hovering over the mountains in the distance. I didn't want to rush back to the house, didn't want to run back to the noise, the kids, the demands. I sat and reflected, needing some time, some quiet.

After dropping my son off with his friends in town, I pushed play on my phone to listen to a speaker from my virtual writing conference. Today's topic, "Making Your Story Compelling."

I focused and hung onto every one of the speaker's words as she talked about the importance of conflict and resolution in any good story. She gave us an assignment that I struggled to mentally complete while driving. The assignment sounded easy—put the conflict of the book you are writing into three words—a noun, an action verb, and a direct object. I pushed pause on my phone and thought for a moment. The conflict surfaced quite easily.

"Habiba searches (for) El Dorado."

I wondered if it was acceptable to have the preposition "for" attached to my action verb, "to search." I also wondered if it was okay if my direct object was a two-part word. I technically had five words, not three, but the conflict was obvious to me.

El Dorado . . . that is why Habiba made a Faustian Bargain and left her family two years ago to board that ship to Spain. That is why she risked it all. Habiba was on a treasure hunt—a search for El Dorado.

The conflict for Habiba had always existed. It started on the day she was born, the day she took her first breath and let out her first cry. The conflict began on the day Habiba was born in Morocco, into the devastating world of poverty. Always lacking, always empty, always desiring, always hungry, always longing. Always wanting, always needing, always pursuing . . . pursuing a way out—a way out of her life of poverty, a way into something better, something bigger, something more.

The door opened, the opportunity arose. Habiba could see El Dorado, she could hear El Dorado. She could smell El Dorado. She could feel El Dorado. She could touch El Dorado. She could taste El Dorado. She could breathe El Dorado. She could dream El Dorado.

When she looked out over the horizon of the sea, she could see the outline of the land beyond. El Dorado . . . it called her; it beckoned her; it lured her; it welcomed her.

The real conflict was poverty. It wasn't just Habiba's conflict. It was the conflict of her people, of her nation, of her family, of all the other women who boarded the boat with her to sail to the other side of the sea. Habiba, like the others, dreamed of a better life with abundant food on the table every day, a steady job that paid well, a house that she could call her own.

El Dorado. Yes, that was the conflict of my story, of my book.

"Habiba searches for El Dorado."

As soon as I stopped the car on the side of the road, I took out my little pink leather notebook stuffed at the bottom of my purse. Scrambling to find a pen in the glove compartment of the car, I jotted down those five words.

"HABIBA SEARCHES FOR EL DORADO."

It was obvious. Her journey to El Dorado in Spain, portrayed through her story, had led her down dirt paths of strawberry fields, to dark alleyways lined with promiscuous women and sex-thirsty men, to highways of risky rescue and freedom, to streets of love and forgiveness with God, to hallways of COVID-infested hospital rooms, to bloodlines of chemo IVs, to hills of friendship and fun . . . to . . .

To what? For what? Was this it? Was this Habiba's El Dorado?

El Dorado—a land of promise, a land of hope, a land of dreams, a land of opportunities, a land of gold.

I sat in my car and looked up the meaning of "El Dorado."

In Spanish, El Dorado means "The Gilded One." It was a term first heard in 1596 regarding a "Land of Gold" in South America.[1]

"In the early 1500s, Spanish *conquistadores* heard tales of an Amazonian king who regularly coated his body with gold dust, then plunged into a nearby lake to wash it off while being showered with gold and jewels thrown by his subjects. The Spaniards called the city ruled by this flamboyant monarch "*El Dorado*," Spanish for "gilded one," and the story of the gold-covered king eventually grew into a legend of a whole country paved with gold."

"Gilded" means "covered with a thin layer of gold or a substance that looks like gold."[2]

El Dorado was just a story, a tale, a legend. Those Spanish *conquistadores* searched for that "country paved with gold," but they never found it.

It wasn't real. It didn't exist.

Just like Habiba's El Dorado . . . it wasn't real. It didn't exist. It was actually a darker land than her homeland of Morocco.

What did this "country paved with gold" look like from afar? When Habiba and the other women looked out over the sparkling blue Mediterranean Sea, what did they see? Did they see gold, or a land that appeared to be shining like gold?

I pondered the five words that I had scribbled on the paper.

"HABIBA SEARCHES FOR EL DORADO."

I pushed "play" and listened to the speaker's words and next assignment.

She explained that we had to finish the story. We had to offer a resolution to the conflict. The same assignment—three words—noun, action verb, and direct object.

I sighed heavily. Anger surfaced in my heart and mind.

There was no resolution to Habiba's conflict. There was no happy ending to Habiba's story. There was no awakening from Habiba's nightmare.

There was no resolution.

Habiba had left it all, risked it all to journey to her land of El Dorado. What she found was the furthest thing from a "Land of Gold." She longed for more, for freedom, for a better life. Rather, she found emptiness, slavery, and a life of deeper pain and suffering.

Was this her El Dorado? Was it all an illusion?

When she landed on the shores of Spain, did she see the colors transform before her eyes from gold to black? Did it happen suddenly? Did it creep in gradually? When did Habiba realize, finally see, that this was no El Dorado?

My story, my ending could offer no resolution to her conflict. I sat in the car wondering, doubting, wallowing in my unbelief.

If I had no resolution, perhaps I had no story. Perhaps I had no book if I couldn't end this drama, end this conflict. Perhaps there was no solution, no ending, no finish. At least not yet.

I stared at the conflict written on the unlined, beige-colored paper of my little pink notebook.

"HABIBA SEARCHES FOR EL DORADO."

The obvious resolution should be . . .

"Habiba discovers El Dorado," or perhaps "Habiba finds El Dorado."

It was still more than three words.

Sadness welled up in my heart, and tears trickled down my cheeks, much like the rain drops slowly dripping down my car windows.

"Will Habiba ever find El Dorado?" I asked myself.

And then, it was as if a light bulb was turned on in my mind. My heart and my soul leapt.

"El Dorado!?" I screamed out loud.

Habiba is on her way to El Dorado. Habiba will get to El Dorado. That "Land of Gold," "that country paved with gold" awaits her. One day, Habiba will walk on those roads, those streets glittered with gold and jewels.

Heaven awaits Habiba. Heaven is her El Dorado.

Distant verses describing heaven in all its glory and color swirled inside my head. I grabbed my telephone, overflowing with joy. I couldn't contain my excitement as I looked up "Revelation," "heaven," "streets of gold."

In describing heaven, the Apostle John writes,

"The city was made of pure gold, clear as crystal. The streets of the city were made of pure gold, clear as crystal."

Revelation 21:18,21—The Bible NIV

Yes, heaven is Habiba's El Dorado!

Habiba is on the way, she is still on her journey. In her final months, her final days, her final hours . . . she waits to enter. I wait with her to cross the threshold, to enter that "Land of Gold."

On that rainy Sunday afternoon, as I sat alone in my car, the conflict, the storm raging inside of me, came to a gentle hush. A whisper, a release, a peace flooded over me. That divine revelation, that holy resolution, calmed me to the core of my being.

As I have journeyed alongside Habiba during this past year and a half, I have wrestled with God. I have questioned His existence, and teetered on the edge of my faith. I have doubted His goodness as I have seen my dear sister face one trauma and crisis after another—a refugee, a sex trafficking victim, a hairless patient battling cancer. I have asked all the "why" questions my mind could muster up. I have emptied myself of tears and grief. I have begged on my hands and knees for a miracle of healing I do not yet see. I have wondered if I am making a difference on this road with my friend.

Habiba's journey to El Dorado has become my own.

As she searched for a better life, I explored and looked with her. As she discovered faith in God, I have rediscovered my own. As she experienced the mighty hand of rescue and redemption of the Divine, I felt it myself. As she looked for a country paved with gold, I searched by her side. As she longed for a heavenly home of her own, I desired the same.

Together, we have been on a journey to El Dorado. I don't know when we will arrive in that "Land of Gold." Will Habiba walk upon those streets made of pure gold, as clear as crystal, before me? I do not know, and I rest in not knowing.

What I do know is that El Dorado is not a mirage, not an illusion, not a fable, not a legend, not a fairy tale, not a dream. El Dorado is real. Heaven exists. Habiba and I will both arrive one day. We will both run and dance together upon those streets of gold. At first, I may not recognize Habiba . . . for her tears and her pain will be no more. She will be made new—with her long, dark flowing hair and physical strength in her frame.

*"He will wipe all tears from their eyes, and there will be
no more death, suffering, crying, or pain. These things of
the past are gone forever . . . I am making everything
new."*

Revelation 21:4-5—The Bible NIV

I can't wait to see Habiba in El Dorado! I can't wait to see her joy,
her peace, her wholeness, her healing, her freedom—all that is not
fully possible this side of heaven.

And that house she has dreamed of for all these years? It awaits
her there. God is preparing now her heavenly home—"Habiba's El
Dorado."

*"My Father's house has many rooms; if that were not so,
would I have told you that I am going there to prepare a
place for you? And if I go and prepare a place for you, I
will come back and take you to be with me that you also
may be where I am."*

John 14:2-3—The Bible NIV

CHAPTER FORTY-SEVEN

TELL THEM!

Habiba and I sat on the edge of her small twin bed. It was hot in the safe house—blazing hot.

The small air conditioning unit on the wall over her bed wasn't turned on. A small fan sitting on her nightstand blew gently on us. It certainly didn't cool us off, but it helped to have some air movement across our sweaty skin.

We had just finished eating a vegetable *tagine* Habiba had prepared for me that morning. I had not intended to stay long, but our late morning visit soon turned into lunch.

We were just hanging out—two friends, two sisters. Lounging and comfortable, my two long legs were propped up on her bed.

"Tell me your story again," I said to Habiba. "I have some questions, and I need you to fill in some gaps."

Throughout the months, I had heard Habiba's story multiple times. I tried as hard as I could to put the random and broken puzzle pieces together, but there were still missing pieces. There were still holes in the tapestry of her story.

I needed to know. I needed to know the truth. I needed to know the answers. I needed to know the facts.

I had been writing Habiba's story for almost six months, and she still didn't know. I was afraid to ask. I was afraid to tell her. I was afraid she would say "No, please don't tell my story."

I'd asked for advice from other writers.

"Since you're changing her name and not using her location, you don't really need her permission to write the book," a journalist friend told me.

"I guess it's more ethics than anything," I told my friend. "I just feel like I need to tell her. I don't want to do anything behind her back. It's her story."

HER STORY.

That afternoon, after Habiba recounted again to me some of the horrors of her journey from the strawberry fields to the brothel, I tried to tell her about the book I was writing. I was looking for an open door to ask her, but I was nervous.

"Do you know that most people in the world have no idea that these kinds of horrors are taking place?" I asked her. "Most people have no clue."

Habiba looked at me surprised. "Really?"

"We have to tell your story, Habiba. People need to hear what has happened to you. There are so many women out there, just like you, and this must stop."

She looked at me, listening intensively. That familiar, yet distant gaze of shock and unbelief still filled her eyes.

"If people hear your story and know what's going on, maybe we can help one innocent girl, maybe we can stop one depraved man," I explained to her. Habiba was silent.

I had the perfect opportunity to ask her. I had her full attention, but I was still too scared to ask. "I'll try again next time I see her," I thought to myself. "Maybe I'll muster up enough courage between now and then."

As I walked on the cobblestone streets from the safe house back to my car in a nearby parking lot, I thought about Habiba. What if her story could be redeemed? What if the healing, restoration, and redemption came through the "telling." What if her journey, her trial, her road of suffering could somehow provide for her family? What if her dream to help feed her poor family could come true? What if God could turn her story around and use it to accomplish something good, something worthy, something true, something powerful? Was it possible?

That day, with each step to my car, my skin burned from the sun and sweat beads upon my brow. My mind wandered, and my thoughts dreamed. I began to dream again for Habiba.

What if her story—the one that I was writing and the one that you are now reading—could somehow bring awareness of the global disease of human trafficking around the world? What if Habiba's broken journey could be a source of healing and rescue for other young girls and women still out there?

Like a winepress that painfully squeezes the grapes to produce sweet wine, what if Habiba's painful and heartbreaking story could somehow bless others around the world? What if her story could somehow change me, my life, and yours, too?

What if...?

That's why I collected Habiba's story. That's why I sat down in a chair at my desk every day. That's why I poured out these words on paper, alongside my tears. That's why I wanted to tell the world what had happened to her and to so many other women like her.

That's why...

When Habiba boarded that boat to sail from her homeland in Morocco to the European continent, she did not know what awaited her on the other side of the sea. She couldn't have known. Her family couldn't have known.

I don't believe that her journey is lost. I don't believe that her dream is dead. I don't believe that her hopes are dashed. I don't believe that her pain is wasted. I don't believe that her story is over. I don't believe that her tears are unnoticed.

Habiba has shed tears—many tears. However, her tears, her story, can be redeemed forever. Her journey to Spain can now provide for her family in Morocco. Partial proceeds of this book, *Our Journey to El Dorado* will be given directly to Habiba to send to her family on the other side of the sea.

Habiba's story is providing for her family today—although not in the way she expected.

Today, as you read this book, as you shed tears of compassion and empathy, you, too, have become a part of Habiba's redemptive story.

———ᵉᵉ———

I sat with Habiba on her bed at the safe house again that afternoon. I couldn't let it go until we talked.

"People have to know. People have to hear your story—all of your story," I insisted. "If we don't tell them, they'll never know."

Every time I brought up the subject, fear gripped my heart. I was afraid to tell her I was writing her story. What if she said no?

Inside, I was struggling. Each time I sat down at the computer to write a chapter of her story, I wondered if Habiba would grant me permission to share her journey. My first full manuscript was almost complete. I had to tell her.

But how?

—— *ele* ——

The following week, I went to the safe house to spend the day. Habiba and I took a walk downtown. After only a few minutes of strolling, she asked me if we could sit on a nearby bench. We watched the people walk by.

"Do you know that these people here, all these people walking by us, don't know what has happened to you, what has happened to all the other women in the south of Spain?"

She looked at me with those same sad eyes.

"In the strawberry fields?" she asked.

"Yes, in the strawberry fields. We have to tell them, Habiba. They have to hear your story so that this will stop. We have to scream it from the rooftops and from the mountain tops so that the entire world hears. We have to tell the secret of what is happening to all the women and the little girls."

"Tell them," she said. "Tell them."

I looked her in the eyes and took her hands in mine. That day, I made her a promise that I will forever keep.

"I'll tell the world your story, but I promise never to tell anyone your name or your location. You'll be safe. Your story will be safe. You can trust me."

"Ok," she answered. "Then, tell them."

That's what I have done. I have finished my task. I have kept my promise. I have done what God called me to do.

I have told you. I have told the world.

CHAPTER FORTY-EIGHT

OUR JOURNEY TO EL DORADO

In God's mysterious and sovereign plan, two unlikely women crossed paths—a tall, fair-complected, light-haired woman from the deep Midwest of America and a petite, dark-skinned brunette from the desert mountains of Morocco.

We may have appeared different, but we had so much in common.

We were both on a journey . . . a journey to a better life . . . a journey to El Dorado. We were both searching . . . searching for deeper meaning and purpose.

Ultimately, we would find it . . . find it in each other.

We don't know when, where, and how our paths will end on this earth, but we know one thing for sure . . .

We will meet again one day in that land with streets paved of gold.

We are both on the journey to El Dorado.

This is our journey to El Dorado.

PART SIX

The Sad Reality and How to Make a Difference

CHAPTER FORTY-NINE

A PERSON OR A PROJECT?

Her name is Habiba.

She has a name. She has a face, a body, a heart, a mind. She has a soul.

She is a person. She is a woman.

Her name is Habiba.

She has feelings and emotions. She has thoughts.

Her name is Habiba.

Somehow, somewhere in the work, in the service, she may lose her name.

Somehow, somewhere in the mix of things, she may lose her identity.

Habiba may become a number, a statistic.

Habiba may become an object, an issue.

Habiba—a person—may become a project.

Oh, the danger!

How do I intentionally keep her name, her face, her identity ever before me?

How do I intentionally remember that she is a person—100% person?

How do I guard and protect her from wearing a number, from being stamped by a statistic?

Habiba, oh Habiba!

I am sorry that we have stolen your name. I am sorry that we have stripped you of your identity. I am sorry that we have erased your face. I am sorry that we have torn out your heart.

I am sorry.

Please forgive us.

You are not a project. You are a person.

You have a name.

Your name is Habiba.

I will keep your name on my lips. I will keep your face in my mind. I will keep your heart next to mine. I will keep your eyes in my sight. I will keep your thoughts in my mind.

You are not a project. You are a person.

You have a name.

Your name is Habiba.

Your name means, "My Beloved."

As I write this book, as you read this book... may we never forget that Habiba is not a fictitious character. She is not a nameless, faceless immigrant fleeing the brokenness of her homeland. She is not a statistic, a number, one more refugee, one more dreamer, about to drown in the boat off the European coastline . . . on her way to El Dorado.

May we never forget that she is a person.

She has a name.

Her name is Habiba.

Please don't forget her name. I beg you. Please don't forget her name.

Her name is Habiba.

CHAPTER FIFTY

THE SAD REALITY OF THE STRAWBERRY FIELDS IN SPAIN

I had heard stories—not just Habiba's story, but so many others. They were all the same sad story of trauma—different chapters and journeys, but similar pain and suffering.

Women lured over from Morocco, often to work in the strawberry fields. However, many of them weren't picking fruit when they ended their journey to El Dorado. Many of them were tempted and drawn away into another line of work—one that would trap and enslave them for the rest of their lives. Even if rescued one day, like Habiba, their souls and their hearts would be broken and wounded forever—outside of a divine miracle of healing.

So, what was the hidden reality of the strawberry fields in Spain?

I became aware of the reality of the labor conditions in the Spanish strawberry fields when a friend sent me a recent article from the Spanish newspaper, *El País*. It told the story of 7,000 Moroccan women—all agricultural workers—stuck in the city of *Huelva* in the south of Spain. When I looked up *Huelva* on the map, I discovered this city wasn't far from where Habiba had first landed in Spain— *Palos de la Frontera*. The article intrigued me, and I wanted to learn more. I thought perhaps it could shed some light into the shadows of Habiba's dark story. Maybe it could fill in some gaps of her narrative. Perhaps it could help me find some of the missing puzzle pieces of her book.

I quickly learned that the strawberry fields of Spain have a long history with Morocco. According to CNN, in 2001, the two countries signed an agreement. This contract grants temporary work visas to seasonal, agricultural workers arriving from Morocco, allowing them to harvest fruit every year in Spain. Boatloads of

Moroccan women—like Habiba—arrive to work in Spain every year. In 2019, approximately 15,000 Moroccans arrived in January to work in the strawberry fields.

"The soft fruits industry, which exports its produce to countries across Europe—including to many UK retailers—is central to the region's economy and generated €500 million in 2018-19."[1]

The soft fruits these women pick, mainly strawberries, are otherwise known as "red gold."{2} Some of these Moroccan workers have been coming back to Spain every winter for over thirteen years to work for the same agricultural cooperative.

"They've been coming to work in Huelva for over a decade, and they are a basic pillar of the companies they work for," said Pedro Marín, the manager of Interfresa, a strawberry trade association in Huelva.{1}

What is so enticing to these Moroccan women? What compels them to come to Spain year after year to work in the strawberry fields?

According to *El País*, "These workers come from small, low-income communities where the money they earn from picking strawberries in Spain is enough to live on for nearly the entire year."{3} No wonder Habiba wanted to come to Spain to work in the strawberry fields. She could easily and quickly provide for her poor family in Morocco. It made perfect sense. We probably would have jumped at the opportunity if we had been in Habiba's shoes.

How are these women recruited for this work in Morocco?

"Several years ago, images emerged of women queuing in public squares, to be examined like slaves for their size, age, and hands during the recruitment drives."{3}

Thankfully, things have changed since then. Today, ANAPEC, the Moroccan public employment agency, handles the initial selection process of the agricultural workers. The Spanish Ministry of the Interior establishes the number of work contracts needed for the picking season, and then each region of Morocco is allocated a quota.

Women between the ages of twenty-one and forty-five, with children, are short-listed by ANAPEC. Single mothers are in greater financial need and, therefore, easier to exploit. Women who are widowed and divorced are often selected as well, for the same reasons. Finally, women who have already worked in Spain are also given priority in the selection process.

Candidates who pass the first screening are then sent to Meknes in Morocco for selection by a representative from the Spanish company. Contracts are then drafted and signed, and the women leave their families and board the boats to sail across the Mediterranean Sea to their so-called El Dorado.

What is the work contract like for these immigrant women?

Most contracts include transportation for the workers from Morocco to the greenhouses in Spain. This includes the cost of the ferry across the Mediterranean and a bus ride. The workers, however, are responsible for paying their way back home to Morocco when the season ends—approximately forty-five euros.

"The workers are promised the legal wage, medical treatment, and free accommodation in return for moving to Spain for the season— but these conditions often go unmet."[1]

New research and statistics have recently exposed the irregularities and illegalities in the industry. According to Spanish law, workers recruited from Morocco should receive a three-month temporary "contracted in origin" agreement. "Contracted in origin" means that the worker was hired in his or her home country—in this case, Morocco. This type of contract guarantees a salary of approximately 42.02 euros a day in Spain, a 6 1/2 hour workday, overtime pay, one day off every week, and safe and decent housing.

According to Philip Alston, a special reporter on extreme poverty with the United Nations, many of the women don't make the promised sum of 42.02 euros a day. Rather, many of them only make 30 euros a day, and many of them work more hours than are documented.

"Contract numbers filed with the Spanish authorities show that of the almost 15,000 workers recruited for temporary employment in the country in 2019, only 0.1% actually received contracts that met their legal rights."[1]

For the 15,000 workers recruited in 2019, only 243 legal contracts were filed. Rather, employers offered the migrant workers "work and service" contracts that exempted them from providing the workers with a salary or guaranteed employment.

"Work and service" contracts are not designed for use with those "contracted in origin." Rather, these types of agreements are used for the occasional Spanish workers. As a result, this type of contract is illegal in this context, in which Moroccans are recruited in their native country to go to Spain to work in the strawberry fields.[1]

In addition, many of these immigrant workers are illiterate and cannot read and write. This obviously limits their understanding of any written contracts they are signing. Many of the Moroccan women also can't speak Spanish. In the case of an emergency, it is very difficult for them to have direct contact with the Moroccan Consulate in Spain or with other authorities in their host country.

"Instead, information reaches them through non-profit groups or through advisors at Prelsi, Interfresa's ethical and social responsibility project," according to *El País*.[3]

What are the living conditions for these women?

Upon arrival, many of these women find themselves in isolated, rural areas with no means of transportation. According to Ana Pinto, a member of the Laborers' Association Jornaleras del Campo, these women "can often be seen walking in groups along the paths near the hamlet of El Rocío, on their way to or from a bus stop that will take them to the nearest municipality to do some grocery shopping."[3]

This is no easy life, and their living conditions are unacceptable.

According to Angels Escrivá, a spokesperson for NGO Mujeres 24h, "The farms that we have been able to access are not suitable for a long-term stay, many are prefabricated modules, they are designed for non-extreme weather conditions, with a large concentration of people in small spaces, which doesn't meet what rules of the hiring in origin agreement."[4]

Immigrant women describe getting wet when it rains, because the accommodations are not properly equipped. In extreme heat, workers often sleep on the ground outside to find relief, and many of the living quarters are without electricity and running water.

The United Nations confirmed these findings. In January of 2020, the UN's Philip Alston visited the region's soft fruit industries in southern Spain for twelve days. He was "stunned" and stated that the immigrants' living conditions "rival the worst I have seen anywhere in the world." Alston described the migrant workers as living in shacks or "tents made of plastic that is used to cover strawberries," with no electricity or running water, and only public squat toilets. [1]

What are the work conditions for these women?

Besides inadmissible living quarters, the work conditions are unacceptable—even deadly.

For those workers arriving in Huelva, the city is considered to be one of the most contaminated in Spain—perhaps even in Europe.

"The earth, air and water are polluted by radioactivity, chemicals and biological waste. The strawberry, blueberry and blackberry fields sit next to a chemical complex built in the 1960s." [2]

Agricultural workers are often expected to continue working even while the greenhouses are being sprayed with poisonous chemicals. They rarely wear safety equipment, and they are even required to take their work breaks in the greenhouses.

As a result, on January 21, 2019, a twenty-seven-year-old worker in one of Nijar's farms died after being exposed to agricultural chemicals. [5]

The work days are grueling and long. Underneath the blazing hot plastic tunnels, women crouch or kneel all day to handpick the "red gold." They often have a plastic box strapped to their back in which to place their delicate treasure. The women are penalized if the fruit they pick is bruised, dropped, or over or under-ripe. [2]

Many of the women I know who worked in the strawberry fields still complain of severe lower back pain because of their history of intense physical labor.

Fatima, an agricultural worker from Nador in Morocco said, "They have to collect a target number of boxes of fruit, and if they do not reach that number, they can be sacked." she says. This type of piecework is illegal in Spain.

Fatima also describes the obvious discrimination between Moroccan and European workers on the farms.

"They send the Moroccan women to work in the fields, leaving Spanish and Romanian women in the indoor jobs." This "indoor" work is much easier and lighter.

"There is a lot of inequality between the different workers," she continues, "and the fact that the Moroccan women cannot speak the language means that they are at the bottom of the heap."

Another worker, Carmen, describes the scene further.

"There is a system: if a worker commits a 'fault,' they get a black mark. In the packing plant, each box of fruit has a number that identifies the picker. If the fruit is damaged, over or under-ripe, the packer registers a mark against the name of that picker." She adds that, "Any fruit on the ground also earns a black mark. Five are a 'slight fault,' but once one has accumulated two 'slight faults,' they are sent home for three days with no pay."[2]

Besides unacceptable living and work conditions on the farms, many of the female workers are lured into sex trafficking. What is the connection between the strawberry industry and prostitution?

In recent years, there have been numerous reports of sexual harassment and other forms of sexual abuse in the soft-fruit industry.

In 2018, female workers went to the authorities to report sexual abuse on several farms owned by Doñana 1998 and Freserrano. Following the charges, Doñana in 1998 attempted to send one hundred of their workers back to Morocco.

In 2019, there was another incident. Three women working in the Las Posedillas farm, owned by Los Arenales de Mazagón, a strawberry production farm, went to the police. They reported they had not been paid their promised salaries, their living accommodations were overcrowded and unacceptable, and they were working extremely long working hours. Finally, these women reported sexual harassment and "coercion to practice prostitution."[1]

As I read the reports of these courageous women, I wept. Habiba had never described her living and work conditions on the strawberry farm, but now I knew.

That's why I wept.

My reading and research certainly shed some light on Habiba's dark story. It filled in some holes in my mind's recollection of her oral narrative.

Perhaps I didn't really want to know the truth about her journey.

Sometimes it's easier to close my eyes, turn my face, hide myself from the truth.

Sometimes, it's better, it's easier, to not know.

When Habiba was first recruited in Morocco to work in the strawberry fields of Spain, she was a prime target. A single mother, a widow—poor, vulnerable, ignorant, naïve.

I don't know if she realized what her "contracted in origin" document said. Perhaps she never even signed a contract. She may not have known what was promised to her and if those promises were fulfilled upon arrival in Spain. It's even possible that Habiba didn't know how much money she made while working in the strawberry fields. Whenever I asked her about money, she didn't know how to count correctly.

Habiba. Prime target.

If Habiba's boss had cheated her on her pay or on the number of hours she worked, she probably would have never known.

I don't know all the connections and networks between the strawberry farms and the prostitution Mafia in Spain. However, they are all tied together somehow.

It's all about money. Everyone is making money in the deal, in the trade, in the slavery.

While they are making money, the women are dying—physically, emotionally, mentally, spiritually.

What is happening to change these conditions and to protect the exploited women arriving from Morocco?

Unions like SOC-SAT (Union of Agricultural Workers/Union of Andalusian Workers), a small independent trade union, and other local NGOs, are working hard to build awareness of this growing global crisis. They walk closely alongside exploited workers on farms to demand their rights from their employers. Active on the frontline, they fight for these workers. They also put pressure on the importers, big companies, local European supermarkets, and the Spanish government—demanding change.

"If they are to follow basic legal requirements, the government must provide more work inspection teams, strengthen trade unionism in the workplaces, and adapt the model of trade union representation in the workplace itself," says Ethical Consumer.[5]

Ethical Consumer is pleading with the local British grocery stores such as Marks & Spencers, Lidl, Sainsburys, Aldi, and others to take responsibility for the workers' rights of those who grow their produce.

Specifically, they are asking them to:

- Publish complete lists of suppliers, tracing back to the farms they source from.

- Establish a whistle-blowing hotline and make this available throughout their fruit and vegetable supply chains, including to farm level and agricultural unions such as SOC-SAT.[6]

- Regularly engage with agricultural unions like SOC-SAT and local NGOs by providing them with grievance mechanisms.

- Commit to fully investigating issues reported by unions and NGOs and demand that suppliers redress the problems raised.

- Put pressure on their suppliers to publish a list of the farms from which they buy produce.

- Put pressure on international certifiers like Global GAP, Naturland, and BioSuisse to improve their audit processes: engage with workers outside of workplaces, away from the hearing and control of the management, where they are not frightened to relate the real labour conditions; and engage with local unions.

What is the reality of the strawberry fields of Spain?

Sad, broken, devastating, traumatic.

But, here's the bottom line . . . most of Spain's berry production takes place in Huelva—97%. That region is actually the main berry producer for all of Europe.

"It means that whenever a box of berries is marked 'Spain' in a supermarket, it is likely to have come from Huelva and risks being associated with the conditions that the UN, as well as many workers, have described."[1]

When I read those words, I wept.

Do you know how many strawberries I have eaten marked "SPAIN"? Not just during the past year while my family has lived in Spain, but during all of our years in France as well. How many strawberries have I eaten? Has my family eaten? Have my children eaten? Were they picked by Habiba's hands, or the hands of all the "Habibas" out there?

I'm sorry, Habiba. Please forgive me. Please forgive us.
I didn't know. We didn't know. The world still doesn't know.

CHAPTER FIFTY-ONE

THE SAD REALITY OF SEX TRAFFICKING IN SPAIN

O ne day, our family was traveling with another family from our boys' school.

We had heard about the beautiful town of Cuenca, a village nestled in the cliffs of the Spanish mountains. Everyone told us we had to visit. Cuenca was at the top of our list.

The drive through the valleys and mountains was beautiful, and our family thoroughly enjoyed the sunny day walking through the cobblestone streets, shopping in the quaint boutiques, admiring the majestic cathedrals, tiptoeing across the high, wooden bridge, hiking up the steep hills, enjoying drinks and tapas at an outside bar in the sunshine. Our boys also had fun playing together with their friends, eating fruit popsicles, and pretend fighting with "stick swords."

It was a great day and one that we will not soon forget.

To prepare for our family's trip, I did my research on Cuenca. I always want to know where I'm going, want to be sure to hit all the highlights in a town. Yes, I'm one of those who never wants to miss an opportunity. I found tourist sites that told us where to visit, where to hike, where to eat. There was plenty of research out there on the little town of Cuenca.

What I didn't know until after our sightseeing visit was that the beautiful countryside surrounding this picturesque tourist town is a breeding ground for prostitution. The Spanish newspaper *El País*, described the National 301 Road as "The Highway of Love." It said that the small stretch of road around Cuenca had six clubs with more than four hundred women working inside. I was shocked![1]

"We probably drove right by it, maybe even right through it, and we didn't even realize it," I texted my friend whose family had gone with us on the family outing.

"I can't believe it!" she replied.

"Me neither. How can this be?"

It's not just the cute, picturesque town of Cuenca that is breeding grounds for prostitution in Spain. The entire country has become infested with this devastating plague.

It's everywhere, on all sides of us, but we don't see it. We don't even realize it's here, because it's so dark, secret, and hidden.

According to *El País,* on the N-IV road that runs from Valdepeñas to Madrid, there are more than 850 sex workers in less than two hundred kilometers. Who would have known? On one of Madrid's busiest shopping streets, Calle Montera, women discreetly stand alone or in small groups. They are prostitutes who are trafficking victims, but most people wouldn't know.

"Many of the women . . . don't look like trafficking victims: it is easy for people to walk past them and not realize . . . many are also acting as human signposts, indicating that there are houses filled with other women nearby."[1]

I'll never know how many times I've walked by prostitutes and had no idea.

Prostitution is hidden behind closed doors in small private apartments that are protected from raids and safe from prosecutors —the police. The apartments are typically rented by a woman who works inside the organization. She usually uses a false identity for the contract in case her workers try to report her.

"She is known as 'The Madam,' and she will usually have had years of experience in sex clubs and will preferably have started out as a vulnerable immigrant working off her debt, which makes her savvy when it comes to exploiting the vulnerability of future trafficking victims."

In the secret places in these apartments, victims are usually groomed and trained for their next big job—sex clubs. An average sex club with 40 female workers will generate an average of 75,000 euros a month of "dirty money," and that's before food and drinks are factored in.[1]

According to *The Guardian*, "To say that prostitution is big business in Spain would be a gross understatement. The country has become known as the brothel of Europe, after a 2011 United Nations report cited Spain as the third biggest capital of prostitution in the world, behind Thailand and Puerto Rico."

Prostitution has been skyrocketing in Spain since 1995 when it became decriminalized. Revenue from Spain's sex trade industry is estimated at 26.5 billion euros a year, with hundreds of licensed brothels and a workforce of approximately 300,000 women.

The difference between prostitution and sex trafficking may be unclear to some.

"Prostitution becomes sex trafficking when one person moves, detains or transports someone else for the purpose of profiting from their prostitution using fraud, force or coercion."[2]

In 2010, the Spanish government recognized human trafficking as a legal crime.

"Spain prohibits all forms of trafficking in persons through Article 318 of its Criminal and Penal Code. The prescribed penalties for sex trafficking is five to fifteen years' imprisonment, and the penalty for labor trafficking is four to twelve years in prison."

The penalties for sex trafficking are commensurate with the penalties for rape.

"The government implemented new legislation in 2007 that increased prescribed penalties for trafficking by two to six years in prison if the offender is found to be part of a criminal organization, and passed additional legislation in 2007 that allows Spanish courts to prosecute cases of trafficking that have occurred outside Spain's borders."[3]

It is now estimated that approximately 90% of women working in prostitution in Spain could be victims of sex trafficking under the control of a third party—such as a pimp—who is profiting from them.

There seem to be several factors why Spain has become the "brothel of Europe." According to Rocío Mora, co-founder and director of Apramp and one of Spain's most renowned advocates for anti-trafficking, the single greatest factor is cultural. In her opinion, the country's sex trafficking epidemic is a gross manifestation of Spain's attitudes towards women and sex.

"There is huge demand for prostitution here. It's become so normalized that it's just seen like any other leisure activity," Mora stated.

In a 2008 survey, 78% of Spanish people stated that prostitution is an inevitable part of modern society. In another survey in 2006, it was discovered that almost 40% of Spanish men over the age of eighteen had paid for sex at least once in their life. Mora says that, in the past, it was largely older men buying sex with prostitutes. However, the trend now is that the sex buyers and the women on the street are much younger.

"The social stigma isn't the same as it was," she says. "We have a generation of young men growing up believing they have the right to do anything to a woman's body if they have paid for it . . ." {2}

José Nieto is the chief inspector and Spain's leading anti-trafficking law enforcement officer in the Centre of Intelligence and Risk Analysis, run by Spain's national police. When considering Spain as a magnet for sex trafficking, he describes it as the "perfect storm."

"First, we are fighting a crime that is socially acceptable, because prostitution is accepted and embraced by many people here. Second there is geography: We are at the center of all major migratory routes," Neito explains. {2}

Most trafficked victims are from Romania, West Africa, and South America, although some organizations are now working with women from over fifty-three nationalities. Spain is easily accessible from many countries, with Africa only fifteen kilometers away. There is also a historical and linguistic relationship between Spain and South America.

According to CNN, another factor for increased prostitution and sex trafficking in Spain is tourism. The country is known for its beautiful weather and sunshine year round, especially in cities like Barcelona.

"Walking hand in hand with the tourists are criminals hoping to make money off of them. People come here . . . looking for recreational activities. Unfortunately, some of these recreational activities that tourists look for are sex. Tourists looking for sex can find it along the highways, in brothels, or clubs, on busy city streets."

Even though sex trafficking in the prostitution industry is running rampant in Spain, it is difficult to identify it and stop it.

"The legality of prostitution in Spain is complicated and it hinges on whether these women want to sell their bodies or if they are forced to. Figuring that out is one of the human trafficking units biggest challenges."[4]

Prosecution is also next to impossible unless a victim is willing to disclose her situation and testify against her exploiters.

"There is great fear among victims that if they tell the police, they will be sent back to their countries with their debts unpaid," Nieto says. "It makes policing very difficult. If the women don't ask for help, there is a limit to what you can do. Here in Spain, prostitution itself isn't illegal, running a brothel isn't illegal, so you have to prove that what is going on is more than meets the eye."

Prostitution and sex trafficking have become a real Mafia with the gangs and pimps controlling the women through fear, debt, and psychological control. For example, some women are forced to get breast implants and then told that they owe a 10,000 euro debt for the operation. Other daily debts may include clothes, rent for their corner of the street, condoms, sanitary towels, etc. If the women don't bring back enough money from their work on the streets, they are often beaten or not given food to eat. Other women are told that their exploiters will kill their mother, sister, or children if their debt is left unpaid.

"People always ask, 'Why didn't you just run away or go to the police?' but they don't know what they're talking about. You can't just stop a random person on the street and ask for help, because someone you love could get killed."

Thankfully, there are people out on the streets looking to help and rescue these women. Since 2010, when Spain passed its first anti-trafficking laws, the government has spent millions of euros in an emergency plan to get on top of the nation's crisis. In 2015, the Spanish government created formal alliances between NGOs, judges, prosecutors, and security forces to rescue trafficked victims and prosecute perpetrators.

"Between 2012-2016, security forces in Spain rescued 5,695 people from slavery but acknowledge that thousands more remain under the control of criminals." Some organizations, like Apramp, are in contact with 280 women a day, with almost 100% of them being victims of exploitation and trafficking.[4]

According to CNN, sometimes it takes months, even years, of undercover research and investigation in the Unitat Central de

Tràfic d'Essers Humans before law enforcement can expose a human trafficking ring and bust up an operation.[5]

There are women such as Marcella and Maria working with Apramp and other organizations who are on the frontlines of this dangerous work. They have been assaulted and threatened more than once, but they aren't giving up. They continue to go door-to-door hoping a woman will dare to open and be set free.

"They keep on knocking, because they have been on the other side of those doors, forced to sell their bodies for a handful of euros, dozens of times a day, seven days a week."

They both seem fearless, full of courage.

"When I'm wearing the Apramp vest at those apartments or on the streets, I don't feel scared," Marcella says. "We know from our own experience they're doing much worse things to the girls and women inside. So it only makes us more determined."[4]

Maria spent eight months on the streets in brothels and apartments. She describes the brokenness in one's heart and soul that happens in such a short period of time.

"The shock and the trauma make you go into survival mode. You don't have time to realize what has happened to you," she said. "You're alive but you're not really existing."[2]

This idea of being "in survival mode" and "not really existing" is common among those who are victims of sex trafficking.

Sara, a prostitute in Johannesburg, South Africa, tells the heartbreaking story of an incident with her seven-year-old son. She tried to hide her work from him at all costs, until one night. After putting him to bed, she changed into her "prostitute clothes" and put on her makeup. As she was walking out the door, her son woke up.

"Seeing her, he stopped dead in his tracks, crying, 'Mommy, I'm scared of your eyes. Where are you?' Sara was devastated. She had switched into someone else in order to prostitute, and her young son saw that. As has been well documented in psychological investigations of other forms of torture, overwhelming human cruelty results in fragmentation of the mind, into different parts of the self that observe, and react, as well as those who do not know about the harm. Sara's disassociation was an escape strategy to handle overwhelming fear and pain by splitting that off from the rest of herself."[5]

"Dissociative disorders are common among those in escort, street, massage, strip club and brothel prostitution, and are frequently accompanied by post-traumatic stress disorder, depression, and substance abuse. The existing data suggest that almost all who are in prostitution suffer from at least one of the following disorders; dissociative, post-traumatic, mood or substance abuse."[6]

Although some women turn to prostitution to support a drug or alcohol addiction, many women will use these substances once they are in prostitution. These substances allow them to detach emotionally and to cope with their fears of feeling and being hurt.[7]

Marcella, a Brazilian, has a similar story of pain and trauma. She was trafficked from her own country after applying for a master's degree in a university in Spain. Her study program turned out to be a trap, and she was forced into prostitution the moment she was picked up from the airport.

"If Apramp hadn't found me, I think I'd be dead by now," she says.

Maria and Marcella, along with other rescued women, are working hard on the streets to rescue women who are trapped in human trafficking. It's part of their own recovery and healing process.

"The mafia take you and destroy your whole identity. Even now, you're recovering but you can never forget your past," Marcella said. "Doing this work really helps."

More and more rescued victims of sex trafficking, like Maria and Marcella, are crying out to be heard.[2]

In 2019, a global conference, "Advances and Future Challenges in the Fight Against Trafficking and Sexual Exploitation of Women and Girls" was held in Madrid, the Spanish capital. Victims of sex trafficking gathered to denounce prostitution as a crime. They pleaded for society to find the courage to come alongside victims to help them heal from this "collective wound for all women."

Amelia Tiganus, a human rights activist, stood up and spoke in the name of women from all over the world who, like her, have suffered the atrocities of the sex industry.

"We need a society that embraces us, believes us and has the courage to look us in the eye and endure our stories," Tiganus said. "If we've managed to survive all this torture, you need to become accomplices in our healing, because what we have is a collective wound that all women, as a gender, share."{8}

Let's dare to look these women in the eye—women like Amelia, Maria, Marcella, and Habiba—and let's endure their stories.

If you read *Our Journey to El Dorado*, that's what you did. You endured Habiba's story—her story, their story, and you became a part of her healing journey—their healing journey.

Let's not stop here. Let's tell others.

CHAPTER FIFTY-TWO

NOW THAT YOU KNOW— MAKE A DIFFERENCE!

By now, you may wonder what you can do to make a difference— right where you are. What can you do to help fight sex trafficking around the world?

After meeting Habiba and hearing her story, I asked myself that same question. I wanted to help. I couldn't remain silent. I couldn't remain idle. I was compelled to speak out about this injustice, this horror. I couldn't just sit back and watch.

I was propelled into action.

For Habiba, for the other women, for the "Silent Ones" . . . that's why I wrote this book. I can't stop talking about this global issue now. It's too late. There's no turning back.

Even while writing this book, I still wanted to do more.

As a result, my family started an online store called "Cultural Threads," (https://culturalstoryweaver.com/shop/), selling the products of survivors of human trafficking around the world. Proceeds go to help them with their artisanal businesses—so they no longer have to go out on the streets to make money to feed themselves and their families.[1]

If we can do something, so can you.

No matter where you are or on what side of the ocean you live . . . you can change the lives of Habiba and so many women like her.

Here are a few ideas. All other suggestions can be shared here— https://culturalstoryweaver.com/contact[2]

1. LEARN: Research to see if there are organizations in your town who are reaching out and helping victims of prostitution and human trafficking. Find out if there are local volunteer opportunities for you to be involved with in this restorative work. Sex trafficking isn't just a crisis in Spain, it is happening all over the world.

Continue to read and grow in your awareness of the reality of human trafficking around the world. Don't close your eyes! Don't hide your face!

Here are some books to help shed light on the reality of sex trafficking.

The Scent of Water: Grace For Every Kind of Broken by Naomi Zacharius[3]

Half the Sky: Turning Oppression Into Opportunity For Women Worldwide by Nicholas D. Kristof and Sheryl WuDunn[4]

Here are some websites that give helpful information about human trafficking.

Apramp (https://apramp.org/?lang=en) [5]

As a consumer, get information about your local grocery stores. Ask them questions about their food chains and regulations. Here are some links and websites to help you get started with your research. Make your grocery store commit to follow regulations.

https://www.ethicalconsumer.org/food-drink/agricultural-workers-rights-abuses-spain[6]

https://www.ethicalconsumer.org/ethicalcampaigns/agricultural-workers-rights-almeria[7]

2. TELL: When your eyes are open to the truth, when you see, and when you know what is actually happening . . . tell others about it. The more people know, the more awareness we raise, and the more people will fight with us in this fierce battle against human trafficking!

Go and tell someone Habiba's story. We need more people to hear her story—the story of the "Silent Ones." We cannot keep this secret hidden any longer!

Encourage your friends and family to read *Our Journey to El Dorado.* https://culturalstoryweaver.com/product/our-journey-to-el-dorado-two-women-two-immigrants-two-worlds-collide-a-true-story-of-faith-freedom-from-human-trafficking/

3. GIVE: Partial proceeds of the sales of *Our Journey to El Dorado* go directly to provide for the financial needs of Habiba and her family in Morocco. Encourage your friends and family to buy a copy. https://culturalstoryweaver.com/product/our-journey-to-el-dorado-two-women-two-immigrants-two-worlds-collide-a-true-story-of-faith-freedom-from-human-trafficking/

You can also support local and online businesses that work directly with artisans who are survivors of sex trafficking, providing them with needed skills and business opportunities.

Shop with a Purpose. Shop for a Cause.

Cultural Threads (www.culturalstoryweaver.com/shop/)[1]

Trades of Hope

(www.tradesofhope.com/culturalstoryweaver)[8]

The Starfish Project (www.starfishproject.com) [9]

Rahab's Rope (www.rahabsrope.com)[10]

Eternal Threads (www.eternalthreads.org)[11]

There are many global organizations aiding exploited agricultural workers. Unions such as SOC-SAT—Union of Agricultural Workers/Union of Andalusian Workers—a small independent trade union, are fighting alongside workers to demand their legal rights from employers.

Find out more about their work on the SOC-SAT website or email them directly at socalmeria@yahoo.es to explore ways you can help and give.

https://www.ethicalconsumer.org/food-drink/agricultural-workers-rights-abuses-spain[6]

The recent COVID-19 global pandemic has added new challenges to this crisis of exploited immigrant workers. Their living conditions were already inadmissible before the pandemic; however, now, they are even more crowded and insecure. Food is scarce, and many female Moroccan women are stranded in Spain—unable to return to their families and children in North Africa.

You can read more about the crisis here, as well as learn about how to give to local efforts, like Crowdfunder, trying to help workers on the ground during this time of great need.

https://www.crowdfunder.co.uk/supportworkers[12]

There are also many organizations on the frontline against sex trafficking.

Apramp (https://apramp.org/?lang=en)[5]

4. ACT: Ask local organizations (involved in sex trafficking / immigration work) how you can help. Or, contact organizations overseas (involved in sex trafficking /immigration work) and see how you can volunteer with them—either from a distance or on the ground.

Ethical Consumer is inviting and calling people to join them in their work. "If you speak Spanish or Arabic, come and help! Fundraise for something specific, like a trade union worker's salary, or petrol for the red van" (belonging to SOC-SAC to go into the agricultural fields of Spain to aid the workers.).

https://www.ethicalconsumer.org/food-drink/agricultural-workers-rights-abuses-spain[6]

Host a fun, online party to encourage your friends and family to get on board with you. Together, we can fight this global battle of human trafficking! By hosting your own party, you can help raise awareness of sex trafficking on a larger scale. Proceeds of the purchases of your party will go directly towards supporting the businesses of survivor artisans around the world. You can sign up and get more information at https://tradesofhope.com/host/?u=culturalstoryweaver[8]

5. BUY ETHICAL: Eating and wearing ethical won't be cheap, but you will be making a strong statement to say no to exploitation —whether it be in food or fashion. Intentionally buy from stores that work with local artisans to sell ethical, fair-trade products— especially those who are survivors of human trafficking. Check out our family's online store, "Cultural Threads." (www.culturalstoryweaver.com/shop/)[1]

6. PRAY: God can intervene. There are so many "God Stories" out there of women being miraculously rescued out of brothels and other dangerous situations. Pray that God will put these women in contact with organizations who are working on the ground to provide a way out. Pray for the protection of the trafficked women and those working with the organizations. Dealing with the Mafia is dangerous business.

Pray for Habiba. Her recent scan showed that the cancer is stabilized and not spreading. Let's join hands around the world and ask God for a miracle. Maybe healing is possible this side of heaven?

7. LOVE: Ask God to fill your heart with His love—His supernatural love—for the unlovely, the unlovable, the stinky ones, the dirty ones, the outcasts, the ones on the streets. Yes, even the prostitutes.

Jesus loved them. Shouldn't we?

JESUS LOVED
PROSTITUTES

It never occurred to me.

It never occurred to me that Jesus loved prostitutes.

I knew Jesus loved everyone.

I knew Jesus loved women.

But it never occurred to me that Jesus loved prostitutes.

How could that be?

How could Jesus touch these women—those among the lowliest, filthiest, most shameful human beings on the face of the earth?

How could Jesus reach out to these women—those among the most sinful, most degrading, dirtiest creatures on the planet?

How could Jesus love unconditionally these women—those who sold their body to the night?

How could Jesus invite these women to come to Him—those who lived in a secret world with men?

How could Jesus embrace these women—those who walked the streets?

How could Jesus entrust these women with His story—those who had given themselves away?

How could Jesus' family heritage come through the bloodline of a harlot named Rahab?

How could that be?

Rahab, a harlot who ran her own brothel in Jericho for traveling men—a prostitute? (Joshua 2:1-24—The Bible NIV)

The woman who washed Jesus' feet with her hair—a prostitute? (Luke 7:36-50—The Bible NIV)

The woman caught in adultery—a prostitute? (John 8:1-11—The Bible NIV)

The promiscuous Samaritan woman at the well—a prostitute? (John 4:1-42—The Bible NIV)

Habiba—a prostitute.

The nameless, faceless woman—a prostitute.

What did Jesus want to show us?

What did Jesus want to teach us?

What did Jesus want to model?

Love . . . unconditional love, borderless love, human love, boundless love, shameless love.

Yes, even love for the prostitutes.

That's what Jesus was all about.

He entered their dark world, reached down his hand, invited them to come, picked them up out of the muck and mire, rescued them from hell, unchained them from slavery.

That's what Jesus was all about.

He entered their space; He brought them out; He loved them; He cared for them; He protected them; He bound their wounds; He healed their hearts.

That's what Jesus was all about.

He redeemed their past; He restored their hope; He fixed their brokenness; He gave them a fresh start; He resurrected their dreams.

That's what Jesus was all about.

He rewrote their story; He entrusted them with truth; He repaved their path; He told them to tell; He sent them out; He filled them with love.

That's what Jesus was all about.

It never occurred to me.

It never occurred to me that Jesus loved prostitutes.

But he did.

And so should I.

So should we.

THE STARFISH PARABLE

One day, an old man was walking along a beach that was littered with thousands of starfish that had been washed ashore by the high tide. As he walked, he came upon a young boy who was eagerly throwing the starfish back into the ocean, one by one.

Puzzled, the man looked at the boy and asked what he was doing. Without looking up from his task, the boy simply replied, "I'm saving these starfish, Sir."

The old man chuckled aloud. "Son, there are thousands of starfish and only one of you. What difference can you make?"

The boy picked up a starfish, gently tossed it into the water and, turning to the man, said, "I made a difference to that one!"

—Starfish Project[1]

"Jesus left the ninety-nine to go and rescue the one."
Luke 15:4—The Bible NIV

───ℓℓ───

Pray for Habiba. Her recent scan showed that the cancer is stabilized and not spreading. Let's join hands around the world and ask God for a miracle. Maybe healing is possible this side of heaven?

ABOUT M.F. RENÉE

Dear Reader,

If you liked this book, would you please kindly leave a review on Amazon and Goodreads? It helps other readers find the book and hear Habiba's story. Thank you for your support!

Along with her French husband, four boys, and dog, Samy, M.F. Renée is a global nomad, who has traveled to more than thirty countries and has lived in the United States, France, Morocco, and Spain. She is a French and English teacher, certified life coach, and an Arabic translator in government-run safe houses in Spain. She and her husband work among refugees and immigrants. She loves to travel, speak foreign languages, experience different cultures, eat ethnic foods, meet people from faraway lands, and of course, tell stories. She also loves giraffes, Dr. Pepper, french fries, and naps!

Sign up for her newsletter by scanning the QR code below or visiting her website, www.culturalstoryweaver.com:

SCAN ME

ALSO BY M.F. RENÉE

Mommy, What's a Safe House?

Pierre's mother works at a safe house. "What's a safe house?" he wonders. In a real-life conversation with his mother, eight-year-old Pierre finds answers to his questions. Pierre experiences the joy of going to a safe house and realizes there's nothing to fear. He wants to go back to help others and make a difference. This story brings a difficult, global topic to a child's level in a heartfelt conversation between a parent and a child.

Discover her other children's books—encouraging children around the globe to explore the great, big world. Available on Amazon worldwide.

*The Boy Who
Weaves the World*

*The Boy of
Many Colors*

———

Also find her book full of stories from her travels around the world
in ...

*Language
Learning Laughs—
Language and
Cultural Bloopers &
Stories from Around
the World*

Find all of her books by scanning the QR code:

SCAN ME

CONNECT WITH M.F. RENÉE

The Cultural Story-Weaver—Stories to Cultivate Cultural Awareness, Understanding, and Appreciation
www.culturalstoryweaver.com
Facebook: https://www.facebook.com/culturalstoryweaver
Instagram: https://www.instagram.com/culturalstoryweaver/
Twitter: https://twitter.com/culturalstory
LinkedIn:https://www.linkedin.com/in/the-cultural-story-weaver/
Pinterest: https://www.pinterest.com/culturalstoryweaver/

Sign up for Marci's newsletter, "Let's Weave Cultures":
Want to stay in touch? Scan the QR code and sign up for the "Let's Weave Cultures" Newsletter!

SCAN ME

BIBLIOGRAPHY

Prologue:
{1}Kristof, Nicholas D., and Sheryl WuDunn. *Half the Sky Turning Oppression into Opportunity for Women Worldwide.* New York City, Vintage, 2010.
The NIV Bible. Bible Gateway, 1993,
https://www.biblegateway.com/.

Ch 1. My Morocco:
[1]Pollock, David C., and Ruth E. Van Reken. *Third Culture Kids: Growing up among Worlds.* Revised edition ed., Boston, Nicholas Brealey Publishing, 2009.

Ch 2. Her Morocco:
"Poverty in Morocco: Challenges and Opportunities." *The World Bank,* edited by Bassam Sebti, 9 Apr. 2018, www.worldbank.org/en/country/morocco/publication/poverty-in-morocco-challenges-and-opportunities. Accessed 1 July 2021.
{1}*The Borgen Project,* 25 Feb. 2018, borgenproject.org/10-facts-about-poverty-in-morocco/. Accessed 1 July 2021.

Ch 4. A Faustian Bargain:
{1}"Faustian Bargain." *Wiktionary,* 30 Jan. 2021,
en.wiktionary.org/wiki/Faustian_bargain. Accessed 1 July 2021.
{2}Nazario, Sonia. *Enrique's Journey.* New York City, Random House Publishing Group, 2007.

Ch 5. The Strawberry Fields:

Billington, Sophie, editor. *Ethical Consumer*. 13 May 2019, www.ethicalconsumer.org/food-drink/bitter-fruit-labour-exploitation-andalusia-morocco. Accessed 1 July 2021.

"Campaign: The Fight for Agricultural Workers' Rights in Southern Spain." *Ethical Consumer*, edited by Sophie Billington, 1 Oct. 2020,
www.ethicalconsumer.org/ethicalcampaigns/agricultural-workers-rights-almeria. Accessed 1 July 2021.

Carlile, Clare. "Agricultural Workers' Rights Abuses in Spain." *Ethical Consumer*, edited by Sophie Billington, 20 Feb. 2019, www.ethicalconsumer.org/food-drink/agricultural-workers-rights-abuses-spain. Accessed 1 July 2021.

Maestro, Laura Perez. "'Please Help Us, We Are Abandoned Here.' Thousands of Moroccan Seasonal Workers Stranded in Spain." *CNN*, edited by Meredith Artley, 11 July 2020, edition.cnn.com/2020/07/11/europe/moroccan-women-spain-trapped-farms-intl/index.html. Accessed 1 July 2021.

Saiz, Eva. "Fruit Pickers Trapped in Spain: 'We Have Run out of Money and Need to Return to Morocco.'" *El País* [Almonte], 4 July 2020. *Prisa*, english.elpais.com/society/2020-07-14/fruit-pickers-trapped-in-spain-we-have-run-out-of-money-and-need-to-return-to-morocco.html. Accessed 1 July 2021.

"UN Condemns 'Inhuman' Conditions for Strawberry Pickers in Huelva." *Ethical Consumer*, edited by Sophie Billington, 14 Apr. 2020,
www.ethicalconsumer.org/food-drink/un-condemns-inhuman-conditions-strawberry-pickers-huelva. Accessed 1 July 2021.

Ch .13 Her Culture of Honor and Shame:

{2}Churchill, Charles W., and Abdulla M. Lutfiyya. *Readings in Arab Middle Eastern Societies and Cultures*. Berlin, De Gruyter, 1970.

{1}Muller, Roland. "Honor and Shame in a Middle Eastern Setting." *Nabataea*,
nabataea.net/explore/culture_and_religion/honorshame/. Accessed 1 July 2021.

Ch. 14 Beauty From Ashes:
The NIV Bible. Bible Gateway, 1993,

https://www.biblegateway.com/.

Ch. 15 Translation Bridge:
{1}Hani, Julie. "The Neuroscience of Behavior Change." *StartUp Health*, Medium, 8 Aug. 2017,
healthtransformer.co/the-neuroscience-of-behavior-change-bcb567fa83c1. Accessed 1 July 2021.

Ch. 16 The Telling:
The NIV Bible. Bible Gateway, 1993,
https://www.biblegateway.com/.

Ch. 20 Broken Women in the House:
{2}Farley, Melissa. *Prostitution, Trafficking and Traumatic Stress.* Binghamton, Haworth Maltreatment & Trauma Press, 2003.
{1}Reimer, Rob. *Soul Care: Seven Transformational Principles for a Healthy Soul.* Franklin, Carpenter's Son Publishing, 2016.
The NIV Bible. Bible Gateway, 1993,
https://www.biblegateway.com/.

Ch. 21 The Strawberry Fields are Calling:
United Nations Office on Drugs and Crime,
https://www.unodc.org/documents/human-trafficking/An_Introduction_to_Human_Trafficking_-_Background_Paper.pdf

Ch. 27 Sartan!:
Google Translate, https://translate.google.com/

Ch. 28 Exposed and Afraid:
{1}Piper, John. *Coronavirus and Christ.* Wheaton, Crossway, 2020.
The NIV Bible. Bible Gateway, 1993,
https://www.biblegateway.com/.

Ch. 32 I'm Tired:
{1}Coles, Tad B. "Compassion Fatigue and Burnout: History, Definitions and
        Assessment." *Dvm 360*, edited by Regina Schoenfeld-Tacher, Oct. 2017,
        www.dvm360.com/view/

compassion-fatigue-and-burnout-history-definitions-and-assessment. Accessed
2 July 2021.

Ch. 33 Lament for Habiba:
The NIV Bible. Bible Gateway, 1993,
https://www.biblegateway.com/.

Ch. 38 Her Family is Starving:
{2}Bearak, Max, and Luis Tato. "They're Back: Trillions of Locusts Descend on East Africa in Second Wave." *Washing Post*, edited by Sally Buzbee, 5 May 2020,
www.washingtonpost.com/graphics/world/2020/05/05/locusts-africa-swarms-kenya-ethiopia/. Accessed 1 July 2021.
{1}Gilliland, Haley Cohen. "Gigantic New Locust Swarms Hit East Africa." *National Geographic*, 12 May 2020,
www.nationalgeographic.com/animals/article/gigantic-locust-swarms-hit-east-africa. Accessed 1 July 2021.
{3}*The Borgen Project*, 25 Feb. 2018, borgenproject.org/10-facts-about-poverty-in-morocco/. Accessed 1 July 2021.

Ch. 46 The El Dorado Revelation:
{1}"El Dorado." *Merriam-Webster.com*. Merriam-Webster, 2021. Web. 1 July 2021.
{2}"Gilded." Cambridge.org. Cambridge, 2021. Web. 1 July 2021.
The NIV Bible. Bible Gateway, 1993,
https://www.biblegateway.com/.

Ch 50. The Sad Reality of the Strawberry Fields in Spain
{2}Billington, Sophie, editor. *Ethical Consumer*. 13 May 2019, www.ethicalconsumer.org/food-drink/bitter-fruit-labour-exploitation-andalusia-morocco. Accessed 1 July 2021.
{6}"Campaign: The Fight for Agricultural Workers' Rights in Southern Spain." *Ethical Consumer*, edited by Sophie Billington, 1 Oct. 2020,
www.ethicalconsumer.org/ethicalcampaigns/agricultural-workers-rights-almeria. Accessed 1 July 2021.
{5}Carlile, Clare. "Agricultural Workers' Rights Abuses in Spain." *Ethical Consumer*, edited by Sophie Billington, 20 Feb. 2019,

www.ethicalconsumer.org/food-drink/agricultural-workers-rights-abuses-spain. Accessed 1 July 2021.

{4}Maestro, Laura Perez. "'Please Help Us, We Are Abandoned Here.' Thousands of Moroccan Seasonal Workers Stranded in Spain." *CNN*, edited by Meredith Artley, 11 July 2020, edition.cnn.com/2020/07/11/europe/moroccan-women-spain-trapped-farms-intl/index.html. Accessed 1 July 2021.

{3}Saiz, Eva. "Fruit Pickers Trapped in Spain: 'We Have Run out of Money and Need to Return to Morocco.'" *El País* [Almonte], 4 July 2020. *Prisa*, english.elpais.com/society/2020-07-14/fruit-pickers-trapped-in-spain-we-have-run-out-of-money-and-need-to-return-to-morocco.html. Accessed 1 July 2021.

{1}"UN Condemns 'Inhuman' Conditions for Strawberry Pickers in Huelva." *Ethical Consumer*, edited by Sophie Billington, 14 Apr. 2020, www.ethicalconsumer.org/food-drink/un-condemns-inhuman-conditions-strawberry-pickers-huelva. Accessed 1 July 2021.

Ch. 51 The Sad Reality of Sex Trafficking in Spain

{4}"CNN: Spain's Hot Spot for Human Trafficking." *YouTube*, CNN, 4 July 2011, www.youtube.com/watch?v=wpXgPhNn5uM. Accessed 1 July 2021.

{6}Colin A. Ross MD, Melissa Farley PhD & Harvey L. Schwartz PhD (2004) Dissociation Among Women in Prostitution, Journal of Trauma Practice, 2:3-4, 199-212, DOI: 10.1300/J189v02n03_11

{8}Diaz, Teresa. "Sex Trafficking Victims Call for Courage to Heal Collective Wound in Madrid." *Agencia EFE*, edited by Alfonso Fernandez Sanchez, 5 Feb. 2019, www.efe.com/efe/english/agencia-efe/sex-trafficking-victims-call-for-courage-to-heal-collective-wound-in-madrid/50000270-3888561. Accessed 1 July 2021.

{5}Farley, Melissa. *Prostitution, Trafficking and Traumatic Stress.* Binghamton, Haworth Maltreatment & Trauma Press, 2003.

{3}"Human Trafficking in Spain." *Wikipedia*, 9 Dec. 2020, en.wikipedia.org/wiki/Human_trafficking_in_Spain. Accessed 1 July 2021.

{2}Kelly, Annie. "'Prostitution Is Seen as a Leisure Activity Here': Tackling Spain's Sex Traffickers." *The Guardian*, edited by Katharine Viner, 11 May 2019, https://www.theguardian.com/global-development/2019/may/11/prostitution-tackling-spain-sex-traffickers#:~:text=Recent%20estimates%20put%20revenue%20fro m,an%20estimated%20workforce%20of%20300%2C000.&text=Bet ween%202012%2D2016%2C%20security%20forces,under%20the%20 control%20of%20criminals.. Accessed 1 July 2021.

{7}Lisa A. Kramer MS (2004) Emotional Experiences of Performing Prostitution, Journal of Trauma Practice, 2:3-4, 186-197, DOI: <u>10.1300/J189v02n03_10</u>

{1}Lozano, Mabel. "Inside Spain's New Brothels: Residential Apartments." *El Pais*, Prisa, 13 Aug. 2019,
english.elpais.com/elpais/2019/08/02/inenglish/1564772155_91720 5.html. Accessed 1 July 2021.

Ch. 52 Now That You Know, Go Make a Difference!

{5}https://apramp.org/?lang=en

{7}"Campaign: The Fight for Agricultural Workers' Rights in Southern Spain." *Ethical Consumer*, edited by Sophie Billington, 1 Oct. 2020,
www.ethicalconsumer.org/ethicalcampaigns/agricultural-workers-rights-almeria. Accessed 1 July 2021.

{6}Carlile, Clare. "Agricultural Workers' Rights Abuses in Spain." *Ethical Consumer*, edited by Sophie Billington, 20 Feb. 2019,
www.ethicalconsumer.org/food-drink/agricultural-workers-rights-abuses-spain. Accessed 1 July 2021.

{12}"Covid19: Food and Vital Supplies for Migrant Workers." www.crowdfunder.co.uk/supportworkers. Accessed 1 July 2021.

{8}"Fair Trade Jewelry and Ethical Fashion Trends." *Trades of Hope*, 1 July 2021,
www.tradesofhope.com/culturalstoryweaver.

{11}"Home." *Eternal Threads*, 10 May 2021,
eternalthreads.org/.

{4}Kristof, Nicholas D., and Sheryl WuDunn. *Half the Sky Turning Oppression into Opportunity for Women Worldwide*. New York City, Vintage, 2010.

{10}*Rahab's ROPE*. www.rahabsrope.com/.

{2}Renee, Marci. *The Cultural Story-Weaver*.
culturalstoryweaver.com/contact/. Accessed 1 July 2021.

{1}Renee, Marci. Weblog post. *The Cultural Story-Weaver*, culturalstoryweaver.com/shop/. Accessed 1 July 2021.

{9}Starfish Project. (n.d.). Retrieved July 01, 2021, from https://starfishproject.com/

{3}Zacharias, Naomi. *The Scent of Water: Grace for Every Kind of Broken*. Grand Rapids, Zondervan, 2010.

Jesus Loved Prostitutes:

Bolinger, Hope. "Who Was Mary Magdalene? And Why Do People Think She Was a Prostitute?" *Christianity.com*, Salem Web Network, 11 July 2019,
www.christianity.com/wiki/people/who-was-mary-magdalene-and-why-do-people-think-she-was-a-prostitute.html.

The NIV Bible. Bible Gateway, 1993,
https://www.biblegateway.com/.

Thomas, Debie. "The Woman at the Well." *Journey with Jesus*, 8 Mar. 2020 www.journeywithjesus.net/essays/2561-the-woman-at-the-well-2. Accessed 2 July 2021.

The Starfish Parable:

{1}Starfish Project (n.d.). Retrieved July 01, 2021, from https://starfishproject.com/

{2}*The NIV Bible. Bible Gateway*, 1993,
https://www.biblegateway.com/.

Made in United States
North Haven, CT
22 July 2023